Praise for *The Last Resort: Taking the Mississippi Cure*

"What a miracle of time travel this memoir is! With the deliciously specific recall of a loving, inquisitive child, Norma Watkins places us inside the Mississippi in which she grew up, yet she exposes at the same time the suppressions and silences that held her world in place. Watkins writes with the irresistible honesty that led her to become the woman who couldn't be quiet anymore."
—**Lynne Barrett**, author of *Magpies* and *The Secret Names of Women*

"Norma Watkins's *The Last Resort: Taking the Mississippi Cure* joins the esteemed ranks of Carson McCullers and Harper Lee. By going through the eyes of the perfect spy, that most marginal of creatures, a young female child, to nail the complexities, hypocrisy, and even dangers in the adult world, Watkins winds up giving her readers a gift of enduring beauty. In language that is stunningly simple yet cogent, the author brings a vanished universe, filled with inequities and passions and good and bad intentions, back to life. Her exacting gaze spares no one, least of all herself. I like memoirs in general, but I adored this memoir in particular: the author is a wise, wry, generous narrator of her journey through the old South to a new world."
—**Madeleine Blais**, Pulitzer Prize–winning author of the memoir *Uphill Walkers*

"*The Last Resort* is an affectionately searing memoir, the story of one woman's coming to consciousness in mid-century Mississippi."
—**Eric Etheridge**, author of *Breach of Peace: Portraits of the 1961 Mississippi Freedom Riders*

"A haunting, beautiful memoir. With the power of a Eudora Welty short story, Norma Watkins reveals intimate details of family and race that shaped her childhood and led to her rebellion from those same worlds. *The Last Resort* is a stunning work of courage that touches the reader's heart in a gripping, unforgettable way."
—**William Ferris**, Joel Williamson Eminent Professor of History, University of North Carolina at Chapel Hill

"In this unflinchingly honest portrayal of personal, spiritual, and political awakening, Norma Watkins brings a rich, rounded presence to a vast array of characters—black and white, young and old—and to a time that, though long past, still resonates behind our own. Gifted with an astounding memory and rare talent for telling detail, Watkins brings many lives to vivid revelation here, and in doing so renders an entire time and place in indelible, resonant detail. Her understanding of character is pitch-perfect, and her devastating self-portrait is both affectionate and withering. *The Last Resort* is a high achievement: a memoir that manages to illuminate a moment in history. It does so with grace, incisive humor, and affection for every one of its wide array of fascinating characters. I've never before read anything quite like it."

—**Michael Hettich**, author of *Like Happiness* and *Flock and Shadow: New and Selected Poems*

"Unflinching, unsentimental, and sly, *The Last Resort* takes us back to the South that was, re-creating that place and time with marvelous wit and insight. Norma Watkins plays no favorites and she calls it right *every* time."

—**Kat Meads**, author of *Born Southern and Restless*

"With *The Last Resort*, Norma Watkins has crafted an exquisite testament to a brave and memorable life—here is the very map that traces the path from an other-era South into the modern day. A moving and illuminating book."

—**Les Standiford**, author of *Last Train to Paradise* and *Bringing Adam Home*

The Last Resort

For
Barbaralee
Enjoy,
preferably with
chocolate.
Best,
Norma

The Last Resort

Taking the Mississippi Cure

Norma Watkins

UNIVERSITY PRESS OF MISSISSIPPI   JACKSON

Willie Morris Books in Memoir and Biography

www.upress.state.ms.us

The University Press of Mississippi is a member
of the Association of American University Presses.

Sketches at the beginning of Part I, Part II, and Part III are by Till Caldwell.

Library of Congress Cataloging-in-Publication Data
Watkins, Norma.
The last resort : taking the Mississippi cure / Norma Watkins.
p. cm. — (Willie Morris books in memoir and biography)
ISBN 978-1-60473-977-0 (cloth : alk. paper) — ISBN 978-1-60473-978-7 (eBook) I.
Watkins, Norma. 2. Women, White—Mississippi—Biography. 3. Mississippi—Social
conditions—20th century. 4. Mississippi—Race relations—History—20th century. 5.
African Americans—Segregation—Mississippi—History—20th century. 6. Racism—
Mississippi—History—20th century. 7. Mississippi—Biography. I. Title.
CT275.W32826A3 2011
976.2′623062092—dc22
[B]   2010043295

British Library Cataloging-in-Publication Data available

For my children: Clay, Allison, Linden, and Thomas, who graciously endured my growing up *after* they were born instead of the preferred way—before.

Everything is as it should be,
nothing will ever change, nobody will ever die.

—Vladimir Nabokov, *Speak, Memory*

Contents

Acknowledgments

I'm grateful for old friends who, over the years, read multiple drafts of this book, both as fiction and as memoir: Meg Laughlin, Michael Hettich, Maggie Silverstein, Judith Hoch, and Margie Klein. Thanks to Ann Starck, who, with pungent comments, helped me type the earliest attempt. To Tom Shroder, who read the memoir and suggested I pull out pieces for the *Miami Herald*'s "Tropic" magazine. To Mike Wilson, John Barry, and Mimi Andelman, who continued that tradition at the *St. Pete Times*.

I'm indebted to my teachers in the M.F.A. program at Florida International University, who helped me pull a thread of story from my thicket of events: John Dufresne, Les Standiford, and especially Lynne ("Where's the conflict?") Barrett, whose sure hand guided me home.

Thanks to my children, who read, commented, and proofed: Clay Craig suggested the title, Starr Sariego, Thomas Craig, and Allison Scanlan (who claimed I made them sound like a litter of puppies). To my niece, Leigh Roberge, for sharing her archive of family pictures. To my cousin, John Fontaine III, who generously provided dates, facts, and invaluable photographs of Allison's Wells. To Julia Latimer and her son, Trey, who helped me get Julia's wedding and my mother's trip to California right; and to my daughter, Linden Craig, who sent the only picture we have of us as a family.

Thanks to my agent, Ron Goldfarb. He took me on even though he doesn't do women's books, then read, edited, and found a home for *The Last Resort*. I'm grateful for all the folks at University Press of Mississippi: Leila Salisbury, who was patient while I wrestled with titles, my editor, Anne Stascavage, Steve Yates, and Valerie Jones. To Carol Cox for her careful copyediting, and for remembering and caring about the people from those days.

Thanks to my fellow Mississippians for cheering me on and for introducing me to other southern writers: Bill Dunlap and Linda Burgess (honorary Mississippian), Patricia Derian, Hodding Carter, Patti Black, and Winifred Green.

I could not have persevered without my writing group, Mixed Pickles: Ginny Rorby, Katherine Brown (responsible for the subtitle), Charlotte Gullick, Jill Myers, and Maureen Eppstein. They reminded me of what I was trying to say; they yelled, "Show us," until I did; and prodded me to answer the question: "But how did you feel?"

Belated gratitude to all the help at Allison's Wells, the people who gave me such acceptance as a child, and who died without being properly thanked. Here's to Mrs. Ora D. Tucker, 91, who still tells me stories; to Miss Annie Carter, 92, who filled our house with good cooking and great humor; and to my second mother, the much-missed Mrs. Marie Austin Henley, who died at 89. Sweet thanks to the long-gone relatives I write about here, the people who completed the unbroken circle of a happy childhood.

Last, and most deeply, I thank my husband, Les Cizek. He provides what every writer needs: unconditional love and freedom.

1943—1945

1

We felt diminished before he left. Mama, my sister, and I bunched on the station platform with Daddy above us in the open door of the train car. His navy dress uniform glittered white and brass, the officer's hat cocked on his blonde hair. He was leaving us to go to war. The train jerked to a start. We cried. He smiled and waved. It was a lesson: leaving was better than being left.

The train disappeared and the platform emptied. "That's enough of that." Mother took a handkerchief from her purse, patted away her tears, then ours, giving a harsh twist to our wet noses.

The house had been sold. Men came and took the furniture. Our clothes and toys were packed. A navy salary did not pay enough for us to live in the Belhaven district of Jackson, Mississippi, in 1943. Our house now belonged to strangers.

My dog, Pal, disappeared before the furniture. Mother said dogs do that when they get old, go off by themselves to die. I didn't believe her. Pal hadn't left my side since I was a year old. He wouldn't leave me now.

Our backyard chickens and pen went to the man from the health department, the same man who came when neighbors complained about the smell. On those visits, he went away with eggs. This time he took it all.

We were moving to Allison's Wells, the hotel where Mother grew up. When I look back over the decades, I see that this was the moment when our lives changed, as if we, too, were put on a train, but shunted off to a different track. I wonder that my mother took it as well as she did. Marrying had rescued her from the hotel once, and here she was, headed back.

In the 1920s, with the country deep in depression, Mother was forced to drop out of college. Both her parents were dead. She and her older sisters and brothers ran the family hotel, struggling during those scarce times to keep the place going.

War had turned the clock back. We were poor again, and the Chevrolet, stuffed with boxes and suitcases, was all we had left. Two pet chickens rode in a crate in the trunk. Mother drove. Side by side in the backseat sat my sister, Mary Elizabeth, four, our nurse, Marie, and furious me.

With Daddy gone, I no longer pretended to be brave. I went through the litany of all I had given up: Daddy, Pal, the house where I was born, every friend I ever had, Power Elementary School, and the good third-grade teacher.

Mother had given up even more and was not sympathetic. After my third whining recitation, she turned on me. "Can you for one minute think of somebody beside yourself?"

Children had no power. I was being dragged away against my will, but I was seven. There was not one thing I could do about it.

We drove thirty-two miles north, through the town of Canton and back into the country. My favorite aunt and uncle lived in Canton, but we weren't allowed to stop. At the place where we turned off Highway 51 to get to the hotel, there was a billboard with a smiling southern belle, dressed in ruffles and a hoop skirt, waving at us. The white words coming out of her mouth said, "Welcome to Allison's Wells." Across the bottom in blue, it read: "Spa-Restaurant-Hotel. Recommended by Duncan Hines." The paint had peeled and part of the girl's face was missing.

Mama shook her head. "Hosford and John ought to do something about that. Makes it look like the place has gone out of business."

Hosford was Mama's older sister. John Fontaine was her husband. The two of them ran the hotel. The store at this corner was

4

called Triangle Inn and had delicious cold drinks. We weren't allowed to stop here either.

Mama took a deep breath. "One more mile."

Marie said something.

Mama turned her head to hear better. "What did you say?"

Marie didn't answer. She said terrible things about us under her breath. You didn't want to know.

Mary Elizabeth sucked her middle fingers and twiddled her hair. A six-syllable name was three syllables too many; we called her Merlizbut.

The road narrowed. We were in real country now. No more Burma-Shave signs, no more cars, fields on both sides, the corn stalks burnt brown. I looked out the back window and watched Triangle Inn, the last sign of civilization, disappear.

My sister started whining.

"I expect she needs to go to the bathroom," Marie said.

"Hold on, honey." Mama pressed the accelerator.

"*Mary Elizabeth wets her pants.*" I sang it, trying to lean over Marie and give my sister a poke in the ribs. Sometimes, if a person had to go to the bathroom bad enough, you could make them do it by tickling.

Mama said, "Will you shut up?"

Marie agreed. "Can't act right for five minutes."

Our nurse preferred babies. She didn't like you as much when you got old enough to talk.

I stared out my window. On the right was the house where Ellis Lindsey lived. He was Miss Hosford's best waiter and one of my favorite people at the hotel. In spite of myself, I felt a bubble of happiness rising inside. The edges of the road were thick with blackberry bushes. We were coming up the last hill. I bounced on the seat. "I see the water tower. I see the gate." Mama slowed and we turned into a gravel road between two brick pillars topped with lanterns. A swinging wooden sign said, "Allison's Wells Hotel and Spa."

5

I yelled. "Here comes the cattle guard. Hold onto your teeth."
The Chevrolet rattled over the metal bars. I slipped my shoes and
socks off. We wouldn't really be here until I felt it with my bare
feet.

"Couldn't make it without the conductor calling the stops."
Mama mentioned trains because Grandpa Latimer was an engi-
neer. He built the Illinois Central railroad from Durant to Jackson.
I never knew him because he was already dead,

We drove past the rose garden, the Annex, and the swimming
pool, gravel crunching under the wheels. Allison's Wells came
into full view. In the late 1800s, Mama's grandfather, Sam Wherry,
bought the property, along with a well famous for its medicinal water, from Mrs. Allison, a New Orleans widow. Mrs. Allison started
the hotel for people who showed up wanting to try the water. There
was one wing then, still the only wing with heat. We called it the
Warm Part. Grandpa Latimer, who married Mr. Wherry's daughter, dug a second, shallower well and hit sulphur water, perfect for
skin treatments, though it stained everything it touched a deep yellow. He sensed a business opportunity. Hotels and spas were becoming popular. In 1904, he bought the property from his father-
in-law, constructed a second wing, and began shipping five-gallon
jugs of well water all over the country. He added a third wing, until
the hotel had ninety-six rooms. We called these added wings the
Cold Part and the Annex. His wife, the first Norma, took care of
guests while he was off working for the railroad. Allison's Wells was
going to be his retirement, but he died when Mama was only three.
Her mother died after a botched operation in New Orleans when
Mama was seventeen.

I hated this story. Losing your parents was the worst thing I
could imagine. I'd already given up one to the navy. Not forever, I
reminded God. Daddy promised not to get killed. I'd seen orphans
sitting upstairs in the Methodist church, looking knobby and ill
dressed. I felt bad about them, but mostly I was glad not to be one.

Miss Hosford was the only sister Mama had left. She ran the

6

place with Uncle John when he was there, but mostly by herself. Uncle John modernized the hotel, turning rooms into baths until Allison's Wells shrank to sixty-six rooms.

The main buildings were two stories high, painted white, with gray, shingled roofs sloping over wide verandas on both floors. I knew exactly the hollow sound my bare feet made running on those green porch boards, and the turpentine smell that rose from them on hot summer days. Upstairs and down, each room had a double-hung window, which could also be used as a door, with a hinged screen leading outside. Using only the porches, you could get around almost the entire place. Downstairs the porches had wooden slat–backed rockers facing the drive. In summer these rockers were filled with comfortably shaped ladies fanning themselves and saying, "Lordy, it's hot. Watch your toes," as I went running by. Today, the chairs were empty. The metal cord clanged against the bare flagpole. Summer was over. There was no one in sight.

Mama nudged the car against one of the peeled pine parking bumpers. During the busy season, we had to park in the family garage behind the Annex, but today we were almost the only car in the lot. She turned off the engine. "Thank goodness."

I was out, running over the gravel and up the walk. I didn't know which way to go first. I could race to any of the rooms, or under the house if I wanted. I could go to the kitchen and see Lena, Ora Dee, and Johnny, or to the office and find Miss Hosford. I could head upstairs where Parthenia might be housekeeping, or to the linen room to see if Savannah was folding sheets. I could go see Alan and the mules in the barn, or check out the nickelodeon in the Pavilion.

Behind me, Mama hollered, "Wait up," but I was gone.

Miss Hosford sat behind her desk in the office, scratching in a ledger with a fountain pen.

"We're here."

She raised her eyes and examined me with a little smile. "So you are."

Miss Hosford was our aunt, but we never called her Aunt Hos-

7

ford. She had always been Miss. Years later, when people asked me why, I found out it was a way of showing respect to an older person. None of our other aunts was a Miss, so Hosford must have been due some extra respect. She never discouraged the title.

She spoke so softly you had to practically quit breathing to hear. I decided it came from running a hotel where things were always going wrong. She developed a voice that reassured. "Everything is fine and dandy," she'd say when a pipe burst, or the lights went out. People in funeral homes have that voice. You listened and thought Miss Hosford could talk out a fire. The trouble was, she never sounded really excited about anything either. According to her, moderation was the companion of wisdom, and a lady had no occasion to raise her voice. She was full of notions like that.

She closed the ledger and rested her hands on top. "Well, if it isn't Norma Latimer Watkins, with bag and baggage, I suppose?"

Of course we'd brought our bags. We were here to live. Why did she say my whole name like I'd already done something wrong?

Mama clicked in on her high heels. She was younger and nothing like Miss Hosford. She perched on the edge of the desk, breathing hard, crossing her legs dramatically, as if we'd driven from China. "I swear, it feels like I've been on the road since yesterday. I'm parched."

Miss Hosford checked the watch pinned to her blouse against the big railroad clock on the wall. Both agreed on five. "I think we could manage a toddy."

Mama pressed her hand to her chest like her heart was going to fall out from gratitude. "Run on, girls. Marie will take you to the kitchen."

Miss Hosford stood. "Not before we have our water." Her voice carried a lilt, as if she was offering a special treat.

There was no way out. The spa water came from a deep well dug between the office and the Warm Part of the house. It pumped up cold, frothy, and vile. A sign in the well house described alphabetically the ailments it was supposed to cure. I made this into a chant and taught it to children visiting the hotel in the summer. You started with a whisper: "Asthma and Arrhythmia," got louder for "Gastric distress and Gout," and shouted the hilarity of "Warts and Worms." There was a warning printed underneath: "Refrain from Imbibing Alcohol While Undergoing the Cure."

For Miss Hosford and Uncle John, Allison's Wells water was serious business. Hundreds of people took the cure each summer, drinking eight glasses a day. Children were supposed to have two. If you were family, it was required. The stuff was disgusting. The only way to get it down was to hold your nose while you swallowed, which made your ears stop up.

Miss Hosford liked to see us down a mug in front of her. We marched out and lined up beside the pump. The well house was a small hexagon with wood siding halfway up, trellis above, and a conical green-shingled roof. It could have been magical, like the house in Hansel and Gretel, except for the witch in the middle: a rusty red pump, beaded with moisture and, beneath it, a dark iron drain to carry away the overflow. Miss Hosford motioned. I held an earthenware mug under the spigot. She gave one downward stroke of the pump handle and the mug overflowed. I waited while Mary Elizabeth got hers. We stared at the frothy water. It looked exactly like pee. Around the walls, left over from summer, hung the mugs of guests, each printed with a room number, row upon row of them. I studied these and the cobwebs lacing the ceiling. I read the chemical makeup of the water on another sign. The wet concrete around the pump felt cold under my bare feet.

"Drink up," Miss Hosford said.

I took a swallow. So did Mary Elizabeth. It was as awful as I remembered.

"Don't stop." Our aunt pressed her hands together like she was praying. "Swallow it right down."

We drank, coughed, wiped our mouths, and drank again. The mug was bottomless. My stomach stretched in protest. I shuffled between swallows and spilled some down my dress.

Mama said, "Now look."

I said, "Why aren't you drinking yours?"

"I'll have mine later."

I knew why, because she was going to imbibe alcohol. I suspected Mama never drank the Allison's Wells water.

Finally, it was over. "Wasn't that nice?" Miss Hosford liked to make you do something awful and then ask wasn't it fun. She hung our mugs on two of the lower hooks. "Where you can reach them. You'll have water in your rooms, of course. Preston will come round and fill up your pitcher every morning."

Mary Elizabeth and I exchanged looks. We knew about that water, waiting outside our door, topped with an oily film. Preston, in addition to being a waiter, was the hotel's water man. Before sunrise in summer, he walked the halls, carrying two enormous buckets suspended from a wooden yoke. He yelled, "Water," except he pronounced it "WAH-duh." Guests were supposed to leave their empty pitchers outside the door, but in case they forgot, they'd hear Preston coming and could meet him in the hall.

Uncle John liked to tell about the man who checked in drunk one night and was dragged out of a hungover sleep the next morning by Preston calling, "Wah-duh, wah-duh." The man stood it as long as he could, then yelled through the transom: "Will somebody *please* give that man a drink?"

Our rooms were on the first floor of the Warm Part, opposite the big living room. Mary Elizabeth and I would share a high double bed. The room was dark. The only window faced an inside porch and courtyard. Mama's room was on the front and had two windows, plus a couch covered with faded flowers, a white bed, and a fireplace. Between us was a tiny, windowless bathroom containing a tub on feet and a toilet with a high tank and pull chain. I ran through our room to Mama's, back to ours, and out the door.

Mary Elizabeth said, "Wait for me."

Marie unpacked our clothes. "You stay here with me, baby."

I ran through the dining room. Miss Hosford let a few guests stay on after Labor Day, but only three or four tables were set with white cloths and flowers. The bare wooden floor felt cool to my feet. At the back were two swinging doors. The one on the right was for going into the kitchen, the one on the left for coming out. Everyone had to use the proper door or, during the season, when the dining room was full and waiters rushed in with trays of food and out with dirty dishes, there would be terrible accidents.

The warm smell of bread hit me before I pushed open the door. "Hey."

"Who's that?" Lena, the head cook, sat in her place at the counter by the woodstove.

"Me."

"Me, who?"

"Me, Norma." She was pretending she didn't know me.

"Come over here, child, and let me get a look at you."

Lena was stout and nearsighted, bent over herself like punched-down dough. Her face was pure Indian with reddish-brown skin, high cheekbones, and a curved nose. Her hazel eyes squinted from under a sloping forehead. She had on a uniform and an apron with a bib. Her hair was covered by a stocking, pulled down tight on her head and rolled at the bottom. "What you doing here? Thought we got rid of you."

"I've come back to live."

"To live?"

"I have a room and everything."

"Naw." Lena put an arm around my waist and tilted her head back to see me better. "Girl, you growing too fast." She felt warm from the stove and smelled wonderfully of snuff and yeast. "I guess we have to let you stay then."

I leaned into her in a way I almost never did with Mama, not because Mama didn't love me, but because she hardly ever held still. "What you making?"

"What it look like?" The pan in front of her was half filled with little squashed pieces of dough. With a floury hand, she pinched a piece out of the bowl, rolled it into a ball, mashed it into a circle, dipped it in melted butter and folded one half over the other. I watched, hypnotized, as she filled the pan. The rolls would rise on the warming shelf over the woodstove, bake for ten minutes, and come out fragrant and brown, to be split at their half-moon crack and filled with butter and plum jelly.

Johnny said, "What you going do here all winter?" Johnny Tucker was Lena's son. He was grown, but he couldn't read or write. A small, shy man, he spent his days following the orders his mother gave from her stool. I liked Johnny. He never got mad.

Lena said, "What you think she be doing? She's going to school."

"I am?" I'd managed to put that out of my head.

"Yes, siree. You starting school next week. I heard Mrs. Fontaine talking about it. School bus going to pick you up out by the road."

Johnny said, "You like school?"

I shook my head. "I'd rather stay here with you."

"And be ignorant like us?" Lena couldn't read either.

I didn't answer. I knew by then that school wasn't what made you smart. From what I'd seen so far, people arrived already dealt brains like hands of cards. You could get a smart or a dumb hand, and there didn't seem to be much school could do about it. I knew all about cards. Before he left for the war, Daddy and Mama played gin rummy every night. They played for back-tickling—the biggest treat you could get—five minutes a hand.

I pulled a stool up next to Lena and watched her work.

She hollered "wood" at Johnny, like she was yelling fire. He went flying down the steep back stairs and came panting back with a huge armload. Wiping his face on his sleeve, he opened the iron door of the firebox and pushed pieces of split oak onto the blaze.

Lena said, "About time. Now take that African soup bone of yours and stir my rice." She meant his arm. It was a joke.

I pinched off a piece of dough and sneaked it in my mouth. Lena popped my hand with the wooden spoon. "Larroes catch meddlers. Get on out of here and let me do my work."

She always said larroes catch meddlers. I didn't know what it meant. Much later, when I took Latin, I found out about Lares, the household gods, protectors of the hearth. Maybe that's what Lena meant, but how could Lena know Latin? I finally discovered the phrase in an Uncle Remus story: larroes was a kind of trap. For me, at seven, the bigger question remained: why didn't she and Johnny know how to read or write? I asked Mama, but she said it was the way things used to be, and I shouldn't mention it or Lena and Johnny would feel disrespected. I misunderstood. I thought she meant the bad old days were over.

That first night, there were six guests left to eat in the dining room. Mary Elizabeth and I had dinner at the metal-topped kitchen worktable. We had roast chicken, rice and gravy, beans, rolls, and apple pie. I ate standing up, which Miss Hosford would never allow, but she and Mama were in the little parlor drinking and eating off trays. After supper, I went and sat on the floor between them. Miss Hosford had two bourbons, but Mama kept drinking until her sister got up and locked away the whiskey.

Mama said, "What's that about?"

Miss Hosford put on the funeral voice. "Let's begin as we plan to end."

"Meaning what?"

"Meaning—" Miss Hosford glanced at me and gave my mother a warning look. "Whiskey is rationed around here along with everything else."

"I'm just so tense." Mama ran both hands through her hair. "Everything in my life turned upside down. It feels like last week that Tom was taking me to a dance at the country club, and now I'm"— she gestured around the room looking disgusted—"here."

The small parlor was the nicest room in the hotel. It had a faded oriental rug and two high-backed couches with lumpy stuffing under worn brocade. There was a coffee table with a silver tray, scratched but polished, holding the aluminum ice bucket, two silver mint julep glasses, and a pitcher of water. Framed flower prints hung between the windows, and over the mantel was a portrait of dead Aunt Thelma.

Aunt Leigh gave the portrait to Uncle Doug one Christmas. Doug was Mama's older brother. Aunt Leigh had it painted by Jackson's best-known artist, from a photograph. In the painting, Thelma wore a white dress with a sailor collar. Her dark hair curled softly around her face and she carried a straw hat with a rose pinned to it. Her cheeks were pink. She stood in front of the hotel, as if she were greeting someone we couldn't see. She looked alive and happy. The painting made Uncle Doug so sad, he couldn't stand having it in the house, so Aunt Leigh sent it up here to Allison's Wells.

Miss Hosford saw me looking. "Such a tragedy." She spoke in the dreadful soft voice. When grownups talked about death, I wanted to put my fingers in my ears. It was horrible to die young the way Thelma did, to never marry or have children, to make people so sad they couldn't stand to look at your portrait. Thinking about it made my chest hurt. It was also terrible having an aunt I would never know and, according to Miss Hosford, could never measure up to. What I meant was, what a shame Thelma would never know me. I listened to Miss Hosford talk about how perfect Thelma had been, how there'd never be anyone like her. If Thelma could talk back, I decided, she'd probably say, "Bull," the way Uncle Sam did when Miss Hosford got sanctimonious.

Thelma died when her car ran into the back of a truck parked without lights on a dark highway. It was wrong of the truck to be there. I hoped the family put the driver in jail. She was with a man, coming home at night from my cousin Doug's christening. Thelma and the man she might have married both died.

I stayed quiet while Mama and Miss Hosford talked. I traced the faint pattern in the rug with one finger. If you wanted to hear any of the good stuff, you kept your mouth shut and tried to be invisible.

Mama was restless. She didn't enjoy her sister's company. She kept sucking at the bourbon-flavored ice. The silver cups were beaded with sweat and the little handkerchief-sized napkins Hosford used were stuck to the sides.

"I could have gone to California with Tom while he trained. The base has housing for officers' wives. The children could have stayed here at the hotel with you and Marie."

My heart bumped against my chest. *She would have left us.*

Hosford shook her head. "I'm sure Tom thought through the possibilities and made the best decision. They also serve who only stand and wait."

"That's—" Mama noticed me and stopped. "He volunteered, a married man with two children. He didn't have to go. I don't see your husband marching off to war."

"John is ten years older than Tom, and he's doing his part for the war effort up in Chattanooga. I hope we're not going to spend our time together complaining about things we can't change."

There was a pause. I took a peep at Mama. She was very white with the birthmark shaped like South America burning on her forehead. It only showed when she got mad. I held my breath waiting to see what would happen, but she just lit another Lucky Strike. As she blew the smoke out, I heard, *"Pharmaceuticals."*

Hosford had her eyebrows up. "What did you say?"

Mama said, "Nothing. Not a word. I'm putting the children to bed." She herded us out of the room, walking fast, clicking her high heels on the wooden floor.

Pharmaceuticals was what Uncle John did for a living up in Tennessee. "Serving his country in a vital industry," Miss Hosford claimed, but it wasn't the same as being in the navy. He didn't have a uniform.

I lay in the dark trying to get used to the strange bed, and thought

15

about Daddy leaving, the way he'd waved from the train door in that glistening uniform. I kept trying to figure it out in my mind. Until he volunteered for the navy, Daddy worked as a lawyer for Grandpa Watkins, and Mama was a housewife. I thought we were content, but he must have been imagining himself out of our lives. War was an exciting place to go and he didn't want to miss out. He called it doing his duty and supporting the country, but Mama was right. In 1943, they weren't drafting thirty-two-year-old married men with two children. He claimed he couldn't live with himself if he didn't do his part. He reminded Mama of the six years he'd spent in military school, and that his great-great-grandfather, the first Thomas Watkins, served as a private in the Confederate army. When he failed the physical the first time for being too skinny, he ate an entire stalk of bananas with cream, gained ten pounds, and took it again. War gave you permission to leave.

Mary Elizabeth was already asleep. She had her fingers in her mouth and was breathing with little sucking sounds that made me want to put a pillow over her face. At the foot of the bed, Marie's cot was made up, but she was back in the kitchen with the others. Telling stories they wouldn't let me hear. During supper, she kept cutting her eyes at Ellis Lindsey, the headwaiter, making him laugh with her smart city talk. When she walked us back I asked if she liked him.

"I'm not studying that man."

But I knew better. I'd overheard her once. She said he was a pretty yellow fellow with a refined way of speaking.

Next door, Mama was banging around in her room. I felt sorry for her. She should go to the kitchen. Plenty happening there.

2

In my memory, we arrived at Allison's Wells in late fall, with gray skies, trees swept bare by cold winds, and the ground as sodden as my hopes. This can't be right because it was September. School hadn't started, and the weather never turns cold in Mississippi before late October. It was only gray in my head. If I got that wrong, what else have I misremembered? In the photographs my father sent, he was always in khaki. I don't think navy officers traveled in their dress white uniforms, but that's how I saw him when I was a child: he glittered.

I mooned around the hotel, wandering from the kitchen to the office to the barn, trying to find some place that felt remotely like home. Marie took my sister, Mary Elizabeth, for long walks to the lake across the road at Rose Hill, and down toward the town of Way, but I wouldn't go. It felt too babyish to be tagging along with a nurse. I hated Mary Elizabeth for being happy. I hated Daddy for leaving us, Mama for bringing us here, and everyone else on general principles. Most of all, I hated being a child. I couldn't wait to grow up and decide things for myself.

Mama wasn't happy either. When she showed us our rooms, Miss Hosford said, "People pay good money for these." That meant we were supposed to earn our keep. "We're getting the family rate." Mama said it sarcastically after Hosford left the room. She meant she'd end up working more than those rooms were worth.

Only a few guests remained, so Miss Hosford invented things for us to do. Mama and Parthenia did an inventory of the linen room, counting the sheets and pillowcases, putting aside the ones that needed darning. That took a day. Miss Hosford decided we should can. The ration board told everyone to preserve homegrown fruits and vegetables so there would be more for the troops. She decided on pears. A pear tree behind the Annex bore large, knobby fruits that hung onto the tree into September and never ripened. Not even birds would touch them. Miss Hosford found a recipe and put everyone to work. Ellis and Preston picked. Ora Dee and I peeled and sliced. Mama and Miss Hosford sterilized jars, boiled the pears, and made a spicy red sugar syrup to pour over them. Lena refused to participate. Said she'd never liked pears and didn't plan to start now. She sat on her stool in the corner with a lip full of snuff, out of sorts over the mess in her kitchen.

Softened by cooking, colored red, flavored with cinnamon and cloves, sweetened with sugar, the pears were just bearable. Miss Hosford was pleased. We'd made something out of nothing, her favorite thing. "So colorful." She lined the jars up on the pantry shelf. "I want to see a slice of spiced pear on every dinner plate next summer."

When I wasn't doing some invented chore, I daydreamed about Monroe Street and our old life. I walked through the house that was no longer ours, remembering every room. The breakfast table where we shared a pint of ice cream after supper. Daddy would drive to my uncle Price Cain's drugstore and come back with the sweet vanilla cream already dripping out of its square cardboard container. The white stove where I ate the entire meringue off a chocolate pie, and where Marie made the one thing she knew how to cook: sliced carrots. The big radio in the living room with its glowing yellow dial. The sofa where we sat in a row on Saturday nights listening to our programs. The hotel was too far out in the country to get decent reception. Miss Hosford and Uncle John had a shortwave radio that squawked and squealed, but it was there to warn us of bombs, not for *Sky King*.

I saw the stepping-stones in the backyard that led to the chicken coop. I saw my bed next to the window, where I propped on elbows and read Tarzan books. There was the front yard where I played with my dog, Pal, and the fence I'd fallen over and broken my arm. The street I walked up to see Cornelia Long, my first best friend. I knew the way to Power Elementary. I could walk there by myself if anyone had let me. I walked home once. The teacher punished me for socking Ross Barnett Jr. in the nose during recess. She left me alone in the classroom while everyone else went to lunch. I walked home, told Mother, and she stormed up to that school. Said I could be punished, but I wasn't to miss a meal.

I did my complaining to Marie when we were away from Miss Hosford's ears. "I never wanted to come here. Why doesn't anybody pay attention to what I want?"

"Because you're neither too old nor too young for your wants to hurt you."

She said that every time I asked for something. I figured it meant you never got what you wanted.

There was no one to play with. Even my cousin Doug Fontaine, who was four years older and a bully, would have been better than nobody, but he'd gone off to military school in Tennessee.

Meals were the worst. We ate at the family table in the back of the dining room. Miss Hosford spent the entire meal teaching us manners, which she claimed we were sadly lacking. Things every young lady should know, like, we were not allowed to say something tasted good. According to Miss Hosford, it was not polite to discuss the food you are eating. I'd never heard this rule, and it certainly took the meat out of the conversation. I missed Daddy telling funny stories and stealing my dessert when I went to get him more milk.

During one of our dinners, Mama started complaining again. "It's not as if he's fighting. He's in Officer Candidates School in San Diego, California, which according to the newsreels, is chock-damn full of excitement."

Mama's nickname growing up was "Me-too," because she hated being left out of anything.

"Language, language," Miss Hosford murmured, meaning the damn. She sipped her soup from the side of the spoon.

My sister, Mary Elizabeth, was the only person anywhere near my size and she was no fun. I tried to make her remember things. "Remember those stomachaches I used to have?" We were lying in bed, waiting to fall asleep.

"No."

"When I had to squat on the kitchen floor it hurt so bad."

"Nuh-uh."

"If I complained, Mama and Marie always said, 'When's the last time you went to the bathroom?' Then they poured huge spoons of milk of magnesia down my throat. Don't you remember? I had to be a milkmaid in the kindergarten pageant because that was the only part where you could squat."

Silence. Mary Elizabeth was asleep. I thrashed around in the bed, but she didn't move except to work those two fingers in her mouth.

I had one thing to be thankful for—the booger man had not followed me to the hotel. When we lived at our old house and weren't good, Marie used to say, "If you don't start minding me, the booger man will get you."

The way she pronounced it sounded just like what we'd better not have our finger up our nose after. She never told us what the booger man would do after he got us. We figured it was too terrible to describe.

In the old house on Monroe, my bed was under an open window and the booger man came tapping down the street every night. It might have been a neighbor with a cane, but I never dared open my eyes to see. I lay there, holding myself stiff, waiting to be snatched through the screen. I knew I wasn't good.

I don't think Marie meant to give me a horror of the dark. Threats were her only weapon. She wasn't allowed to hit us—that was one of the unwritten rules—but she could tell. Marie was not just good help, she was superior help, and she knew it. The last thing Mother wanted was to be left to do her own washing, or to swap bridge and tennis for looking after us. All Marie needed to say was that we'd been disrespectful and Mother would have us out at the hedge picking switches.

Up here at Allison's Wells, I was free of the booger man, but I started having Nazi dreams. Every night I ran up a dark path in the mountains with German soldiers chasing me. It was like a movie. I ran, but the camera panned back and I saw a clump of them in their dark uniforms and scary helmets, heads bent, boots clomping, guns with pointed bayonets. I couldn't get away. It was only a matter of seconds before I was caught and stabbed. I woke up as they reached me with my heart jumping out of my chest. No matter how much I told myself to dream about Tarzan or Sleeping Beauty, the Germans came.

I had a hard time falling asleep at the hotel, and hated my sister that she didn't. Staring at the ceiling, I thought about the second floor above us, and the attic over that. The weight of it all and what held it up. I wondered if it could crash down on us and if I'd have time to get under the bed. Too bad about Mary Elizabeth. Being asleep, she'd get smushed. Dead at four. It was so sad I almost liked her. If we got killed, Daddy would be sorry he left. War was more important than family, more important than staying with the people you loved.

Next door, Mama rattled her magazine. She was restless, too. I could tell because she jiggled her leg and smoked too much.

Marie slipped into our room and undressed without turning on the light. She said her prayers and climbed under the cover.

"Tell me about the tornado." I loved this story. I couldn't hear it enough.

"I can't be bothered with any story this time of night."

"Come on, please." We whispered so Mary Elizabeth wouldn't wake up.

Her voice was tired. "I fell asleep in my bed. A big old storm came with a black cloud sucking up everything and twisting it around, thundering across the ground like a hundred freight trains. It tore our house right off the foundation and flung it through the air. When I woke up, I was on the other side of the cornfield, still on that mattress. Nothing left of the house but broken sticks and a chimney. Nothing left of that bed but the mattress. Covers gone, the clothes torn off my back, and I didn't have a scratch on me."

Each time I heard the story, I thought Marie would get killed. Her escape was always a fresh miracle.

"The good Lord spared me for a reason."

To work for us? That didn't seem fair. "You're Mrs. Marie Austin. What happened to Mr. Austin?"

"Gone."

I figured gone meant dead, but Marie never used that word. All I knew about the husband was he wasn't around anymore. There must be more to it. "Didn't you ever have children?"

I heard her breathing in and out of her nose. She was getting sick of me. "When in the world would I have a minute to take care of my own child?"

I lay back feeling guilty. We were stealing her life. But I knew she wasn't telling me everything. Had she been by herself in that house when the tornado hit? What happened to the rest of her family? What happened to the husband? I wanted to know the hidden things, the parts white people never got to hear. If I asked, she found a dozen ways not to answer. Colored people were full of secrets and next to them our lives seemed flat and obvious.

During the day, I crept around the hotel, flattening myself against the wall outside the linen room where Marie talked to Ora Dee. "Girl, I flat out told that woman—" The voice stopped. Marie saw or sensed me, closing her mouth like a trap on the rest of the story.

"What? What'd you tell that woman?"

Ora Dee rolled her eyes in my direction. "Little pitchers sure got big ears."

I wasn't allowed to know because I was little and white. It wasn't fair. I tried listening from behind the swinging door in the dining room, holding my breath. But they talked so low. I only caught a word here and there and something always alerted Marie. It was like she had ears in the back of her head. "Where is that child?"

I whispered now in the dark. "Do you love me?"

Marie shifted on the cot, putting her back to me. "You'd do better to forget about love and think about minding."

I lay down on my stomach and pretended I was back in my bed on Monroe Street. Every night, Daddy came in to tickle our backs and tell us a story. By the light from the hall, he sat first on one twin bed, then the other. We waited, jealous of the one chosen, yet dying to be last. Tickling was pure ecstasy. Some people called it scratching and said, "Scratch my back," but they were Yankees and this was nothing like that. He pushed our pajama tops up and began a gentle circular stroking with the pads of his fingers. No fingernails, no getting too near the ribs, just a silky caress up to the shoulders and down to the waist and around again, while we swooned with pleasure. When he was done, always far too soon unless you were the one waiting, he pulled down our tops, patted us on the back, and said, "That's that." Mary Elizabeth and I jealously accused each other of getting more time.

While he tickled, he told us stories about Jake. Jake was a wild man Daddy used to pal around with. Tom Watkins might spend his days reading dry law books, but Jake went from one fantastic adventure to another.

Once Jake found a gorilla caught in a trap. Using his smart dog, Tim, to distract the beast, Jake snuck and opened the trap. This story involved gorilla noises. Daddy would give a terrible howling scream. From their bedroom across the hall Mama would say, "Tom, *please*." Part of the fun was making Mother use that exasperated voice.

Lying in the dark at Allison's Wells, I could almost feel Daddy's hand on my back.

Mary Elizabeth kicked me in her sleep. I kicked back, hard.

23

She whined.

"Be still," I hissed.

I lifted up. Marie was asleep, a dark mound under her comforter. I curled back into the warm nest of the bed. Maybe I was wrong about the ceiling falling. It was good having the big building with all those rooms around us. Nothing bad could find its way in.

3

"You will like this school and they will like you," Miss Hosford said. We were in Mama's room the night before I started. I turned in a slow circle while Mama marked the hem of the brown and green plaid dress I'd wear the first day. "It will be a treat for them to have a little girl from the city," Miss Hosford said. Mama smiled in a way that was meant to be reassuring. I didn't feel reassured.

The school was called Pickens Consolidated and I would go into third grade in a room with one teacher and three grades, third through fifth. I'd never heard of anything so peculiar. In Jackson at Power Elementary, we had two rooms and two teachers for each grade, plus art and music instructors and a school nurse. Pickens Consolidated didn't even have a cafeteria. I'd have to take my lunch in a black pail with a round lid and a thermos that clipped inside. The thermos was good, but I'd miss the lunch line at Power, with the kind ladies in hairnets, glasses steaming as they ladled food. Dishes of quivering red and green Jello waiting to be chosen. I'd started school a year early to get to eat in a real cafeteria.

Daddy agreed with me. His favorite restaurant in New York City was the automat, where all the food was behind little glass doors. I'd never been, but he told us about it. You put in a quarter, the door opened, and you got macaroni and cheese or a slice of pie, whatever you wanted. Having a thermos in no way replaced the cafeteria.

Miss Hosford and Mama took me in the car the first day, using rationed gas to help ease the strangeness. We drove out to the highway and turned north up 51, eleven miles to Pickens. The school, one flat story of yellow brick, sat squarely in the middle of a treeless pasture. I looked around suspiciously. "We had trees at my other school."

"This one's brand new." Miss Hosford held my hand in both of hers over the seat back while Mama pulled up to the front door. I hated having my hand held that way. It felt like bad news. Miss Hosford said, "Consolidated schools are the latest thing in education. Students are bused here from all over the county." So would I be after today, riding the yellow bus from Allison's Wells to Pickens and back again, the second student on and the next-to-last one off.

I cannot remember exactly why I was so unhappy in that place. I can't see my tormentors' faces or recall their names. I do remember a wall of hostility, which included the teacher, and was aimed, not so much at me, as at people like me and my family. These were the children of plain, hardworking white people. My family had pretensions. We had colored people waiting on us. My family drank and ran a hotel where people spent good money doing nothing. And worst, I suspected, people like us, who thought ourselves fine, didn't associate with people like them. We bought gas from them and seed for the garden. We called them to come see about the frayed wiring or the balky furnace, but none of these people were ever invited as guests to the hotel or hired to work alongside the Negroes. They wouldn't have, of course, would have thought themselves insulted to be asked. They might be poor, but they were white. They lived their hardscrabble lives furiously, worshipers of an angry Old Testament God. "Dirt eaters," my cousin Doug called them. "White trash," Mama said when they didn't show up fast enough to fix whatever had broken.

A large boy sidled up to me that first week on the scraped dirt playground. "Think you're better'n us, doncha?"

"No." That was the truth. I didn't. I felt worse. They treated me as if I had a loathsome disease, turning their backs if I approached, the girls whispering and giggling over their shoulders at me during recess. I was left completely alone. I thought I would make up for my social failure by being smart the way I'd been in second grade,

26

but I wasn't. Fear froze my brain. Everything that had seemed easy about school became difficult. In the large, rectangular room, third graders faced the teacher's desk, fourth graders were turned toward the side wall in the middle, and the fifth grade sat at the rear, facing the back wall. There was a blackboard for each grade. While the third grade did sums, Miss Etheridge, a stone-faced woman, wrote math problems on the board for the fourth grade and word problems for the fifth. Instead of working my sums, I kept turning to look in dread at the impossible things I would someday be expected to know. Far from being the smartest, I almost failed. I could not concentrate on my reader when another grade was reciting. My eyes were drawn to the back rows where some of the boys were as large as my father, held back until they reached sixteen, the legal age for quitting school in Mississippi. Miss Etheridge delighted in catching me with my head screwed around.

"What do you think you're looking at, missy?"

I jumped in fear and snatched my head back to my book.

"Somebody's going to fail and find herself right back in third grade."

I felt my face go red and in spite of my determination not to cry, tears blurred the letters of my book into insects.

Around me, the other girls snickered. "Crybaby's crying."

The shame of it, the humiliation. I rubbed my face with both hands. "Got something in my eye."

In late fall, when it turned cold and the last straggling guest checked out, the five of us, Mama, Miss Hosford, Marie, Mary Elizabeth, and I, shrank into the Warm Part. We lit fires in the bedrooms at night and slept under piles of blankets so heavy I could hardly turn over.

When we lived on Monroe Street, on the nights Mama and Daddy went out, we'd have Marie's sliced carrots for supper, floating in yellow butter, then sit in the glow of the big console radio, listening to *Mr. District Attorney*, *Sky King*, and *The Shadow*. Marie wouldn't let us hear *Inner Sanctum*. We only got to the creaking door part and that was scary enough. Marie turned off the set, we said our prayers and went to bed. Marie turned out the light before she put on her nightgown and I always tried to see her brown body in the dark. I never did. I saw only the white shape of the gown coming down over her outstretched arms, falling around her like a tent. The last thing I heard before falling asleep was Marie on her knees, muttering under her breath to God. Here at Allison's Wells it was the same except no radio programs and Marie shivered while she prayed.

Every morning Ellis and Alan worked to coax more heat out of the ancient coal furnace, but none of us were ever quite warm. I lay in bed with my sister in the early winter darkness, listening to the radiators clank and echo, wondering what my daddy did on that island where it was always summer. He was somewhere in the Pacific. He'd crossed the equator in a ship. He sent us pictures of the crossing party, a lot of men dressed up and acting silly.

Suddenly and for no good reason that I could see, Marie was gone. I think it was early November. Mama said she had business to tend to back in Jackson, but I knew that wasn't the whole truth. Eavesdropping in the kitchen, I heard Ora Dee say something was "not right." Parthenia said, "That pitcher was bound to get broke." It made no sense.

Another one of the people I counted on had vanished. The cot at the foot of our bed was taken away. I'd lie there at night trying to fall asleep feeling lonelier than ever. First Pal, my dog, then Daddy, and now Marie—everybody I loved was leaving.

I had to wait until Thanksgiving when my cousin Doug came home from military school to find out what happened.

We stood outside on the front walk, our knees turning blue from the cold.

"Marie's gone."

He gave me a look. "Bet you don't know why."

I squirmed with resentment, hating to ask him anything. He was pale and skinny and still sucked his thumb when he thought no one was looking, but he was Miss Hosford's son and I was only a niece. He was twelve and went off to Baylor in a gray uniform. I went to the Pickens Consolidated. Still, information was information. I couldn't afford to be choosy.

"Tell me."

He took his time, cleaning something out of his big front teeth, looking down at me like I was too dumb to live. "She was messing around with Ellis, that's what. Ellis's wife, Gert, told him to make a choice, so Marie had to go."

He stared at me. I didn't know what to do with this information.

"You don't even know what an affair is."

I walked away, giving him a disgusted look over my shoulder. "Do, too." I would not ask him one other thing. He was right. I didn't know what an affair was, or what Marie and Ellis did to make his wife so mad. Gert was a handsome woman with a long, proud neck. She straightened her hair and twisted it into a bun. She dressed like Mama or Miss Hosford and never worked at the hotel. She bragged that Ellis wouldn't allow his wife to hit a lick for anybody. The rest of the kitchen thought she was stuck up. When Miss Hosford needed extra help and Gert wouldn't come, Ora Dee called her a "high-yellow heifer."

"What's an affair?" It was late Thanksgiving afternoon and I was in Mama's room. The day was cold and gray. A leaden sky sat on top of the hotel like a bad mood. The uncles and aunts had left and Miss Hosford and Uncle John were taking a nap.

Mama walked back and forth in front of her sofa smoking. "Who have you been talking to?"

"Nobody."

"Good, because I better not hear you using language like that again."

I went to bed knowing no more than I'd known before.

In winter, Alan slept in a storeroom behind the kitchen. With Marie gone, he was in charge of getting us up. Every morning in

29

the frozen dark, he tapped on the door, stuck his head in and whispered. "Time. I got a fire going in the stove."

In the freezing room, I reached to the bottom of the bed and pulled up my clothes. I slept with the next day's outfit under the cover, which kept things warm if somewhat wrinkled. Marie would never have put up with this, but Marie wasn't here to see. I dressed under the covers, not coming out until I had on my panties, long socks, a pleated wool skirt, an undershirt, blouse, and two sweaters. Mary Elizabeth moaned when the blankets lifted. She was too young for school and could stay in bed until the hotel's furnace warmed things up. I ran through the icy hall, across the North Pole of the dining room, into the kitchen, where I waited, shivering, until the wood stove turned from oily gray to pink with a heat so fierce I had to back away and warm first one side and then the other.

Alan scrambled me two eggs, fried toast on the griddle, and I ate standing at the metal-topped worktable, which was exactly the right height for me to scoop the eggs directly into my mouth.

"That's not how decent folks eat. You ought to sit down." Alan never criticized. It was just a statement.

"It's too cold to sit."

"Don't say I taught you them manners."

Alan was the best man in the world next to my father, and he liked me, too. He was six and a half feet tall, with broad shoulders and muscular arms. He did the hard outdoor work at the hotel when he wasn't looking after Mary Elizabeth and me. He milked the cow, chopped wood, kept the garden, slaughtered the hogs in the fall, and ploughed the pastures with the hotel's two mules. In winter he wore overalls over long-sleeved flannel underwear. I never saw him dressed in a white coat and black pants like Ellis and Preston. Feeding me scrambled eggs was as domestic as Alan got.

After breakfast, I brushed my teeth at the sink while Alan made me a sandwich. I stood between his knees and let him pull the tangles out of my hair. "You tough-headed." It was a compliment. We put on our coats and reluctantly left the warm kitchen, walking out the long curved driveway, me taking two steps to his one, past the rose garden and the water tank, across the cattle guard, between the brick columns with their broken lamps, to the road where we waited together for the school bus. Neither of us was sure of clock time and the thought of being late made us nervous. It would be a terrible thing, we agreed, to miss the bus. To be safe, we went out as much as an hour early. We stood in the still-dark morning, me jumping up and down in the gravel to keep warm, Alan with his shoulders hunched, a tall shadow against the dawn. We talked until the headlights of the bus appeared like cat eyes far down the road. I pulled up my socks and picked up my satchel. We got quiet as the bus pulled up. Alan handed me my lunch box. I gave him a little backwards wave good-by. He stood watching until the bus drove out of sight. All the way through third grade, Alan was the last good thing I saw until I got home.

At school, a girl finally spoke to me. She got on the bus at the stop after mine, in front of a dilapidated house. She sat in the desk behind me, and one Monday outside at lunchtime, she settled silently beside me on a wooden bench. I'm ashamed to say, I don't remember her name. I'll call her Ida. She was large as a grown-up with small blue eyes and oily blonde curls she kept pushed behind her ears. She wore the same two faded gingham dresses, one red checked, the other blue. They hung on her oddly.

She saw me staring one day at lunch and smoothed the cloth across her lap. "These was Mama's. Made them over to fit me."

I nodded, not knowing what to say.

She sat with me despite the others' looks and whispers, staring them down. She wanted me to talk about the hotel, how many rooms we had, how many colored people worked there, what the guests ate, and what sort of clothes they wore.

She said, "Your mother's beautiful. Like a princess." I was astonished. I'd never thought about how Mama looked. Ida described the farm they leased and listed the chores she did every morning before school: milking, slopping the hogs, feeding the chickens, fix-

31

ing breakfast. She had a favorite pig she'd named Gwen, short for Gwendolyn, and would name a daughter that if she ever had one. She planned to quit school after sixth grade or when she turned sixteen, whichever came first. "My brothers are off in the army and Daddy needs me. If we can get enough money together, he'll buy us our own place after the war."

"What's all that stuff in your yard?" I hesitated asking, embarrassed to call attention to the broken-down cars and appliances I saw when the bus stopped to pick her up.

"Daddy collects. He gets together a load and we sell it for scrap. Except for the good stuff. We keep that."

She took great interest in my lunches, a sandwich made of potted ham or tuna fish with lettuce, on light bread with a piece of fruit and a cookie. I felt an equal fascination with hers, which came out of a tin bucket and were wrapped in a greasy cloth. It was always the same: two biscuits broken open with patties of cold fried sausage between and molasses poured over the top. Ida's mother was dead and she made these biscuits herself. I thought this was a marvelous talent for a third grader and told her so.

"I've been held back," she said. "I'm not much for school."

"I think you're very smart," I said. "You can cook and sew."

"And dress a hog," she said.

One noon as I unfolded the wax paper from around my lunch and Ida placed her biscuits side by side on her lap, I noticed her looking at my sandwich.

"Want to swap?" I said.

"Don't mind," Ida said. She took half my sandwich and I took one biscuit. We found each other's food delicious and exotic. We traded entire lunches from that day on. Biscuits and molasses with cold, heavily peppered pork sausage were the best things I'd ever eaten, though I knew better than to mention this at home.

On the school bus, we sat together and I watched from the window as she crossed the littered yard and vanished into her house. She would turn and wave to me from the door, a solemn wave with no smile. Some days, her father waited for her, leaning against the doorjamb. On those days, Ida didn't wave. She never invited me to her house and I never asked her to the hotel. We knew without saying that our friendship was a secret.

Even with Ida, school was a bleak and lonely place. As winter deepened and I continued to do badly, I used the afternoon drinking time to complain to my mother and aunt. "They all hate me."

"Of course they don't hate you," Miss Hosford said.

"They *do*. Even the teacher hates me."

"You will have to learn to get along with all kinds of people in this world." Miss Hosford had on her silky, reprimanding voice.

Mama bit a length of thread off a spool. "I'm sure the child is exaggerating."

"They were lovely the day we took you in," Miss Hosford said.

And they had been, the teacher nodding and smiling, putting her arm around my shoulders, telling my aunt how much they looked forward to having me. She introduced me to everyone in the class. All the children smiled and said, "Welcome" when she told them to.

"That was just one day." I started crying. "Because *you* were there. They've never been nice again."

Mama and Miss Hosford were stern. I was to be good and keep a stiff upper lip. Being good supported the war effort. With so many terrible things going on around the world, children must do their part without complaining.

"Listen to this." Miss Hosford read out of her magazine. "Your loved ones may be riding the high seas in inky darkness or pitching through the shell-pierced air. Shall we allow this to tear our temper ragged and shatter our morale?"

I was horrified. "I didn't know Daddy was riding the inky seas."

"He's not. For heaven's sake, stop frightening the child." Mama put down her sewing and hugged me. "Your daddy's sitting under some palm tree, happy as a toad. Hosford just means you need to be brave and stop pestering us about that school."

33

I tried, but one day in early March I'd had enough. When I got home, I told Mama I wasn't going back. The playground had been muddy from cold spring rains. At recess, I slipped or was tripped, and fell heavily against the metal swing set, cutting my knee and coating my dress and legs with mud. Miss Etheridge snatched me by the arm to the washroom, scrubbed at my knee with alcohol, painted it with iodine, and said to "stop that ruckus" when I cried. That afternoon, I failed a spelling test and came home with wet clothes and red eyes.

"I won't go back," I told Mama and Miss Hosford.

Miss Hosford said, "Of course you will."

"No, I won't. I will never go there again." I refused supper and cried so long and hard that the two of them whispered together, and came to tell me I was to stay at home the next day. They would go to school and look into things.

The next morning they put on their good wool coats, felt hats, and kid gloves and drove away looking grim. I wandered from room to room in the Warm Part, feeling lost and out of place. I waited by the glass front doors most of the afternoon watching for the hotel's station wagon to come around the curve of the driveway. Finally, they were back, but refused to say a word until they had settled in the main parlor in two large chairs on either side of the fire with cups of hot tea. I was jumping out of my skin by that time.

Miss Hosford said, "Sit, please."

I dropped to the floor between them.

Miss Hosford spoke first, her voice almost a whisper. I had to lean forward to hear. "There is nothing really wrong with the school. We had a long talk with your teacher and told her how you felt."

They told Miss Etheridge? I would get killed when I went back.

"She was quite sympathetic."

I'll bet. I knew what would happen tomorrow: *death to the squealer.*

"There's nothing seriously wrong with the place or the children." She and my mother exchanged glances. "But I have made some calls.

If you'll finish the year at Pickens without complaining, next year the bus route will change and you can go to Canton Elementary instead."

I felt lightheaded with relief. One deep breath and I could float up and bump my head against the water stains on the ceiling. My aunt was more powerful than I knew. She could change bus routes.

"You'll be in the same school where I went as a girl." Mother stroked my hair. I leaned against her knee, feeling good in every part. "It had twelve grades back then." Her hands lifted and dropped strands of my hair, giving me goose bumps. "I used to catch the Banana freight back and forth from down in Way. The train stopped just for us kids. Canton's larger than Pickens, so the school has a room for each grade. You'll be friends with the children of people I grew up with."

I was hardly listening. Canton was where Momae and Uncle Sam lived, my favorite aunt and uncle. Canton was a real town with a movie theater, a five-and-dime, and a drugstore. I jumped up. "I have to go tell them in the kitchen."

Miss Hosford held me back. "One more thing. We'd prefer you not play with that large child, the one who sits behind you."

I stopped. Not play with Ida? "Why not?"

"She didn't look clean. We'd rather you didn't. We spoke to the teacher about it. She said you've been eating her food."

I looked past my aunt's head, keeping to the only life philosophy I'd developed so far: never admit to anything.

Miss Hosford spoke carefully. "There's nothing wrong with having little friends who are different. But you must trust our judgment on this. The child may have lice."

Lice. That brought me up short. Sometimes the traveling nurse found nits. She took the guilty children to the cloakroom, pulled a sharp-toothed comb through every inch, then soaked their heads in something that smelled like coal oil. The victims screamed. I couldn't bear to watch. We'd never heard of lice at my old school.

Plus, if they found nits on you, you had to take a letter home and boil your sheets. If you had them real bad, they shaved your head like they did Elsie Winger's and nobody spoke to you until it grew out. Almost nobody spoke to me anyway, but I couldn't take the chance.

All the way on the bus the next day, I tried to think of some way to tell Ida, but I couldn't. I sat as far apart from her as I could. At school, Miss Etheridge moved me to the front row and, from that fresh vantage, gave me looks that combined wariness with dislike. At lunchtime, she called Ida to her desk and I left the room quickly. Ida came out a few minutes later, her face blazing. She never sat next to me at lunch again. Once in a while, I caught her looking at me, but when I looked back, she lifted her head and turned away. On the bus, she walked by me without a glance. I was filled with a sodden guilt. I had traded my only friend for the promise of Canton Elementary.

The problem was soon solved. Ida's father took her out of school to help with the spring planting. Most of the larger children disappeared. Miss Etheridge gave us a piece of her mind the day the class shrank. "It's a crying shame, taking children as if they were plow horses, and it's a misbegotten law that allows it. No wonder the whole state is illiterate."

I was glad. I didn't want to have to look at Ida anymore. I wanted to think about next year.

4

I figured the bad times were over, until Mother called me into her room. "I got a wire from your father today."

It seemed like a miracle that Daddy could reach out and find the hotel from across the Pacific. My chest filled with happiness. I waited for Mama to tell me how much he missed and loved me.

"He's got a leave. I'm going out to California to meet him."

I came down with a thud. "You're leaving?" This was it. I was losing my last person.

"It'll just be a couple of weeks. I'll be back before Easter."

"Take me with you."

"I can't do that, baby."

"Who'll be here for me?" I started to cry, picturing interminable dinners with Miss Hosford, silent except for the rules: don't hum, don't eat so fast, elbows off the table, leave something on your plate.

"Stop acting like a baby. Hosford will be here. You love Alan. He'll still be taking care of you."

I howled and stomped the floor. "You can't go away and leave me here. I won't let you." I was so impressed with the noise I made, screaming and throwing myself around, I failed to notice the red map of anger blossom on my mother's forehead. She slapped me hard across the face. The sound was like a shot and my head ricocheted. I felt the sting and went deaf. The sound of her hand silenced everything, including my crying. I saw her lips move, but I couldn't hear a word. As my hearing came back, the place where she hit me started to sting.

"See what you made me do? Haven't I got enough on my mind without you carrying on? You are a child. You have no say in the matter." She caught her breath and quieted down. "Go wash your face."

I went into the small, dark bathroom and turned on the light. Lifting myself up by my arms, I studied my face in the medicine chest mirror. My left cheek had a perfect handprint in stinging red. I was too astonished for tears. I'd been switched on the legs and spanked on my bottom, but I had never before been slapped in the face. I turned my head to examine the mark. Everyone I loved was leaving and I would be scarred.

That night in bed, I tried to figure things out. Daddy left because of the war. Marie left because she did something bad. Mama was leaving because of Daddy, and I was going to be left, period. I touched my face. It still hurt. That slap meant that no matter how much people claimed they cared about you, they would not put you ahead of their own desires. That was the plain truth and also the trouble with being a child. You had to live by other people's rules. If I were grown up, I could pick my own school. I could move back to Jackson and not share a bed with anybody. I could leave like Daddy. My cousin Babee had joined the Waves. Women could go to war. But right here, right now, there was not a single person I could count on.

Mother left. Miss Hosford turned out to be an absent-minded dictator, stern about table manners and prayers, but letting us slip from her mind at other times. We were cared for but not about. The weather settled into a steady run of cold rain. The servants were gone except for Alan and Lena. Lena stayed in a warm room down from the kitchen because of her rheumatism.

I thought I couldn't bear it, but I did. I went to that terrible school and came home, ate supper with Miss Hosford, and let her put us to bed. When Mary Elizabeth was asleep, I cried, but not too much. It occurred to me that a lot of the crying I did was for other people's benefit.

Mama came back after twelve days. Though I was desperately glad to see her, I punished her for leaving. When she told stories about the wonders of California, I pretended to be busy. When she talked about Daddy, I got very still so as not to miss a word, but I didn't respond. She had betrayed me and I wouldn't let myself be won over by trinkets and funny stories. A part of me held back, cold and watchful.

She tried to make up for it. On Easter weekend, she gave me my favorite treat. I could spend two nights in Canton with Momae and Uncle Sam, the best aunt and uncle in the world.

Doug and Sam were Mama's older brothers and the very opposite of my father. They were big, loud men with plenty of money. They wore their bellies proudly, firm watermelons of success parting the unbuttoned coats of their suits. Neither one of them had finished college, but they made a lot more money than lawyers. Sam traded cotton and Doug bought and sold oil leases. These mysterious occupations didn't take nearly as much time as the law and paid a whole lot better. When I mentioned this once to Daddy, he said it was better to have a profession than money.

Even I could tell Uncle Sam and Uncle Doug were rich. Their wives drove Buicks and Cadillacs instead of Chevrolets, and they wore lovely starburst brooches, pearls for day, diamonds at night. The uncles had enough money to gamble hundreds of dollars on Ole Miss football games, calling in their bets long distance to bookies in New Orleans. Everything about them was immoderate, their cars and voices, their appetite for food and whiskey. I could tell from the way Daddy's family spoke about Doug and Sam, they were suspect. Without professions, they weren't as common as tradespeople, but close.

I liked their jokes and big belly laughs and the wads of cash they carried folded in money clips. Uncle Doug and Aunt Leigh had moved to Key West for the war, but Canton was only eleven miles south of the hotel. Pickens, with its horrible school, was twelve miles north, in what I considered the bad direction, and Canton was the good way—toward Jackson and home. It was the county seat and where Mama or Ellis went to pick up supplies from the wholesale grocer.

Mama drove us in. We parked in front of Uncle Sam and Momae's peaked-roof house. The Cadillac was already in the driveway. Uncle Sam worked in an office around the corner, but he drove to work in the morning, home for lunch, back to work, and home again in the afternoon.

Inside, Momae was stretched out in a canvas recliner on the glassed-in porch. She had a bad back and needed to do a lot of reclining. Uncle Sam cooked on the nights Mateel didn't leave supper. He specialized in steaks. No potatoes, no salad, just meat.

Mateel was their scary maid. She did not think I was adorable. She watched me like she was waiting to see what I'd break next.

Mama threw off her shoes and put her feet up. Uncle Sam mixed drinks for the three of them, scotch and soda in tall glasses with lots of ice and little socks on the bottom. I got a cold bottle of Coke with the same stretchy sock. He made open-faced cream cheese and olive sandwiches on dark bread. I'd never seen an open-faced sandwich. I liked it. You could see what you were biting into. I'd never eaten an olive either. They were sliced and the red centers looked like screams.

He said, "Try one, Little Angie."

The uncles called me Little Norma or Little Angie. Mama was Big Norma, and her nickname was Angie. When she was small, she couldn't get enough pancakes, and Aunt Jemima got shortened to Angie. Everybody said I looked just like her, and we had the same name, and wasn't that cute? I didn't want to look like Mama or anybody. I wanted to be an original.

"Come on, Little Angie, it's good." Uncle Sam held out the cream cheese and olives.

I made a face. I hated trying new food.

He said, "Olives are the kind of thing you have to develop a taste for. You may be too little."

A challenge. I was not too little for anything and I was desperate to get bigger. I took a bite. I liked the way my teeth left a scalloped semicircle in the cream cheese. If you chewed fast, you couldn't feel the slimy red parts. The olives tasted green and salty. I took another bite; a new ragged half-moon overlapped the first. "Good." Spoken with my mouth full.

"How about that?" He ruffled my hair to show how proud he was.

Another man might have hugged me, but not Uncle Sam. Hair-ruffling was as personal as he cared to get. He liked me, I could tell, but from a distance of a foot or two. He didn't encourage physical contact. I knew, because I'd made the effort. We'd been taught to hug relatives, but I could feel him holding back, stiffening in the chest and arms. I tried not to bother him with it.

Mama needed to head back to the hotel, but she'd had three scotch and sodas and didn't want to leave. The laughing and talking got louder. Momae laughed with a low ripple like a creek. Mama went "ha-ha-ha" with her head thrown back, her mouth open and her fillings showing. Sam kept his in his belly, a grumbly "heh-heh-heh." I couldn't figure out what was so funny, but when I asked, Mama squinted like she didn't know who I was. "Don't interrupt when grown-ups are talking." Her eyes looked different. When she kissed me good-by, it was all smoke and whiskey.

Uncle Sam fried us a steak. Momae put me to bed in the guest room. Of all the rooms I'd ever slept in, this was the best. It had red walls and a bed with four posters and a pleated thing up high in between. There was a peach satin comforter and stacks of matching taffeta pillows, pink shaded lights on the night tables, and a whole wall of mirrors so you could see yourself from bed.

The next morning, I got breakfast in my room. Nobody in that house got up for breakfast. Everyone ate in his own bed and enjoyed being alone. Momae and Uncle Sam had separate bedrooms, a thing I'd never heard of married people doing, but which I filed away to consider. Mateel brought in a wicker tray that rested over my knees.

She raised my shades. "Don't be bothering Miss Mae."

I shook my head. I wouldn't.

I got the same breakfast I always got, the same as Momae and Uncle Sam. It made me feel grown up, although it was not a breakfast anyone in our family would recognize: a tiny glass of fresh orange juice with lots of pulp, little thin pieces of dry toast with the ends cut off, marmalade, bacon, and real coffee in a thin china cup. I tried to strain the juice through my teeth, and the coffee tasted black and bitter no matter how much sugar I added. I made bacon and toast sandwiches and ate and drank everything.

When nobody came for the tray, I slipped out into the hall where Momae kept a cedar chest filled with old clothes and costume jewelry. I was allowed to play with anything in it. I dressed myself in navy silk with white polka dots and a string of pearls that reached to my knees. The dress pooled around me on the floor. I was admiring myself in the hall mirror when I noticed Uncle Sam's door cracked open. I peeped in. He was standing in front of the dresser in striped undershorts and a white undershirt, the kind with no sleeves. He was lacing a corset over his undershirt, an enormous band of canvas and elastic with stays. It gripped his stomach, shaping it into the flat hard curve I felt under his shirt when I tried to hug him. I'd never imagined such a thing existed, or heard of a man wearing one. It was as if I'd stumbled on a dark adult secret. I felt ashamed for knowing and darted back into my room.

Mateel was there getting the tray. "What are you up to?"

"Nothing."

"Better be nothing."

Midmorning, when Momae was awake and receiving, I watched from her bed as she put on her face. She sat on a brocade bench in front of her dresser, wearing a pink satin slip with a little white cape

42

tied over it to catch any loose powder. It was like watching an artist paint. I couldn't wait to be able to do that. I never got to watch Mama make up. She put on lipstick and powder the way she did everything—on the fly.

The telephone rang in the hall. It was Mama calling from the hotel. "You were not drunk," I heard Momae say. "You tell Hosford to mind her own business. Besides—" She gave a trill of amusement. "You're a better driver drunk than she is sober." There was a pause while she listened. "Well, you didn't have the child with you, did you?"

Drunk. That was the word. When Mama laughed too loud, when her eyes got hard and she looked at me like she couldn't remember who I was, she was drunk.

This was my introduction to what turned out to be the Latimer family curse, the disease that would kill Uncle Sam, his son, Sam Junior, Uncle Doug, Mama, and people who hadn't even been born yet.

Canton was a small town and I was allowed to wander freely. Late Saturday morning, I went to Uncle Sam's office, upstairs in a building on the square. The square was filled with colored people, in town to do their shopping. I walked by them, saying hi-dey to anybody who said hi-dey to me. When I stuck my head in the door, Uncle Sam's secretary acted like it was the second coming.

"Mr. Latimer, look who's here."

He grabbed his hat and coat off the rack. "Me and Angie going for a Coke-Cola."

We walked across the square, past the courthouse to Mosby's drugstore, and sat in wire chairs at a little marble-topped table. None of the colored people outside could come in here, but I didn't notice that.

The man behind the counter said, "Who's your girlfriend?"

Uncle Sam knew everybody. I felt famous being with him. I ordered a large cherry Coke with lots of crushed ice. Uncle Sam drank black coffee and smoked Chesterfields while he talked to people at other tables. When we were done, he set his hat well back on his head and we retraced our steps.

He told the secretary, "Heading home for lunch." We got in the Cadillac and drove three blocks.

Mateel had a hot lunch ready in the shadowy dining room. Momae waited, sitting at the head of the table dressed in white silk with her pearl starburst pin and red lipstick. Her dark hair fell in perfect waves around her long pale neck. She smelled wonderfully of tobacco and Lily of the Valley dusting powder. We ate without speaking, the only sound our forks clinking against the china. Mateel walked around the table, silent and somehow disapproving, holding out silver serving dishes of vegetables and biscuits while her raisin eyes watched me. Momae smoked all through the meal, using a pearl holder, tossing her head back to blow smoke toward the chandelier and flicking ashes into a tiny crystal dish. After lunch, Uncle Sam went to his room for a nap and Momae went to hers, lying on top of the cover in the pink satin slip. "Momae needs to rest her head, baby." She had a low, husky voice, and lay in an underwater gloom with the shades pulled down against the afternoon sun and a damp cloth over her eyes. Mama said my aunt was plagued by headaches.

I was expected to lie down too, but I didn't have to sleep. I sat on top of the quilted satin comforter and read the books I checked out of the one-room library in the courthouse. When naps were done, we each drank a Coke-Cola. Uncle Sam and I had ours in bottles. Their refrigerator kept drinks so cold there were little chips of brown ice floating at the top of each bottle. Momae had her Coke in a glass with ice and a spoonful of spirits of ammonia. "A little pick-me-up," she called it.

In the midafternoon, Momae had ladies over for canasta. They played on the sunporch, a glassed-in room on the front corner of the house off the living room. I'd never heard of a sunporch. It seemed extremely elegant. Four of them sat around a wooden card table with little dishes of candy and nuts on the corners. The game used so many cards, they had a machine to shuffle them. I liked to watch them play because they said nice things about me.

"You are such a cute little girl."

"Isn't she an angel?"

Momae would agree that I was indeed one of the heavenly hosts.

"And smart, too, I'll bet."

I ducked my head, acknowledging the truth.

"Look at that smile. Have you ever seen anything so adorable?"

I could take a lot of this before I got bored.

Late in the day, I rode with Uncle Sam out to the farm. His land was leased to a black tenant, who lived with several small children and no visible wife in a cabin by the edge of a dusty road. While he and Uncle Sam talked about corn and soybeans, I played in the dirt with the man's children. One little girl didn't wear underpants, so I pulled mine off and gave them to her. Nobody noticed until we got back to town.

"Where are your underpants?" Momae was laughing so it was okay to tell the truth.

"I gave them to a little colored girl."

Uncle Sam said, "Why in the world did you do that?"

"Because she didn't have any."

"Don't that beat all?" He slapped a thigh and did his belly laugh.

Momae said, "Keep that up and you won't have any either."

The best part of being with them was they never got mad. They didn't hand out blame, which meant I never needed to lie. Neither of them had a poisonous soft voice like Miss Hosford or yelled like Mama. They thought I was fine just the way I was. And they taught me things, like how to play hearts and eat olives.

I loved sleeping in that house. The bed was so high, I had to use a little wooden step to climb in. Under the peach comforter, there were pink sheets. I propped myself on two pillows with the entire bed to myself. No Mary Elizabeth snuffling next to me. Uncle Sam and Momae let me decide when to turn off the light. I stayed awake as long as I could, reading and listening to the faint sound of Uncle Sam's radio. Then I reached under the ruffled lampshade, clicked the light off and curled like a shell under the covers. I always felt safe there. I still had the dream about German soldiers, but it didn't scare me as much.

In the morning, I lay in bed, looked out at the day, sipped the awful coffee and thought about things. I heard church bells. It was Easter Sunday and I would go to the Baptist Church with Momae. Uncle Sam was Methodist like us, but he didn't go to church. Their son, Sam Junior, didn't either. Momae said they were heathens.

When I started school at Canton Elementary, I'd get to see Momae and Uncle Sam all the time. I could play in Momae's cedar chest and visit the library whenever I wanted. The lady in charge had let me rearrange the books by a system I invented: the color of their covers. We agreed this was a terrific idea. A person could come in and say, "I feel like a red book today," and there they would be, all together.

Mama was back and life looked pretty good. I was so happy I didn't mind Pickens Consolidated. My grades improved. I wouldn't be held back after all. In class, I squinted my eyes and looked around, thinking, I will never have to see a single one of you again. This was my first experience of solving a problem by leaving.

5

It was summer and I forgot all my reasons for hating the hotel. Summer at Allison's Wells was paradise.

The season began on Memorial Day. In the weeks before, we did housecleaning. The worst of the furniture got hauled outside to be scrubbed and painted. Iron bedsteads, dressers, four-drawer chests, bedside tables, and chairs were deposited on the front lawn. I considered myself artistic, so Miss Hosford made me a painter. Ora Dee, Preston, and I dutifully slapped two coats on each piece, aqua, pale yellow, or off-white. At first, I loved it, the smell of the oil paint when the lid came off the can and the way the brush looked, thick and dripping. All day we piled new paint over old, covering the chipped places, cigarette burns, and water spots. My enthusiasm faded.

Miss Hosford came by at regular intervals to revive our flagging spirits. "Keep up the good work. Everything's looking just grand." She believed in paint.

Once the paint dried, I was allowed to decorate. At eight, I specialized in daisies, tulips, and rosebuds, painting them relentlessly across the fronts of drawers and headboards. My pink, red, and yellow flowers were surrounded by dabs of green meant to be leaves. This was not just painting; this was art. I fantasized that guests would be struck by the beauty of their furniture. They would ask Miss Hosford, "Who painted this?" "Not a child? You don't mean it. Come here, child, and let me give you a quarter." Or even a nickel.

My flowers grew more abstract, their leaves floated further away. I slumped. Miss Hosford took over. She didn't do flowers. She painted V-shaped swoops, like bird wings, and wavelike curves in loud primary colors. She called it her Mexican motif. The furniture was declared done and hauled back into rooms onto freshly painted green wooden floors.

Everyone at the hotel except Lena, the cook, gave up regular chores to help with spring cleaning. Under Parthenia's supervision, rusty springs were carried out and scrubbed, stained mattresses hung over the banisters to air. Windows and screens were washed. New straw mats were placed by the beds, starched cotton bedspreads smoothed into place, and two thin towels folded on rods next to the basins.

Ora Dee told me about the time Miss Hosford went away during the annual cleanup and a couple arrived early looking for a room. "You know how we look when we're cleaning." She pointed to her stained uniform. "Here comes Parthenia, limping along on her bad leg. She's going to talk to them. They see Ellis carrying one of them nasty mattresses and Savannah walking with that lope of hers. Preston comes up grinning like a mule, his waiter's jacket black as dirt. Not a white person in sight. Those people jumped in their car and just flew out of here. They thought the whole place was run by niggers."

I snickered nervously. Ora Dee had used the forbidden word. They were colored or Negroes, but never the other. We weren't allowed to say it. It was a mouth-washing offense. I knew the rules were different if they called themselves that, but I felt odd laughing. Miss Hosford wouldn't like the story anyway. She would be upset over losing the business.

When everything was done, we stood back and admired our work. We were filled with hope. "It's going to be a good season," Miss Hosford said. "I can feel it." We weren't a fancy place, and we didn't charge fancy prices—seven to twelve dollars a day, for lodging and three meals. The hotel brochure boasted, "Running water in every room." Every room did have a sink, but in some the toilet and tub were shared or down the hall.

None of us admitted the truth. No matter how good the season looked, the cash coming in would never match the cash going out, or slow the inexorable decay: the failing furnace, termites, dry rot, worn wiring, the thousand plagues that used all of Miss Hosford's energy and Uncle John's salary. Except for Doug's school, every cent they made was poured into the black hole of possibility that was Allison's Wells.

The hotel filled up on Memorial Day weekend and stayed full through Labor Day. That summer I was eight and allowed to work in the office for the first time, operating the enormous nickel-plated cash register. I stood on a wooden stool and rang the drawer open officiously, made change, sorted the paper money by denomination, fastened the bills under clips in the correct slots, and dropped coins into the cupped metal sections. To my eyes, the cash register held a fortune. I couldn't understand why the family worried. We were rich. Sometimes I got to register new people, filling out a card with their names printed at the top, last name first. I rang a big bell that hung outside so that Ellis or Preston, who were bellboys as well as waiters, could come get the bags. Registration cards were kept in slots on a wooden board, one slot for each room. I loved looking at the board when there was not a slot open and Mama would say on the telephone: I'm sorry, we don't have a thing.

All charges were put on the card. The room came with meals, but guests could buy water mugs, hot sulfur baths, massages, horseback rides, and tennis balls. Nobody paid or tipped until they checked out, though if they were staying longer than a week, Miss Hosford might clear her throat and suggest a little something on account.

Mary Elizabeth and I were supposed to do whatever we could to help. Miss Hosford believed in work even more than paint. She liked to see people doing something useful every minute of the day, especially children, who could be made to work for nothing. Silently she'd come upon us where we were not exactly hiding but keeping out of her way and, in her silky voice, she'd say: "There you are. Ora Dee needs help with the peaches." Or, "Run out to the garden before the sun gets hot and pick enough beans for dinner." Or, "It rained last night. Why don't you get those weeds out from around the roses before the ground dries out."

My sister and I would be on our knees in the rose beds, legs covered with damp red sawdust, and she'd come smiling by wearing a straw hat and carrying her basket and clippers. "Aren't we having fun?"

We mocked her when she'd passed safely out of hearing. *Aren't we having fun?*

On Saturdays, we killed chickens for Sunday dinner. This was not nearly as disgusting as it sounds. Our pet chickens, Reddy and Brownie, came to the hotel with us in a crate in the trunk of the car. They'd been put into a big pen with the hotel chickens. After a week, neither of them seemed to know me. After a month I couldn't find them. I ran crying to Mama.

"We've eaten Reddy and Brownie."

She said, "Don't be ridiculous. Of course we haven't."

I knew we had. There went something else I loved. I minded, but I blamed myself. I had not paid attention to them the way I did back home. I tried not to fuss. Being at Allison's Wells had not improved Mama's disposition. Too much carrying on could get me switched—or even slapped.

Once our pets disappeared, Mary Elizabeth and I had no personal feeling for chickens. Allen brought the ones to be slaughtered around behind the kitchen. Each of us grabbed a bird and held it by the neck with one hand. I shouted, "One-two-three-go." We swung the chickens, flapping and squawking, around our heads. It only took two or three swings for the heads to separate from the bodies. The rest of the chicken went flying, feet clawing the air, turning somersaults in the woodchips where it landed, and running around in headless bloody circles until it fell over dead. We had two contests. The first was to see whose chicken could flap the longest without its head. The second, after we gutted them, was to count the eggs inside. Whoever found the most soft, yellowish, half-formed eggs won. In between these two contests, we had to dunk the chickens in water, boiling blackly in a cast-iron cauldron over an open fire. Holding the headless carcasses by their horny yellow feet, we dipped and dipped, then tugged the feathers out in clumps. I hated that part. Wet chicken feathers smelled nasty.

We carried the picked chickens upstairs to Jimmy Lee, who worked in a dark, stinky room on the west side of the kitchen. Dirty dishes were brought here to be scraped free of leftovers, which went into the slop barrel. The dishes were then rinsed, soaped, and scalded. Jimmy Lee was in charge of every plate, bowl, and glass used for the hundreds of meals we served. He was not like Ellis and Preston. Jimmy Lee was young and carefree. He danced around telling jokes, acting like working in this hot room was nothing. Miss Hosford said he had a lot of outside children and that he couldn't be trusted. We knew about that. Jimmy Lee helped unpack the moving van when my aunt and uncle shipped their furniture from Chattanooga. Missing items turned up at his house. Nobody called the sheriff. Jimmy Lee was not hauled away to jail. He was given a stern talking to by Uncle John, and marked as untrustworthy. He would never be promoted out of the dark side of the kitchen.

Free of the chickens, Mary Elizabeth and I turned our attention to the slop barrel. Mesmerized, we stood on our toes, holding our noses, and gazed in fascination at the liquefying scraps of everything not eaten. That summer my sister carried a little purse with her everywhere. Peering into the slop barrel, she dropped it, and sobbed as it sank into the brownish goo. Hoisting herself up the side of the barrel, she leaned in to try and retrieve it. I observed this as if from another planet, knowing what would happen. Her weight toppled her over the edge and in she went, head first. When she could get her mouth free, she screamed. I thought, *Help, murder, police. My sister fell in the grease.* Except it was worse than grease. She sat there with terrible stuff dripping off of her and I laughed so hard I was paralyzed. Jimmy Lee came running from the sinks, and Ellis and Johnny from the kitchen. They pulled her out and wiped off the worst of it. They thought I pushed her, and I was laughing too hard to defend myself.

Every night, Alan wrestled the full slop barrel down the back stairs, put it on the wagon, and drove it up to the pigs. Everything went in a circle at Allison's Wells, because after the first hard frost, the pigs got fed back to us.

On the days we didn't kill chickens, we picked blackberries or plums for dessert. Blackberries grew along the road to Way, the vines thick, dusty, and prickly. We came home with full buckets and scratched arms, our legs covered in chigger bites. Plums grew on the path to the gullies, which was an entirely different thing.

At least once a week during that summer of 1944, Mary Elizabeth and I walked the mile to the gullies barefooted with our tin buckets banging against our shins. We went past the barn and over the hill. The wild plums grew on either side of the path. In June and July, they ripened on bushes not much taller than our heads. There were two kinds: tart pink plums with big pits, and fat, sweet yellow ones with small pits. We trailed our toes in the dust or ran through the cooler grass between picking. We talked, getting quieter as the buckets grew heavy. First we got the fruit we could reach. Dragging the buckets, we squatted and worked our way under the low branches, through and around to the other side. We ate the choicest plums, tight and shiny in their skins, smooth on the tongue. When bitten, they squirted a stream of tart juice in your mouth and left sweet pulp and a bitter skin. We sucked the pits clean and spit them far out into the grass. The heat felt good on our backs. We liked the floury dust of the path and being free from grown-ups under the white summer sky. Nobody to boss us, and nowhere to be until lunchtime.

When the buckets filled, we left them in the shade of a plum bush and climbed under the barbed-wire fence to cross the field to the gullies. A cow or bull lived in this field. I couldn't tell which because it was always sitting down. It had enormous horns and eyes that followed us, the slow head turning to watch our approach. I was terrified of the beast and pushed Mary Elizabeth along ahead of me. We walked slowly across the immense emptiness toward the safety of the gully's edge. The cow looked us over deciding if we were worth getting up for, worth chasing and goring. I knew better than to wear red. Red aroused its killer instincts. We wore white, dusty white by now. I knew better than to run because that would make the cow get up and gallop, and galloping was faster than running. In my worst fantasy, the cow caught up with us. I imagined its sharp yellow horn going through my back and me screaming as it came out in front through my shirt, a bloody ivory curve just to the left of my navel. Mary Elizabeth and I acted extremely casual, never meeting the cow's eye, cutting a wide path around where it sat in the shade of the only tree, picking up the pace as we got past halfway.

"Slow down," I warned my sister. "You're practically running."

"It's getting up." She pulled out of my grasp.

"No, it's not. Stop shouting. Are you trying to make it mad?"

Sprinting the last few feet, we flung ourselves over the edge into the gully where presumably cows couldn't follow.

Miss Hosford said the gullies were once part of the old Natchez Trace, an ancient Indian trail. We didn't care about that. The gullies were our personal Grand Canyon. Erosion from a stream had cut abrupt fissures in an otherwise normal pasture, as if a hand had reached down and split the earth into a network of red wounds, ten, twenty, thirty feet deep. We scampered down the sandy banks and played on the bottom. There were layers in the sandstone cliffs, red, salmon pink, white, and yellow. The bottom was a checkerboard of cracked red clay.

The twisted formations were perfect for games. The high walls echoed and made our voices enormous. We played king and castle, climbing the buttes, slipping and sliding, the winner declaring herself king of all she surveyed. We played Indian and settler with blood-curdling screams and lots of scalping. We played princess and evil fairy godmother. I much preferred being the evil godmother, casting spells that froze my sister in place or turned her into a frog. Some days I put her to sleep until the prince arrived and then I turned into the prince.

We had no gender in those summer days. We were small beings, neither male nor female. We became whatever our imaginations stretched around, unbothered by the blistering heat or the red sand coating our skin and clothes.

One day, while we rested, I spotted a snake, the monster snake of all creation. It must have been ten feet long and bigger around than my leg. I held my breath and watched as it eased itself, foot by foot, into a hole in the opposite cliff. When it was gone and only the hole remained, I couldn't believe my eyes. No snake could be that big. Mary Elizabeth hadn't seen it. I tried to show her, stretching my arms, but she looked skeptical.

On Saturdays, Miss Hosford ran what she called the Canyon Express. Preston drove guests in an open-bed truck with a fake steam engine made of plywood nailed to the front. Guests sat on benches in back and were hauled out to the gullies for a picnic lunch. It was one of our aunt's many ideas to make extra money. We thought it extremely dumb to bump out there and eat dry sandwiches in the sun. We didn't go near the gullies on Canyon Express days.

During the week, when the sun moved straight over the Gullies, we climbed back up the sandstone walls. The distance to the fence seemed only half as far going home, and the cow always looked the other way. Safely under, we brushed off as much red sand as we could and picked up our plum buckets, each with a hover of gnats. These plums would be cobbler with hard sauce by suppertime. Guests left polite piles of plum pits on the sides of their plates. We walked slowly back, not talking much, past the barn, the smokehouse, woodshed, and up the steep steps to the kitchen.

We could hear Lena screaming, "*Wood, wood.*" Johnny and Jimmy Lee came running past us on their way to the woodpile. Lena was president of the kitchen, the boss of everyone. She was famous for her terrible temper. "I'll take an axe to your head," she'd say. "I'll bust your hide off." "I want to see that wood box *full.*" Everybody ran when she yelled, but not fast enough to suit Lena. According to her, they were all lazy and shiftless and made her life a misery.

In my opinion, the kitchen at Allison's Wells defined good cooking. I was proud of our Duncan Hines recommendation because Miss Hosford said we should be, not because I had any idea who Duncan Hines might be. My aunt claimed he was a famous food critic and everybody who was anybody respected his opinion and coveted one of his recommendations.

The portions we served weren't large, but they were exactly right for a child. It was wartime, but as a hotel and farm, we got extra rations. The sugar went into desserts. Guests no longer got seconds on coffee, and there wasn't a lot of fancy meat, but Miss Hosford never believed much in meat. Too expensive.

We raised chickens for eggs, frying, and broiling. Vegetables from the garden were plentiful all summer. Ora Dee skimmed cream off the milk and churned it into butter. The leftover milk sat in a covered dish in a dark corner and turned into something disgusting called clabber, which people who didn't know better sprinkled with sugar and ate. Alan killed a hog or two in the fall and we cured bacon, hams, and sausage in the smokehouse. Ora Dee made blackberry and plum jam. Alan carried cane to a nearby mill to be squeezed and boiled down into sorghum.

For breakfast, Lena cooked cornmeal pancakes and each table had a silver pitcher with a hinged lid, full of thick, golden syrup. For lunch and dinner there was always a first course of soup or a fruit cup. Guests were served salad and homemade bread—flaky biscuits, crisp corn sticks, or soft, buttery rolls—with their main course. I don't remember much about the real food: lots of homegrown vegetables, chicken, pork chops, one of the cheaper cuts of beef. Guests could order steak if they wanted, but that cost extra. Both lunch and dinner ended with dessert, sometimes a choice of desserts, twice a day, seven days a week.

There were enormous pans of blackberry cobbler with a tender doughy crust and sweet purple syrup bubbling over the sugary top.

Cobbler was served warm, in squares, with a dab of hard sauce. Miss Hosford made the hard sauce because it contained whiskey. She whipped up a fluffy mixture of butter, sugar, and bourbon that melted slowly over the top of a warm cobbler. Lena made yellow cakes with thick caramel icing that broke like fudge under a fork, and lemon meringue pies tart enough to bring tears. Fresh peach cobblers were served when peaches came in season, or homemade peach ice cream with Lena's pecan-topped sugar cookies. When there was no fresh fruit, we had peppery gingerbread with lemon sauce. The only dessert I didn't care for was something called the Allison's Wells Special, a wet cake floating in a floury brown sauce. It was disgusting.

When lunch was ready, Ellis rang a large bell attached to a post on the front lawn. The first bell was for children, and everyone under twelve took off for the Children's Porch, a narrow screened room running the length of the main dining room. Visiting children were my responsibility and I commanded all meals, telling people where to sit and, like a ship's captain, putting my favorites near me. I explained the food and monitored behavior. No rule breaking unless I initiated it. Occasionally, maybe once or twice a summer, I allowed food throwing. It caused loud screaming which attracted the attention of grown-ups in the next room. Freedom on the Children's Porch depended on keeping a low profile, and food throwing put Ellis and Preston in a foul mood for days.

I never stopped to think, in those blind days, that these were men—brown, but grown men like my father—waiting on us and cleaning up our messes. I lived inside a dream.

After lunch, Mary Elizabeth and I were supposed to take a nap. In the summertime, when the hotel filled up, guests were given first choice of the oscillating fans. There was seldom one left for us. We took our naps on the screened porch where we slept in summer, at the back of the family quarters, down the porch from the kitchen and far away from the paying customers. Outside the kitchen there was a one-story wing, containing Lena's room, an ironing room, linen storage, my cousin Doug's room, Mama's, our sleeping porch, and a dark, mildewy bathroom. The building turned a corner and Miss Hosford and Uncle John had a living room, bedroom, and bath. The family wing was built high off the ground and, underneath, Uncle John had his shop. In one corner, under their living room, he built a special place for Miss Hosford, a screened room with a brick floor, where she retired for naps, and where special guests were invited for drinks in the late afternoon. We called this the Retreat. Only Lena's room, with its ancient gas heater, could be used in winter.

We hated naps. We'd lie on our cots on the screened porch in the baking stillness after lunch, watching heat waves rise off the cornstalks in the garden below. Wearing only cotton underpants, we complained listlessly about the way sweat glued our legs together. We put pillows between our knees. We breathed through our mouths in the thick air and brushed flies away. We were sure we would never fall asleep. We woke hotter than ever.

In spite of the heat, I loved summer. Allison's Wells was popular during the war. With gas rationed, thirty miles was as far as families could travel for a vacation. The rooms were cheap and the food good. Most people arrived with children, children I could boss around or ignore. We spent all day outdoors and I could run the full length of the gravel driveway barefoot without feeling the rocks.

One day, Mother sent one of the help's daughters along to make sure we went down for our nap. I'll call her Rosalie. She was maybe twelve and already working at the hotel during the summer. There was no cot for her, so she curled up at the foot of mine. Mary Elizabeth and I took off our shirt and shorts and we made Rosalie take off her dress. Lying there in our cotton underpants, I was fascinated by the difference in our bodies. I laid my arm next to Rosalie's. "Look."

She nodded. "I'm colored."

"Colored what?" I was teasing her.

"Black."

"You're not black, you're kind of purple."

"I am not purple."

"Just where the sun hits."

Mary Elizabeth watched from her cot, sucking her fingers.

I put my palm next to Rosalie's. They were the same color. We looked in each other's mouths. Both pink, except Rosalie didn't have any dark fillings.

She had just started to get breasts. Instead of flat nipples like ours, hers were soft and puffy.

"Can I touch?"

She nodded without looking at me. I reached out and pressed one. It was like velvet, like a cow's udder. I touched it again. Rosalie watched my finger without comment. I felt swollen with power. She would do anything I asked. What I did next, I'm ashamed of to this day.

"Take off your underpants." Would she do that?

She looked at me crooked.

"I want to see." I tried to sound like my mother.

She pulled her pants off and sat cross-legged on the bed. Mary Elizabeth got up to look. We were totally quiet, awestruck. Between Rosalie's legs, growing from her purple-black skin, was the lightest covering of fuzz. Between her split, I saw pink, as pink as the inside of her mouth. It looked wet and complex.

"Pull it apart," I said.

She held open the lips of that secret place. I bent and looked as far up into her as I could. There was no end of pink complication. A lazily circling fly landed there. Mary Elizabeth and I sucked in our breath. Rosalie watched with interest. Another fly arrived, then another. They crawled around inside her. We watched, hypnotized.

"Don't move," I said. "Let's see how many come." I felt dizzy with excitement. Seven flies now explored Rosalie's depths, flexing their iridescent wings, rubbing their front legs.

Footsteps sounded on the porch. Rosalie dove for her underpants. Mary Elizabeth and I hit our pillows and squeezed our eyes shut. The steps passed by. My heart pounded so hard that for a few seconds I couldn't speak. I was horribly afraid.

I said, "Don't ever tell. If either one of you says a word, I'll do something terrible." I looked hard at Mary Elizabeth.

She nodded, sucking her fingers again.

Rosalie rolled her eyes like, what's to tell, and turned away.

I lay back down. The world felt dangerous. I didn't like thinking about what I'd made Rosalie do. It was my biggest wrong yet. But the power was like a new muscle. Something I didn't recognize and didn't like had stretched and tested its strength. I could still see Rosalie, sitting cross-legged and obedient. The feeling I got made me press my legs together. Stretched across the end of my bed, Rosalie had her eyes closed pretending to sleep.

I spoke into the hot quiet. "You can't tell a single soul for the rest of your lives. Swear?"

"Swear." They said it without looking at me and I was still afraid.

6

For days, I watched Rosalie. Wherever I caught sight of her, working in the kitchen or helping Savannah with the rooms, I tried to read her face. Had she told anyone? Was she going to tell? Did she hate me? I didn't dare ask. Asking would re-create the event. If I kept quiet, maybe she'd keep quiet. Maybe we'd both forget.

I didn't worry so much about Mary Elizabeth. She was only five and she forgot a lot. She was also terrified of me. Guilt hung like a cloud over every day. The bad thing had happened. I couldn't wish it away. If either one of them talked, I'd be deep in what Parthenia called "the cup of shame." In one instant, I would go from being a darling child to a terrible person. It made me feel sick to think about life turning on you like that. It was the first thing I thought about when I woke up and the last thing before I fell asleep. The fear of being caught nibbled at all my pleasures. I went to a war movie in Canton about soldiers creeping inside dark buildings, expecting the enemy around every corner. I crept around inside my life like that. Yet I saw nothing bad in Rosalie's eyes. A month went by and she hadn't told. I started to relax. But I'd learned a lesson. If you do a bad thing and someone knows, you're never safe.

One afternoon I found Rosalie sitting on the steps outside the kitchen, the ones leading to Uncle John's shop. We were allowed to play together here, out of sight of the guests, when Rosalie didn't have a job to do. Our friendship, if that's what it was, was the back-door kind.

She had a big square of cold cornbread left over from lunch. I sat down and watched her chew, my mouth watering.

"Want a piece?" She broke a chunk off.

The cornbread passing from her hand to mine felt like forgiveness. I opened my mouth to take a bite off the far side, a place with no chance of having Rosalie spit on it.

"I hope I don't see what I think I'm seeing." I hadn't heard Mother coming up behind us. "You know we don't eat other people's food." Her heels clicked away.

I put the cornbread down on the step between us. We didn't look at each other. She finished her piece, brushed the crumbs off her hands and stood up. "Parthenia needs me to sweep."

I sat there feeling ashamed. We didn't eat other people's food, that part was true. At the dinner table, Miss Hosford not only forbade talking about the food; she wouldn't allow sharing, swapping, or even tasting off another person's plate. But that was not what Mother meant. Hadn't I tried to bite as far as I could get from where Rosalie's mouth had been?

I'd been taught by indirection that colored people didn't keep themselves clean the way we did. Contact outside of service was abhorrent. The disgust, which we never admitted to, came inextricably mixed with admiration, a tangle of emotions that beamed over Lena's cobbler, but backed away from sharing a bite with the dark hands that made it. I never tried to sort things out. I accepted life the way I breathed the air.

Picking pole beans early one morning with my sister and cousin Doug, he kept hinting about something he knew and I didn't. Much as I wanted to find out what he was talking about, I couldn't stand giving in to his bossiness. We moved along the rows, lifting the wet leaves, pinching off the beans, which hung in the dusky shade like green fingers. Doug didn't usually do chores with us. Miss Hosford spoiled him on account of his weak chest. For some reason he was out here, showing her he didn't need to be coddled, but his mouth worked more than his hands.

Curiosity won. I said, "What is it?"

"Wouldn't you like to know?" He loved lording it over us.

I waited.

He leaned toward me and whispered. "The Blue Geese arrive today."

I pictured a flock of large blue birds descending onto the front lawn, which, I had to admit, would be amazing. "How do you know?"

"They made reservations. They're insurance people."

I slumped.

"Mother says they can get a little crazy, but the money's good."

Miss Hosford was always thinking up new ways to make money. "Crazy how?"

"You'll see."

"Tell me now."

He made his voice a whine. "*Tell me now.*"

I truly hated Doug Fontaine. I moved to another row to put some distance between us.

Before lunch, Miss Hosford put me to work on the screen porch on the east side of the kitchen. This was where salads were made, fruit peeled and chopped, tea poured into ice-filled glasses, and hooked with lemon slices. When I helped in the kitchen, this was my place.

I was peeling peaches for fruit cocktail alongside Ora Dee and her cousin Bessie May, almost hypnotized by the way the skins slipped off with a nudge of the small, dull knife. My head was filled with the smell of ripe fruit, my hands dripping with juice.

Next door, the kitchen was all dark heat and hollering as lunch approached, but out here it was peaceful with the three of us working side by side. The air was still except for the buzzing of a fly and the click of our knives on the peach stones.

A rare and blessed thing happened: Bessie May and Ora Dee forgot I was there.

"He married down," Ora Dee said. "She's a black little thing."

I didn't know who he or the black little thing was, but I knew enough not to ask. I pulled in my elbows to make myself smaller, and practically quit breathing.

Bessie May said, "It's a shame."

Two words, not "ashamed" like Mother kept saying I should be.

"Not like Ellis," Ora Dee went on. "Him and Gert made them some pretty children."

They nodded agreement over their bowls. Ellis's children were light, almost yellow, with freckles. Light was better. Dark was bad.

I had never thought about how colored people got light or dark. I didn't know how any babies got made. I stood there, silent as the peach stones, with something new to figure out.

The answer came a few years later when I read a novel by Frank Yerby. (My mother and her friends passed his books around, but I don't believe one of them knew the writer was a Negro.) *The Foxes of Harrow* talked about a quadroon, and truth arrived like a knife—white people and colored people had sex. That meant the same people who wouldn't share food with Negroes for fear of being contaminated managed to overcome their disgust enough to mix bodily fluids. I thought of it as white men doing it with black women (fear of black men had been implanted in us girls along with the other taboos, and I couldn't imagine the reverse). I saw it happening in the dark—lust overcoming the forbidden—the deed never seeing the light of day. The results, the lighter children, were kept on the colored side of the barrier.

No one in my family ever spoke of why Ellis was lighter, or that his great-great-grandfather might have also been ours. The very idea would have been loathsome, and yet there it was, staring us in the face every day.

New questions didn't keep me from showing up outside the office to watch the Blue Goose people check in. That's what they were called, not Blue Geese. They looked ordinary enough, middle-aged men, heavy around the stomach, with chirpy, sweet-voiced wives in damp traveling dresses. To my disappointment, they didn't look a bit crazy.

"You'll see." Doug gave my arm a twisting pinch.

"Stop it." I grabbed Mary Elizabeth. "Come on, let's find Mama and get a nickel for a candy bar." Doug was allowed to ring open the cash drawer and take a nickel anytime he wanted. I would never dare, even when I was alone in the office. One false ring and every grown-up on the place would come running, probably with the Canton police.

We found Mama in Miss Hosford's bed with her legs up and begged for a nickel.

"It's too close to supper for candy. Rub my feet, baby."

She always wanted me to do this, and I hated it, but I knew the places her feet had been. Mary Elizabeth and I did the chores we were forced into, but we spent the rest of the time swimming and playing. Miss Hosford and Mama divided the work of managing the hotel. Miss Hosford never seemed to hurry, but Mama woke up running and ran until she fell into bed. Her feet always hurt. I grabbed one and started to rub.

Mama leaned back against Hosford's bed pillows, giving an appreciative groan every now and then to keep me at it. Mama was proud of her feet. She wore size four and a half, triple-A shoes, but when you rubbed her feet, you saw that her toes were bent double, and each one had a corn on top. The condition was called hammertoes. She had high arches and had worn heels for so long, her Achilles tendons shrank and she couldn't put her feet down flat. Even her bedroom shoes had wedge heels. The tiny white foot with its bent toes and yellow corns looked awful and felt awful to touch, but I saw how much pleasure the rubbing gave her.

In those days, the smaller a woman's foot, the more darling you were. Miss Hosford claimed her feet were size three and a half, but Mary Elizabeth and I figured she was just trying to stay ahead.

I continued rubbing Mama's feet, listening to Miss Hosford in the bathroom splashing in the tub. Ellis arrived. He stood in the half-open bathroom door, staring at the floor, taking orders about the Blue Goose people.

"It's a Backwards Dinner," Miss Hosford said. "Remind Lena or she'll forget and get upset."

"Yes'm."

Ellis left.

Mama laughed.

"What?" Miss Hosford pulled the plug and water sucked down the ancient pipes.

Mama raised her voice. "Talking to him while you're bathing."

Miss Hosford said, "Don't be silly."

I could see her toes on the mat and imagined the rest: pendulous white breasts with enormous brown nipples, wide hips, round, birth-wrinkled stomach, dimpled thighs. A thatch of light brown hair between her legs. Mary Elizabeth and I had taken orders from that bathroom door. I could never bring myself to look at my aunt straight on. I took darting glances so my eyes wouldn't have a fit.

"You have to admit it's a little strange." I could tell Mama didn't care.

"Ellis would never look at me," Miss Hosford said. "Nor would any of the other servants."

Mother made a doubtful noise.

Miss Hosford was talking about the rule—a colored man could not look a white woman in the eye. Not ever. When Miss Hosford told Alan what to do in the garden or Ellis in the dining room, they stared at a spot on the ground in front of her shoes. No matter what she said, they said, "Yes'm" and didn't look up.

Mary Elizabeth and I used to giggle about it at night on the sleeping porch. We agreed that although Ellis, Preston, and Jimmy Lee might appear to be staring at the floor, they probably knew what every inch of Miss Hosford looked like.

It was time for drinks in the Retreat. That hour before dinner was the closest Mama came to relaxing. Miss Hosford unlocked the liquor cabinet. The three or four invited guests arrived and everyone talked and sipped bourbon or scotch and water from silver mint julep cups. Mary Elizabeth and I knew how to mix and pass drinks before we were tall enough to see over the table. Mama enjoyed chatting with guests, asking them where they were from and what they did. It gave her a taste of the world, and was as close as she got to being back at the Jackson Country Club.

I slipped away to see what was going on with the Blue Goose people. For the banquet that night, Ellis and Preston had set up long tables on the front lawn, covered them with white cloths and put out napkins, silverware, and flowers. A sign on an easel said "Blue Goose Backwards Dinner."

I approached the lady putting place cards around the table. She had little beads of perspiration above her top lip. "What's a Backwards Dinner?"

"Just like it sounds, honey. Dessert first, soup last."

"I never heard of that."

"Well, you should just come, shouldn't you? What's your name?"

I told her.

She filled out a blue card. "I'll put you right here next to me."

When I looked, she'd made me "Norman."

I didn't ask Mama. She might have said no. I was trying to grow up and a Backwards Dinner was a new experience. When seven o'clock arrived, I was standing behind my place. The woman, who said to call her Miss Verna, was dressed in pink with an artificial pink flower pinned to her dress. She even smelled pink.

She caught me sniffing. "It's Carnation."

She was married to the head goose. The men had on dinner jackets and were sweating, either from the dressy clothes or the drinking. The Fishes Club, where grown-ups went to drink, had been packed all day. Extra waiters had been hired to carry trays of drinks and snacks back and forth to the pool. Preston and Parthenia were booked solid with massages. The hotel was full and everybody was spending money. Miss Hosford was in heaven.

Miss Verna's husband got up and made a speech about character, charity, and fellowship, which were the watchwords of the Honorable Order of Blue Goose International since 1907. He addressed the others as ganders. These geese were from the Tennessee Pond and the meeting was called a Grand Nest.

I wanted him to hurry up because Rosalie had just put a piece of lemon meringue pie in front of me. When she was working, Rosalie pretended she'd never set eyes on me. I wondered if any other people at this table had secrets they couldn't bear to hear spoken.

Finally, the head goose finished, there was a prayer, and I could start. I tried to eat really slowly, letting the sourness make my mouth draw up. I loved lemon meringue pie. For Christmas, somebody sent Miss Hosford a jar of lemon curd and she let me have a spoonful. It was divine, like lemon pie without the crust or meringue. I could have eaten the whole jar, but she said it was a delicacy and we could only have one spoonful. Sweets were my weakness. They always had been. When I was five, I ate the meringue off an entire chocolate pie. I tried to stop myself and afterwards I told Mama there'd never been a meringue, but it didn't work.

I wasn't as good at lying as Clever Gretel in my favorite fairy tale. She was roasting chickens for her master's dinner guest. As they turned on the spit, they smelled so delicious and looked so brown and crisp, she couldn't resist eating a wing, which had begun to burn. The chicken looked unbalanced, so she ate the other wing and then the legs. A wingless, legless chicken looked ridiculous, so she ate the rest. One roast chicken was not enough to feed the guest, so she ate the second chicken, too. When the guest arrived, Gretel warned him not to go in, saying the master had invited him as a ruse and was sharpening his knife to cut off his ears. Hearing the sound of sharpening as the master prepared to carve his chickens, the guest fled. Gretel said, "Master, master, your guest has stolen your roast chickens and run away." The master went after him, knife in hand, shouting, "One, only one," meaning leave me one chicken, and the guest, thinking he meant to take only one ear, ran faster. I shared Gretel's knack for getting into trouble, but lacked her invention.

Around the table, tipsy, red-faced men and their dressed-up

wives scraped their pie plates clean. Down came plates of steak with baked potatoes and beans, probably the beans we picked the day before. Steak was a treat, but it didn't look nearly as good after pie.

Verna said, "There's one rule for a Backwards Dinner, honey. You have to eat everything on your plate."

Mama walked by. She stopped and gave my shoulders a squeeze that looked like affection, but hurt. "Look who's here?" Using her false happy voice.

Miss Verna said, "I invited her. She's just darling."

I smiled up at Mama. I'd hear about this later—me and a steak. I ate it, along with some of the potato. I pushed the beans around. Rosalie passed a basket of rolls and wouldn't look at me. More than one thing at this dinner was backwards. There were two worlds, the friend world and the servant world, and they never overlapped.

Dinner plates were removed and salads arrived. I really didn't want salad. I ate a few pieces of lettuce because Miss Verna was watching. I didn't want her to think she'd wasted a dinner on me.

Her husband got up to talk again. There were toasts. People were recognized for this and that. Salad disappeared and soup appeared, vegetable soup with chopped stuff floating in it. I couldn't possibly swallow soup. I stirred it with my spoon, watching bits surface and sink, waiting for dinner to be over. I felt imprisoned between Miss Verna and the anonymous backside of the man on my right. It had gotten dark.

I said, "May I be excused? They need me in the kitchen."

"Why sure, honey." Miss Verna's eyes didn't quite focus.

"Thank you for inviting me."

"You're very welcome, sweetie." She pressed the pink ring of her mouth into her napkin.

Keeping an eye out for Mama and Miss Hosford, I went to look for more pie. A Backwards Dinner wasn't bad. It just needed to end with pie. I wondered what Daddy would have thought. He had never been crazy about the food at Allison's Wells. He said he always got up from the table hungry. He wasn't crazy about anything at the hotel. I didn't know why, except it was Mama's place, not his, and running a hotel wasn't a profession. It might have been because Miss Hosford stood too close and tended to touch people while she talked. Whenever she asked me to do something and told me how much fun it would be, I pretended Daddy was listening. We laughed to ourselves like hyenas.

Whatever I was doing, I asked myself what Daddy would think. Like I was living in a play and Daddy was the audience. Except, of course, he wasn't. He was so far away he couldn't imagine me.

7

After Labor Day, we closed the place down, washed the linens and stored them for the winter, latched the windows, and unplugged the lamps in the unused wings. The halls of the Cold Part and the Annex echoed under my feet and even the air smelled forgotten. Alan emptied the pool for the last time and dead leaves began to fill the diving well. Preston went back to his family; Ora Dee and Ellis came only on weekends. Bee-Bee, the bartender, left, putting the chairs upside down on the tables and locking the Fishes Club until next summer. Rosalie went back to wherever she went to school without tattling on me. The kitchen felt deserted with only Lena and Johnny there. Lena didn't yell as much.

By this time, my cousin Doug should have left for Baylor, his military school, but Dr. Durfey in Canton told Miss Hosford he was one of those children who failed to thrive. Doug *was* puny. He got sore throats and infections. Every cold settled into his chest and turned into bronchitis. No matter how much Miss Hosford fed him—cream on his oatmeal, pancakes floating in butter and molasses—his ribs stood out like barrel staves.

One day we got into the woody, the hotel station wagon, and took Doug away to Preventorium. Nobody remembers these places anymore. They were modeled on tuberculosis sanatoriums, except they were for children—white children who might get TB.

I don't know how far away Preventorium was. We drove south and it seemed to take all day, but the atmosphere in the back seat grew grimmer with each mile. Usually Doug entertained himself by tormenting me. He was four years older and, in spite of his skinny body, strong enough to win every battle. He liked to give me twisting pinches, contact burns, tickling that turned to torture, all punctuated by a high insane laugh. But today, he stared out his window, morose, refusing every bait I offered. He wouldn't play car games or I Spy. When I poked him, he moved away.

Up front, Mother and Miss Hosford were just as quiet. Mother rolled down the window to smoke. Hosford frowned and made motions toward the back seat, reminding her of Doug's weak lungs. Mother smashed the cigarette out in the tiny car ashtray and drove faster.

We pulled up to a large two-story building, gray and ominously quiet. Nothing moved and the windows reflected trees and sky. A bunch of children came running around a corner of the lawn, chasing and laughing. They wore nothing but underwear. I stared at them all the way up the walk, with Doug trailing, until the big front door closed behind us. I would never be allowed outside dressed like that. We stood in an almost empty lobby. Miss Hosford signed Doug in. Somewhere a door opened and closed. Whatever went on in this place was hidden and muffled. I pictured operating tables with leather straps, knives, and giant needles. A bigger boy came and took Doug away. He went, head down, giving us one backward glance. He was too much like his mother to beg, but the look said, *How could you?* I thought the same thing—how could any mother, even Miss Hosford, leave a child in a place like this?

In the car, we turned back north. Miss Hosford did not cry—I never saw her cry—but she looked beaten. She found nothing to be cheerful about. Doug was her baby. Everything was not going to be fine and dandy.

"I'm sure it's for the best." She wiped her nose on her handkerchief.

"Of course." Mother had visibly brightened once Doug's lungs were out of the car and she could smoke in peace.

"The place has an excellent reputation."

"I've heard the same thing," Mother said.

"But it seems harsh not to let the parents visit."

Mother nodded, touching a ring finger to her tongue to remove a speck of tobacco, and flicking it away.

"And the way they make them dress. Dr. Durfey says it's modeled on sanatoriums in Europe, but running around outside in cotton underwear through a Mississippi winter. It's barbaric."

"They give the girls two bobby pins, did you notice?" Mother's voice held a grin. "It's the only way I could tell them apart."

Miss Hosford ignored her. "All that fresh air and exercise, combined with good nutrition. They must know what they're doing. It's supposed to work wonders."

I spoke up from the back seat. "Where do the puny colored children go?"

"Don't say puny," Mother said.

"Colored children don't get run down." Miss Hosford had on her reprimanding voice. "They thrive on a diet of cornbread and turnip greens cooked in pork fat. I've read that they don't even need to go to the dentist, because the grit in cornmeal keeps their teeth white and strong."

Why didn't Doug live on *that* diet? I did not say this.

The sun was getting low. Mother hiked her skirt up over her knees and jiggled her legs. She was ready for her drink and we were still a long way from home.

I thought about Doug in that scary place as dusk folded around us. I felt pitiless. Looking down at my own plump, healthy body, I was just glad it wasn't me. With him gone, when next summer came, I'd get to be boss of all the kids.

Ordinarily, with the fun over and the hotel deserted, I got depressed, but pretty soon I'd be on a school bus headed south to Canton. That thought kept me happy. Besides, I'd learned to like being alone. I poked around upstairs in the Warm Part and discovered a staircase and a trap door leading to the attic. I climbed into a large dusty space, lit by clouded dormer windows and filled with the abandoned possessions of several generations. A large trunk sat under a dormer. "Ali Baba and the Forty Thieves" was one of my favorite stories. Lifting the lid, I held my breath, hoping for ropes of pearls and piles of gold pieces.

I did find treasure. The trunk was filled with books that must have belonged to Mother, Hosford, and Thelma when they were growing up. I found the entire "Little Colonel" series, thirteen novels about the aristocracy of old Kentucky. The heroine was called the Little Colonel, because her bullying ways reminded the family of her grandfather, who'd been a Confederate colonel. I read every book three times, longing for the Little Colonel's life and my own plantation.

My particular favorite was *The Little Colonel at Boarding School*. In their cozy firelit room at school, the Little Colonel and her friends made fudge in a chafing dish. I couldn't imagine anything more gratifying than making fudge in your own room, and eating as much as you wanted without adult supervision. I had no idea what a chafing dish was. The Little Colonel heated hers with alcohol. I pictured a pan on a tall, three-legged stand with a campfire underneath. When my father returned from the navy, I would ask him to send me away to boarding school. He'd gone to a military school in Tennessee for six years. He never mentioned fudge, and I wouldn't tell him the real reason I wanted to go, but if I got to boarding school and could get my hands on a chafing dish, I knew how to make fudge. I'd watched Mother do it.

I found other books in that trunk, novels where men and women pined, wept, parted, and found each other again. They were my first grown-up books, if you didn't count Tarzan. When we lived on Monroe Street, Daddy bought me a new Tarzan book every time I got sick. We went through the whole set, him reading aloud, me reading to myself after I learned how. When we finished Tarzan, we moved on to Edgar Rice Burroughs's other books like *The Warlords of Mars* and *Pirates of Venus*.

I was enchanted by the pining in those novels from the trunk.

I wondered if it would ever happen to me. I couldn't imagine who might want to kiss me passionately, but I was ready.

When I got tired of being alone and needed someone to talk to, I walked up the hill and visited Parthenia, who lived with her husband, a preacher, in a small cabin. This was the cabin where a band used to stay back in what Miss Hosford called the "glory times," when the hotel made enough money to hire a full-time orchestra for the season.

Parthenia was short with grizzled gray hair and piercing eyes behind rimless glasses. One of her legs had stiffened and she walked with a limp. I'd take them drawings or a story I'd written. Inside the cabin, the weathered silver boards were papered with pictures from magazines. The room had a warm, peppery smell, different from ours. In good weather, Parthenia's husband sat on the front porch in a rocker, dressed in a starched white shirt, buttoned to the neck, and a black suit. He spent his days staring out at the trees with a Bible open in his lap. His pupils were milky and he wore bottle-thick glasses.

When they shooed me off, I'd go back to the kitchen and worry Lena. I climbed onto a tall stool to watch her work. "Parthenia's husband was a preacher before he retired. That's why he always wears a suit."

Lena sniffed. "Some kind of preacher."

There was a rivalry between Lena and Parthenia. I wasn't sure what it was about, but I could never say anything nice to one about the other without being contradicted.

"What kind of preacher was he?" I pinched a piece of batter from the edge of the bowl.

Lena swatted at my fingers with the spoon. The stocking that covered her hair shaped her head like a bean. I sneaked another pinch.

"I'll skin you bald." This time the spoon got me.

I sucked my fingers. "What kind of preacher was he?"

"None of your beeswax, that's what. Get on away from here."

74

Johnny said, "You can help me put up these dishes."

The nice thing about living at Allison's Wells was you could always find somebody glad to see you.

Years later, after Parthenia and her husband were dead, I learned she'd worked at a Negro college. She came to Allison's Wells to nurse her aunt during the 1918 flu epidemic, and stayed on. Her husband was an itinerant preacher and infected her with syphilis. It was a sadder story than any of those novels I found in the trunk.

8

Even when I was impatient for the war to be over, so Daddy would come home and my real life could begin, there were time-outs, stretches that felt open and inviting.

Canton Elementary was like that. It was everything Pickens Consolidated hadn't been. The building was two stories of time-softened red brick with an impressive white marble entrance, and it sat on a grassy lawn shaded by enormous oaks. When Mama went there, it had twelve grades, but the big kids had moved to a new school near the Piggly Wiggly. Eight grades now filled the old, high-ceilinged classrooms. At Pickens Consolidated, my spirit shrank to the size of a raisin. At Canton, I expanded. I colored the best Thanksgiving turkey in fourth grade and won savings stamps. If you collected enough of these, you could buy a war bond. I was selected to present an award in the auditorium to the retiring librarian. The fact that I forgot my lines and stood onstage in mute embarrassment, deaf to prompting, and burned in my bed for weeks afterwards, reliving the event, did not erase the honor. I had been chosen.

I failed to win the school talent contest in spite of a spirited, perhaps too spirited, rendition of "I Wish That I Could Shimmy Like My Sister Kate." I sang breathlessly, wriggling across the stage in what I hoped was a shimmy, trying not to step on Miss Hosford's beaded chemise. A tall, blonde classmate named Sandra Sullivan won, dancing to "I'm a Yankee Doodle Dandy." Dressed as Little Miss Uncle Sam in a star-spangled blue leotard, a red and white striped tailcoat, and a white top hat, wearing shoes covered in silver glitter and tossing a silver baton, she tap-danced her way into the judges' hearts and out of mine. This was my first bitter taste of envy.

I became a scholar again. I didn't have to try harder; in fact I found school much less trying. Fourth grade turned out to be a breeze. I understood everything the teacher said, read books as fast as I could check them out of the library, wrote inspired paragraphs about each one, and flapped my hand like a drowning man, begging to be chosen to read aloud. I never wondered where the colored children went to school. They went somewhere else and it wasn't a question we thought to ask.

I tried making a friend. She was the daughter of Mama's closest childhood pal, so we were supposed to like each other. Her name was Mary Alice. She had shiny black hair and freckles like rust spots on her white skin. She wore large plaid taffeta bows in her curls and lace-edged petticoats under her dresses. She owned a collection of Story Book dolls, which couldn't be played with, only looked at through the cellophane of their boxes. She never got scabs. Our friendship was a prickly business. I couldn't find the words to explain to Mama why I didn't want her to come spend the night at the hotel, but being with her made me feel bad. At her house, in the middle of cutting out paper dolls, she'd say something like, "I think you're nice. I don't care what the others say."

My skin got cold. "What others?"

"Never mind." She'd smile to herself, folding the little paper tabs perfectly over her doll's cardboard shoulders.

I would smart for days, watching my classmates suspiciously.

Our teacher was Miss Ransom, a young woman so full of romance, I watched her in a delirium of desire. She wore her brown curls pushed up in front into a pompadour and dressed in full cotton skirts, cinched around her tiny waist with a wide black patent belt. Her bust swelled wonderfully under her starched blouses and she smelled like violets. One day, as she gave us a lesson on the Allies and the Axis, using her pointer on the pull-down map of the world, there was a knock on the door. Miss Ransom opened it. A handsome soldier stood there, his hands filled with gardenias. She gasped. He gave her the flowers, took her in his arms, and kissed her on the lips. What glory.

When he left, she said he'd asked her to marry him. The scent of gardenias filled the room. I wanted a man like that, so crazy in love with me he'd walk into a crowded room with his arms full of flowers and propose.

Actually, I was torn. My cousin Babee, on Daddy's side, had joined the Waves. She came to Allison's Wells on leave wearing a glistening white uniform studded with brass, a black leather belt with a shoulder strap, a holster, and a *pistol*. Before that, my fantasy was to be a drum majorette, but I dropped that one in a flash. I wanted a uniform, a holster, and a gun. I wanted respect. Could I have both? Would a man fill my arms with flowers if I were wearing a pistol?

I did not excel at the war effort. "Buy that Extra War Bond!" the signs said. "Support War Bonds and Stamps." No matter how many stamp books I started, I never managed to finish one. After two or three pages, the book slipped into some crack in my life and vanished. My fellow students collected tin foil and string, rolling the stuff into baseball-, even basketball-sized lumps. Not me. I'd roll a lump as big as a marble and lose it. I didn't have follow-through and I worried about this. I prayed my failure wasn't like "loose lips sink ships." I didn't want my carelessness to keep Daddy from coming home. I probably had loose lips, but except for the thing with Rosalie, I didn't know any secrets—nothing that would sink ships.

Uncle Sam heard about my nightmare with the Germans chasing me, and took me to visit a prisoner of war camp. We drove a long way and pulled up next to an open field, surrounded by a fence with barbed wire on the top. We walked up and down the fence looking at the prisoners and they looked back. They didn't have uniforms, just shirts and pants with "PW" printed on them. Uncle Sam said they were Germans, captured in Africa, and sent here to hoe and pick cotton. I didn't go close. I was afraid one might try and snatch me inside, but they didn't feel scary. They looked younger than Daddy and smiled and said words I couldn't understand. Uncle Sam gave them cigarettes through the fence. Then we left. They waved until we drove away. I felt sorry for them and quit having the dream.

At school after lunch one day, I rested my elbows on the ledge of one of the big classroom windows and looked out. On the other side of the playground stood a row of small unpainted wooden houses where colored people lived. I was thinking fire. There was going to be a fire. I stared and stared until, sure enough, one of the roofs started to smoke. Flames burst through around the chimney. "Fire, fire," I yelled. There was a good wind. Pretty soon the whole row of houses flamed. We watched from the window until the fire engines finished and there was nothing left but smoking ruins. I was stunned and pretty sure I'd done it.

There had been another fire. Marie and I used to ride the Trailways bus from Jackson up to the hotel. Riding that bus, I felt just as free and superior as when we sat together in the balcony at the Paramount movie theater. We got the big seat across the back. The other ladies made a fuss over me. Marie shrugged off their compliments. Didn't do to praise a child. Made them too big for their britches.

On this particular trip, the seat got really warm under my legs. I told Marie.

"It's the engine," she said. She didn't like causing a stir. I learned a lot about being invisible from her.

I started bouncing up and down. "It's really hot."

"Keep still."

I stood up and looked out the back window. Flames and black smoke were shooting out the rear of the bus. I poked Marie and she turned to look. She yelled louder than I'd ever heard. "*This bus is on fire.*"

I jumped up and down on the cracked leather, yelling with her.

All the colored people started yelling "*Fire*," and the white people up front turned around and frowned like we were making it up. Then they started yelling, too, and the bus driver pulled over to the side of the highway. We piled off the bus, white people first, and stood in segregated clumps on the dusty shoulder watching the bus burn (I counted as colored and stayed with Marie). At first it was exciting. Cars stopped, people got out, saying, "Would you look at that?" The driver shook his head like the bus was a member of his family. A fire truck came from Canton and unrolled big hoses from a tank. They shot water until the engine was black and dead. The firemen left and it got boring and hot waiting for another bus.

Here was another fire and what I wanted to know was: did I cause fires? Was it a magic power? I wouldn't have minded possessing a magic power, but I didn't want to burn down poor people's houses, or even a bus. I told no one and awaited further evidence.

About this time, I got my first taste of love. It wasn't as exciting as my teacher's, but it was mine. His name was Kenneth Ray and he was top boy in the local Cub Scout troop. He wasn't better looking or brainier than the other boys, but he had the one quality that would always draw me to a man: he admired me. He listened when I talked. He laughed when I said something funny. One day he told me that his Cub Scout troop had elected me their pinup girl. I felt my face get hot. I was incredibly pleased. I knew I was smart, but what I really wanted was to be pretty. My mother and Miss Hosford had little patience for such silliness. A young girl was expected to be obedient and polite. Time enough for pretty. Mama dressed me in colors to match my olive skin: rust, khaki, brown. I walked around looking like an acorn.

"You're not the type for ruffles." She stood behind me one morning combing my hair, both of us looking into her dresser mirror. "You're more the tailored type." That's what she made me: plain, practical dresses with no lace or wide sashes. I had no curls and

Mama would have laughed if I'd asked her to roll my hair in rags every night the way Mary Alice's mother did.

Kenneth Ray said they wanted me to come to their wienie roast on Saturday so the troop could give me the award.

"I'll ask my mother." *Pinup girl.* I went and sat alone at my desk to savor the joy.

Miss Hosford said no, so of course Mama said no. There would be no other little girls present and it wasn't proper for a young lady to go alone to a boys' function.

"But I'm the one they elected." I wept, I begged, but they were firm.

Miss Hosford said, "Let the honor suffice."

Their refusal lent fire to my love. When I told Kenneth Ray I couldn't come and he saw how sad I was, he told me he liked me, and I said I liked him, too. That was all, but it was enough. I thought of him constantly, dreamed of him at night and forced my sister to practice kissing just in case. We moved from mashing lips to letting our tongues touch in midair. Mary Elizabeth tasted metallic, like tinfoil on a filling. Mama walked in on us. She said what we were doing was nasty and she'd better not catch us doing that again.

Kenneth Ray got influenza and was absent from school for two weeks. I despaired. What if he died? He'd never know I loved him. With my allowance I bought six comic books and asked Mother if we could take them by his house. I wrote a secret letter: *Please get well. I love you and I will never love anyone else. When we are older we can get married.* I hid it inside the top comic.

The night before we were to go, Mother stood over my bed with the birthmark shaped like South America flaring on her forehead. In her hand, she held the letter. "What's this supposed to be?"

"Nothing."

"A young lady does not write letters like this. No boy will ever respect you. I will deliver the comic books. You will stay here and think about what you've done."

I hated my mother and hated myself for getting caught. I vowed to run away from home and find people to live with who understood what real love was and would not read my mail.

Frost was hard on the ground and it was time for hog killing. This was much worse than chicken killing. Pigs were more like people. They reminded me of my uncles Sam and Doug, fat and loud, their eyes looking at you shrewd and a little mean.

Down the steep back kitchen stairs was the yard where we did the chicken murdering, along with a smokehouse and a woodshed. Against the wall of the smokehouse Alan killed the hogs, hoisting them by their heels with a pulley and slitting their throats. After the first time, I never watched again. When it was about to happen, I ran as far away as I could, to the far side of the rose garden, and squatted under the water tank with my hands over my ears. It didn't help. I could still hear the screaming, horrible human shrieks of terror and pain, trailing off into gurgles.

When the noise stopped and the hogs were totally dead, I came back. I liked the next part. Every ounce of pig got turned into something. The blood was caught in buckets and brought to the kitchen. The long metal-topped table became a hog-processing factory. The skin was scraped and pieces of crackling fried on the woodstove. Hams, bacon, and fatback were sliced off, salted, and taken to the smokehouse. Hog parts steamed and boiled in every pot and the meat grinder stayed busy with the leftovers. This mixture, heavily spiced, was squeezed into intestines that had been turned inside out and scraped. Strings of sausages joined the hams and bacon in the smokehouse. For several days we feasted on fresh pork chops and pork roast. Miss Hosford ate the brains scrambled with eggs, which was so disgusting I couldn't even watch. Everybody came for hog killing and the kitchen was thick with meat smells and laughing.

And then it was Christmas, which was not the same without Daddy. No matter how much fun we had, there was an empty space where he belonged. He couldn't even call. The telephone company said, "The War Needs the Wires." He sent presents. There were packages from him waiting on Mama's closet shelf, wrapped in thin brown paper, pasted with colorful stamps, but the woven straw dolls and carved coconut heads we'd gotten last year made him seem even farther away.

This was my second Christmas at the hotel and I knew what to expect. Alan brought a tree in, not a bought tree like we had in Jackson, but a pine from the woods with its trunk cut off. I thought pine made a strange Christmas tree. The branches were too far apart. But it was tall, so tall the top bent against the ceiling. Miss Hosford, Mama, and Ora Dee decorated it from boxes of old ornaments and hung it all over with silver icicles. The front hall smelled like a forest.

Uncle John came home from wherever he did pharmaceuticals. They let Doug out of Preventorium, no fatter, but more cheerful. Uncle Doug and Aunt Leigh drove up from Key West. On Christmas Eve, Miss Hosford made eggnog with a dozen eggs, two pints of cream, bourbon, and sugar. It was so thick we had to eat it with spoons, and everyone, children and servants included, got a small cup sprinkled with nutmeg. We ate Christmas Eve dinner around the family table, alone in the big dining room. I could hardly sit through the baked ham and spoon bread I was so eager for bedtime.

Each child was allowed to open one present from under the tree before we went upstairs. This was a terrible choice. It couldn't be a big present, but we wanted something meaningful enough to get us through the night. After much shaking of packages, I opened a yo-yo from Sam Junior, black with a silver spiral. I was thrilled, but the gift lost some of its luster when Doug proved far more adept than I. He made it swing, still spinning, through a little triangle of its own string. I could hardly get it to go up and down twice without tangling.

He pinched me on the way upstairs. "Yo-yos aren't for girls."

The scariest part of Christmas was when Uncle John pretended to be Santa and his reindeer, galloping across the roof over our heads yelling, "Ho-ho-ho." The first winter, I was fooled. I thought it was actually him, but I was bigger now, almost nine. Besides, Doug had taken me outside last Christmas and told me the truth about Santa: it was his father.

We slept in an upstairs room in the Warm Part. Mary Elizabeth and I were tucked into bed and warned that Santa wouldn't come unless we went straight to sleep. There was a terrible racket overhead, like a hundred feet running. "There he is now." I grabbed Mary Elizabeth. She shrieked in fright. I giggled nervously. Even though I knew it was Uncle John, I wanted to believe. I wasn't ready to give up on Santa. When I opened Mama's closet and saw packages, which later appeared under the tree, I closed the door quickly and tried to forget.

On this Christmas Eve, I woke at some unknown hour from sounds out in the hall. When I opened the door, Mama, Miss Hosford and Uncle John were carrying lumpy brown packages down the stairs. Mama was laughing and I could tell she'd been drinking.

When she saw me, her face turned angry. "Don't you know Santa won't come if you're awake?"

I closed the door and stood in the cold dark. Who were they fooling? *They* were Santa.

On Christmas morning, we found our stockings bulging at the end of our bed. These we could plunder until Mama woke up. Oranges, apples, and nuts filled the top and we discovered a gold-wrapped chocolate coin in the bottom. As soon as everybody was ready, we went downstairs in our bathrobes, hollering "Christmas gift" at anyone we saw, and gawking at the presents under the tree. When I spied my blue bike, the dish set, and a new doll arranged around the shining tree, my faith was restored. Who but Santa could create such wonder? Mary Elizabeth got a red tricycle and a doll like mine, except dressed in blue. Doug got a basketball net and a tennis racket. Uncle John and Miss Hosford were always trying to make him more athletic.

We sat in the big parlor to open presents. I looked around. It was wonderful to be in the place where you belonged, surrounded by people who loved you. The only thing missing was Daddy.

Present opening had rules. We could only open one gift at a time, which meant I had to sit through a lot of boring sweaters and cologne before I got to another one of mine. The second rule was, the person opening closed her eyes and guessed at the gift by feeling, which made the rest of us, who could see, laugh. When we finished, the servants came in to get their Christmas bonus and sing. They made a semicircle on the far side of the parlor: Ora Dee and Johnny with Rosalie, Preston, Ellis, Parthenia, and Savannah. Everyone showed up except Lena, who was too stiff, Alan, who wasn't an inside singing kind of person, and Bee-Bee, off in Memphis for the winter. They sang carols. I thought we were supposed to sing along until Mama jerked my arm. Not singing made me feel funny, but Miss Hosford loved what she called "the pageantry." She said it was a family tradition and one of the things Allison's Wells was known for. When the singing was done, we clapped and everybody got an envelope off the tree.

Preston brought more logs for the fire. We left the wreckage of paper and ribbon and went in to breakfast, which was quail shot by Ellis. Mama started worrying a month before Christmas whether Ellis could get us enough quail, but he always did. Broiled in a heavy skillet, weighted with flatirons, the birds came out tender and juicy. We got a quail each, along with grits, quail gravy, biscuits, homemade plum jelly, and coffee. Everyone chewed cautiously around the birdshot. I squirmed in my chair, dying to go outside and try my bike. I could only ride on the sidewalk. Between breakfast and lunch, I fell off eleven times and skinned both knees.

Momae and Uncle Sam came from Canton for Christmas dinner, along with their son, Sam Junior, and Great-aunt Hattie. We dressed up in our best clothes and the grown-ups had drinks. We didn't eat until four o'clock, when we had turkey and dressing, rice and gravy, peas and mushrooms, sweet potato casserole, Lena's rolls, cranberry sauce, and three desserts: coconut cake, charlotte russe, and ambrosia.

By the time dinner was over, I was in a foul mood. I envied Doug because he could already ride a bike, an accomplishment I privately decided was beyond me. I liked Mary Elizabeth's blue doll better than my pink one and thought they must love her more to give her the best one. I ate too many pieces of chocolate candy from the boxes Uncle Sam and Great-aunt Hattie brought. Doug and I had lingered in the parlor before dinner draining every silver cup left on the tray. The contents tasted vile, but it was my first liquor and I wasn't about to pass up the opportunity to try a new sin. Now, at bedtime, I really missed Daddy. If he'd been here, I could have learned to ride the bike. He'd sent us necklaces made of polished cowry shells, which didn't in any way make up for his absence. I snuffled with self-pity. It was terrible being half an orphan.

That winter of 1944, between Christmas and my birthday in January, everything changed again. Mama had to go to the hospital. I noticed she'd grown a big stomach. I asked about it and Momae took me into a corner and whispered about the new baby. It had to be whispered. Nobody said the word "pregnant" back then. Women were "expecting," and it wasn't necessary to prepare the children unless they did something rude the way I had, hollering, "Why are you so fat?" in front of company.

I didn't get upset the way I had about Mary Elizabeth's arrival. I was almost nine. But there was more to it than a new baby. Everyone acted worried. Mama had to go all the way to Jackson. The baby was going to be cut out. I had no idea how babies emerged, so cutting one out didn't sound far-fetched. In the kitchen they shook their heads and looked serious. Miss Hosford was going with her and they would be away for several weeks.

All I knew was, Mama was going off to have a baby instead of giving me a ninth birthday party. I had been promised a wonderful party, a celebration of how well things were going at Canton Elementary. I could invite everyone in my class to a formal dinner at the hotel. Mother would make me a new dress.

"With lace?" I had pleaded.

"And taffeta," she promised.

We would sit at the King and Queen's table, with me in the King's chair and I could have all my favorite food: roast chicken, rice and gravy, Lena's rolls, and chocolate cake with ice cream for dessert.

I tracked Mama down. "What about my party?"

"Adele Renfro is coming to stay with you and your sister. We'll tell her exactly what kind of party you want." Mama held my face in her hands. "She'll see to everything. It will be the same as if I were here."

Adele Renfro lived in the town of Way, a mile down the road. Way had a gas pump and post office in one run-down building, with an iron hook out by the track so the train could grab the mail sack without stopping. That was the whole town. Mrs. Renfro's husband worked the gas pump, or sat in a straight chair, canted back against the wall, waiting for a customer or for the Illinois Central to pass by and toss the mail off.

Mama and Miss Hosford left three days after Christmas. The baby would be born January 2.

Mrs. Renfro installed herself in the upstairs corner room, and spent most of the day in the kitchen, standing in front of the big range, telling everyone what to do.

The servants couldn't stand her.

"She never bossed nobody," Ora Dee said to Parthenia.

Parthenia agreed. "Trying to get it out of her system in one go."

The Renfros were country people and Mrs. Renfro didn't feel comfortable in her new role. The way she showed this was to get crosser and meaner every day. Never had our faces and ears been scrubbed so red and raw. Never had we eaten so early and been put to bed with the lights off before it got dark.

I'd heard Mama talking about my birthday to Mrs. Renfro before she left. "Now, Adele." My mother liked to pretend things were equal by using first names. "I've told Little Norma she can have a great big party for her ninth birthday. She'll tell you what she wants to eat and Lena will cook it. You just give Ellis a list of what you need from town and he'll pick it up the week before."

Mrs. Renfro nodded like she understood. She had one of those peeled faces, as if she'd been scrubbing herself with a rough rag her whole life.

Mama said, "She'll need to take invitations to her little friends a week before the party. You two can make them together. She'll give you the names."

"Yes, ma'am." Mrs. Renfro gave me an unfriendly look. She kept her hands under the skirt of her apron. She must have had her fingers crossed.

As soon as Mother left, I started talking about the party. "Roast chicken," I told Mrs. Renfro, "or maybe fried, with rice and giblet gravy and Lena's rolls. Peas, I guess for a vegetable, the little bitty ones that come in the silver can. A great big chocolate cake, three layers, with double thick icing and nine blue candles. There are twenty-two people in my class so we can sit ten to a side down the table. I'll sit at the head and Kenneth Ray can sit at the foot."

Mrs. Renfro just looked at me. Almost a week went by and though I brought up the subject of the party several times, she didn't take the names or suggest that we write invitations.

On the second of January, Parthenia got news by phone from Miss Hosford. Mother and our baby sister were fine, but Mary Elizabeth and I could not visit. Children were too germy to be allowed inside hospitals. We could each write her a note.

I reminded Mrs. Renfro again. "We'd better invite people. It's only ten days off."

She brushed at her lap. "I don't think you want to be giving a fancy party like that with your mother in the hospital."

"But she said for me to."

"That was before the operation. It wouldn't be right now."

"But I'm supposed to have a party." My voice climbed to a whine.

Mrs. Renfro was implacable. "Four or five children maybe, for hot chocolate and toast."

"*Hot chocolate and toast?* I don't want hot chocolate and toast. What kind of party is that?"

"The right kind of party for a little girl whose mother is in the hospital."

Maybe Mama was sicker than I knew, dying even, but Parthenia said no. Miss Hosford told her everything was fine. Our new sister was named Sydney, which was Hosford's middle name, and Thelma for their dead sister. Mary Elizabeth and I thought Sydney Thelma was a terrible name, practically a curse, but we agreed it could have been worse—it could have been Hosford.

None of the servants would cross Adele Renfro about the party, not even to do what Mama wanted.

Parthenia said, "She left that woman in charge, baby. She didn't leave it to us. There's nothing we can do."

The birthday grew nearer and even the idea of hot chocolate and toast was dropped. "There's too much responsibility around here with you and your sister and all these coloreds." Mrs. Renfro twisted her hands in an angry way. "I can't take on any party."

On the day of my birthday, Mama called, but Parthenia warned me before handing over the telephone not to say anything that might upset her. The voice on the other end sounded tiny, like it was coming from the other side of the world.

"Happy birthday, sweetie, are you having a wonderful day?"

"Sure." I tried not to cry over long distance.

"Did Mrs. Renfro give you the present I left?"

"Yes, ma'am." I'd gotten the package with my breakfast: three Nancy Drew mysteries. "Thank you."

"You're welcome. That's just the little surprise. I'll have a bigger one for you when I come home. In fact, I'll bring *two* surprises."

"When are you coming back?"

"The doctor says a couple more weeks."

I hung up without crying, but that night in bed, with Mary Elizabeth safely asleep, I wept into the pillow over the failed promise of my ninth birthday.

On the day Mother returned with a tiny baby and Marie—Marie coming back as Sydney's nurse was one of the surprises—Adele Renfro packed her things and returned to the store in Way. I could hardly wait for Mama to be installed in the downstairs bedroom, propped on two pillows in a new bed jacket, before confronting her with the crime.

"I didn't get a birthday."

"What do you mean, baby?"

"Mrs. Renfro said I couldn't have a dinner because you were sick, that I could have four people for hot chocolate." I gulped with tears. "And then she said I couldn't have any party at all." I put my head down and sobbed into the bedspread.

I felt Mama's hand on my hair. "We'll fix that. As soon as I'm up and around, you'll have the biggest party you ever saw. Look what I brought you." She opened a cardboard box and unwrapped blue tissue from a beautiful dress, a dress from a store, pale yellow silk with tiny blue flowers and lace around the neck and hem.

I could hardly breathe. It was exactly the kind of dress I'd always wanted.

Marie slept on a cot in the baby's room instead of in ours, but as soon as I got her alone, I asked the question I'd been wanting to know. "Why did you leave us?"

She gave me that Marie look, the one that warned me not to try and get too close. "I'm back, aren't I?" Which left me right where I started.

I had my party in April. I didn't get presents because it was too late to be a birthday, but everyone from school dressed up and came. I felt like a princess in my new dress, with curls for once. I told everyone where to sit, and put all the best people near me. We had a brocaded linen tablecloth, flowers in a silver vase, and lighted candles. Ellis and Preston waited on us as if we were grown-ups. Everyone liked the fried chicken and we threw the rolls, laughing hysterically, bouncing pieces of bread off each other's heads down the full length of the table. Kenneth Ray brought me a camellia corsage and kissed me on the cheek out by the Pavilion. I found Mary Alice crying. Kenneth Ray had told her no, he didn't love her; I was his sweetheart. I lay in bed that night going over the whole party with great satisfaction. It was one of those rare triumphs of life over expectation.

9

One rainy morning during late spring in 1944, when Alan took me to catch the bus, I tried a trick. We went out early as usual. I left my raincoat open and stomped around in puddles until I was thoroughly soaked. Alan told me to button up, but I had a plan. When the bus pulled into Canton, I went up to the driver. "Could you drop me by my aunt, Mrs. Latimer's, house? I'm too wet to go to school."

It worked. I showed Momae my sodden clothes. She called the school and I got to spend the day trying on outfits out of the cedar chest. I was standing on her dressing table stool admiring myself in the triple mirror when she told me about Sam Junior's wedding. I had on an old evening dress of hers, cream satin with lace inserts, and two long strands of pearls.

I must have heard about the wedding from Mama and Miss Hosford, but my attention in those days was like a flashlight, clicking on to illuminate a random moment of adult life, then off and back into the velvet darkness of self-absorption. Mother's pregnancy had been that way. The light came on and there was that enormous stomach under her blue crepe dress.

Sam Junior was Momae's and Uncle Sam's only child, and he was getting married. I wasn't clear how he could still be in the States when everyone else his age was off fighting. He looked perfectly fit to me, even overfed. He was a storekeeper in the navy, and he and his bride would live on a base in California after the honeymoon.

I'd never given much thought to weddings until Momae saw me in the cream satin. She said, "You'll make a darling flower girl."

I paid attention.

"You'll walk down the aisle in front of the bride strewing flowers out of a straw basket."

"Strewing?"

"Sprinkling flower petals, baby." She made a gesture to show me.

I went flying into Mama's room that night. "What'll I wear?"

"To what?"

"To be a flower girl in Sam Junior's wedding."

"You'll need a special dress."

"A new one?"

"Long, to the floor. It's a formal wedding. I'll pick out the fabric as soon as we know what color the bridesmaid and maid of honor are wearing."

I'd stopped listening. *A long dress*, like a princess. My head swam. I became intensely interested in weddings. I drew pictures on the flyleaves of my books of what the dress might look like. I wanted rhinestones.

"No rhinestones," Mama said when I asked.

"Why not?"

"Tacky."

The dress turned out to be blue taffeta to match the bridesmaid. The maid of honor would wear peach. Mama made my dress off the shoulder with a ruffle around the top, a tight waist, a big skirt, and another ruffle at the bottom. I was overcome. I didn't even fidget during the fittings.

Sam Junior was marrying Julia Posey from Yazoo City, the most beautiful girl in Mississippi. She was dark haired and full lipped, with pale skin and huge blue eyes. She had a contagious way of laughing. Everything we said was funny to her. The night before the wedding, we rehearsed at the church. Julia wore red lace and sat in a pew while Mama came giggling down the aisle, playing the bride. It was bad luck for the bride to rehearse. I walked in front of Mama pretending to throw flowers out of an empty basket. I did my part quickly and efficiently.

"Not so fast," the lady who bossed us said. "This isn't a race. Walk like this." She showed me a funny hitching step, walk and wait, walk and wait. It felt dumb. She showed me how to throw rose petals, a few this way and a few that. I hadn't seen any petals yet, but I thought I could handle it.

On the night of the wedding, Mama dressed me in the ladies lounge at the Baptist church. Once again, I had curls. They bobbed like hope beside my face. I felt totally transformed. Mama put rouge on my cheeks, powdered my nose, and gave me a touch of pink lipstick. It was strange having her dab at my mouth with the tube, like neither one of us knew where my lips were. I studied myself in the full-length mirror with great satisfaction. This was my best yet. My nose was still too long and my mouth too wide for my chin, but I was almost pretty.

The door opened and Julia came in with her mother. I stopped breathing. In her wedding dress, Julia was gorgeous, better than a queen. I had never imagined anything like it. The dress glistened and sang when she moved. The long sleeves had points over her hand and many tiny buttons. The top was lace and satin and I could see her skin through the lace. The skirt billowed over her hips and moved along the floor behind her with a shushing sound. Her mother had to carry it when they went through doors. She wore a wreath of white rosebuds and a lace-trimmed veil longer than the skirt. I was too astonished to speak.

She bent over me smiling. The dress rustled as if it were layered with secrets. "Don't you look like an angel? Here are your flowers. You have a wreath." She lowered a circle of pink rosebuds onto my head. I sucked in my breath. Mama jammed in a couple of bobby pins, which woke me up. "Cat got your tongue?"

I shook my head.

"Thank your cousin Julia."

Julia's mother said, "Here's your little basket." It was decorated with roses and ribbons and filled with rose petals. I fingered them, softer than silk. My head swam. What was it I was supposed to do? We went out into the foyer, crowded with the bridesmaid and maid of honor, twittering like birds, and men smelling of wool and mothballs. I was eye-level with hips, too short to see.

The bossy lady said, "Stand right here. I'll tell you when to go."

Mama gave me a final warning look and walked down to her seat on a male arm. The music started with great wheezes of the organ. I could see past the attendants. The church was filled. The bridesmaid and maid of honor started down, carrying bouquets of gladioli. Each girl took a deep breath and stretched her lips into a smile before she stepped out. Eyes, hair, teeth, lips, all glittering. I looked back at Julia. She stood nervously with her uncle, not smiling.

"Now." The woman gave me a little push. I took a step and remembered to pause. And took another.

She hissed. "Flowers."

Flowers?

"Throw them."

Oh, yes. The people on each side smiled. I flung a few petals and looked up. In a side balcony, I saw Ellis and his wife, Gert, Parthenia, Ora Dee, and Johnny. Sitting beside them in a dress I'd never seen was Rosalie.

"Flowers." The woman hissed again.

I threw a few more petals. The music swelled. That meant Julia had started down the aisle behind me, but I wasn't supposed to turn and look. People murmured as she passed. I threw a few more petals and looked in my basket. I was almost out and not halfway to the altar. I made my hitching steps a little longer. Mama leaned out of her pew and looked back. She made motions for me to slow down. I threw the last of my petals and made it to the end, turned and stood beside the maid of honor. It was strange seeing everyone's faces. I looked up at the balcony instead. The light reflected off Parthenia's glasses. Ellis gave me a little wave.

Everyone was staring at Julia now. She seemed to come down the aisle without taking steps, as if the dress moved on its own. She smiled at Sam Junior who made a face back. He liked to turn everything into a joke. Julia's uncle handed her over and sat next to her mother, who was crying into a little handkerchief. We turned and faced the minister. I couldn't see Julia's and Sam Junior's faces except when they looked at each other. He towered over her like a building. The preacher went mumble, mumble. I liked the ring part. Sam Junior kissed Julia and we all walked back up the aisle. I went behind the bride and could go as fast as I wanted.

Mama said, "You threw your flower petals too soon."

According to Mama, I never got anything quite right.

The reception was at Julia's house. The men kept slipping into the kitchen to drink. I was supposed to drink only the lukewarm fruit punch, but Doug and I found the men's used glasses and tasted what was left.

I rubbed my nose. "I like it." Lying.

"You should taste champagne."

I looked at my glass with its smudge on the rim. "We're probably going to catch something."

"Leprosy," he said.

Leprosy was one of the things I was really afraid of, along with lightning and rabid dogs. "Mama says all the lepers are locked up in Louisiana."

"These are secret lepers." He grinned at me. Doug had really big front teeth, probably from sucking his thumb for thirteen years. He'd worn braces practically since he was born, but he still couldn't close his mouth.

I put down the glass and wiped my lips hard to get rid of the leper germs. I studied the guests. In the kitchen, Sam Junior and his friends sang a song about being the drunkest rebels of Ole Miss. He certainly looked like the drunkest. When the war was over, Momae and Uncle Sam were going to buy him a Ford agency.

Doug said, "You know what he's doing to Julia tonight, don't you?"

"What?"

He made one hand into a fist and stuck a finger in it like he was churning. "Poke, poke."

"What's that supposed to mean?"

"You're too little to know."

"I'm almost nine and a half."

He turned and walked away. I had to eat two pieces of wedding cake to recover my temper. The floor seemed to be slanting.

The woman serving cake said, "Put a piece under your pillow tonight and you'll dream of the man you're going to marry."

"Did it work for you?"

She went into a spasm of giggling. "Not yet."

I took a piece anyway and wrapped it in a napkin with gold letters that said *Julia and Sam*.

I looked back at Sam Junior. He was still young, but already working on his belly. The men were laughing and slapping their thighs. Sam Junior could hardly stand up. I found Julia in the crowd. She was smiling and smoking. Her skirt had two burn holes where sparks hit, but she didn't seem to notice. Whatever Sam Junior did to her tonight, he'd be doing it drunk.

"Come on, we've got to go." Mama took me by one hand and Mary Elizabeth, who was half asleep, by the other. She jerked my arm. "Stop stumbling around."

Miss Hosford said, "Do you think you should be driving?"

"I drive ten times better than you." Mama sounded angry. She didn't have as much fun at parties with her sister next to her watching. I didn't think the women were drinking, but she had been. I could tell by the way she ran her words together. Still, we got in the car, Hosford in the death seat and me and Doug and Mary Elizabeth in back. Mama shoved her skirt up over her knees to give her legs some air and took off toward the hotel.

Miss Hosford said, "Lovely wedding."

"I'd hate to be climbing into bed with Sam Junior tonight," Mama said. "I'll tell you that."

"Shhh." Miss Hosford tilted her head toward us in the back seat.

Doug poked me in the ribs and made the finger and fist motion again.

I ignored him. "Mama?"

She turned an ear toward me.

"Why didn't Ellis and Parthenia and them come to the house for the party?" I was pretty sure I knew, but I wanted to make her say it.

"They're servants," Miss Hosford said.

Mama said, "It's not how things are done."

Doug pinched me and whispered. "You are so dumb."

It didn't seem right to drive all the way to Yazoo City and not be at the reception, or at least in the kitchen with the help. Ellis and Parthenia weren't allowed to sit downstairs at the wedding, or come by afterward and give Julia a kiss, though she'd be welcome in the hotel kitchen greeting them. Maybe sitting in the balcony at a wedding was like watching movies upstairs at the Paramount with Marie. You got a better view. I was pretty sure that wasn't why we did it.

My piece of cake was getting squashed, but since I was going to sleep on it, that didn't matter. I looked over at Doug. He had a thumb hooked behind his top teeth and his eyes were closed.

Mama took a curve too fast. He and I fell toward Mary Elizabeth.

Miss Hosford said, "Will you watch where you're going?"

I prayed we'd make it home with no parked trucks on the dark road. That we wouldn't end up dead like Thelma.

Lying in bed with my head on my cake, I went over the wedding. Even though Sam Junior had been awfully drunk, he was my favorite cousin, and Julia was lucky to be his wife. She would be part of our family now, the best family in the entire world. I liked walking down that aisle in a long dress, and I loved the way Julia looked. Getting married was like a door into another life, like being Cinderella in the pumpkin coach, except real and forever. I filed it away as something I definitely wanted to try, along with being a drum majorette and carrying a gun. I was having so many experiences, Daddy wouldn't know me when he got back.

I went to sleep hoping to dream of Kenneth Ray, but I didn't.

10

Fourth grade was almost finished and summer was on the way. Germany surrendered. Miss Hosford held a celebration in the kitchen with little juice glasses of champagne for all, including servants and children. With V-E Day behind us and only the Japs to go, everyone said the war was all but over. That meant Daddy would come back. It looked like downhill coasting to me. I hadn't quite got the concept of home ownership. I thought we'd go back in our house on Monroe Street, and I'd be with my old friends, as if two years hadn't slipped by underneath us.

When the hotel opened, I carried on with my favorite summer job, which was being boss. As new children arrived with their parents, Miss Hosford let me show them around. I gave a tour of the place that was not at all the same one my aunt gave the grown-ups. Mine included the coal cellar, a dark, thick-aired labyrinth with spider webs, blackened beams, and a dirt floor. I showed them a secret way to disappear into an almost invisible door by the side steps, run through the twisted passages under the Warm Part, and come out in Uncle John's shop or within running distance of the garage. I showed them where to stoop to miss the low beams and how to avoid nests of what I described as deadly black widows. "One bite and your parents won't recognize your body."

I took them to the swimming pool with its ice-cold, dark green mineral water, and to the sand box, which I knew to be heavily mined with deposits from the hotel cats. I pointed out the badminton court where I excelled, the lumpy tennis court, and best of all, the Pavilion, which had Ping-Pong, a pool table, and a nickelodeon.

From the porch of the Annex, I proudly pointed out the windows of the Bridal Suite, our best accommodation. It boasted an upstairs corner view and a dressing room.

We ran up to the barn and I made them climb into the hayloft and lean dizzily out. I showed off the hog wallow, our cow, and the two worn-out mules. The climax of my tour was the well house. Grabbing the sweating red pump, I swung vigorously and sent a rush of clear sulfur water into their mugs.

"Drink," I said to today's batch of initiates, freckle-faced twins about my age and a smaller boy. I spoke the way Miss Hosford would, making it an order, not an option. I liked to watch their faces when they took the first swallow.

They howled and spit. "People drink this?" It was one of the twins, I couldn't tell which.

I nodded triumphantly. "People taking the cure drink eight glasses a day."

Mary Elizabeth and I poured our morning and evening doses down the sink. "Yes," we told Miss Hosford when she asked if we'd had our water today, becoming talented if guilty liars. We weren't sure if adults had a way of telling from the look of the sink or the smell of our breath. We took one swallow for insurance and ran a lot of tap water down the drain.

In the South, during the hottest part of a summer day, everyone who could (meaning the white people) took naps. After ours, we looked for someone to watch us swim. Doug was usually the best we could do. At thirteen, he ate in the big dining room and counted as an adult. He spent most of the hour trying to drown us. He crept around the side of the pool, dove on top of me, plunging me to the soup green bottom, then stood on my back to keep me there. I fought, aching for air, convinced this time I would die, until he relented and I got loose. The hour was filled with chases, in the water and around the slippery moss-covered brick edges. The artesian water was numbingly cold, drained and refilled once a week from a deep well. We had to move fast to stay warm. Black green on top and yellow green underneath, the pool water was so thick with minerals we could hardly see. I came up, brushing my eyes and trying to get my bearings. Doug was gone. Mary Elizabeth, playing calmly in the shallow end, screamed and disappeared. Our lifeguard had struck again. Other children joined in and we fought long, furious splashing battles, throwing so much water nobody could see to breathe. Most of the swim was spent screaming in fright or gasping for breath. We loved it.

Afterwards, Mary Elizabeth and I were supposed to bathe and dress for dinner. Dressing meant a clean pair of shorts and a fresh shirt. As for bathing, we felt perfectly clean after a swim. Mother and Miss Hosford were too busy running the hotel to notice. Marie was taken up with the baby. We could make it three or four days before Marie looked behind our ears (threatening to pull them off in the process), threw us in a tub, and scrubbed us.

People left, that's what I'd learned. New children arrived at the hotel, I made friends, and then they left. There was nothing you could count on to stay the same, except family, and I counted on that. As soon as Daddy got home, we'd be a family again, instead of parasites like we were now, depending on Miss Hosford's good will. *Parasites is all we are.* That's what Mama said when she was feeling beat.

With wet hair and clean clothes, Mary Elizabeth and I presented ourselves to Mama in the office. She questioned us about our day and gave us each a nickel out of the cash register. A nickel bought a cold drink and we raced to the Fishes Club. It was dim and cool inside and smelled sugary like the water in the coolers. This was where guests gathered to drink whiskey. It was fixed up like a small nightclub with a bar, tables, and straw-bottomed chairs. Everything was painted in Miss Hosford's bright Mexican colors, the walls decorated with straw hats and maracas. Bee-bee was behind the bar in his starched white jacket. He was blacker than black with a bullet-shaped shaved head and a gold tooth. We thought him very sophisticated. When people started drinking, no matter how rowdy things got, Bee-bee stayed dignified. At four o'clock in the afternoon, there were no serious drinkers and he was glad to see us.

"What can I get for you ladies?"

We presented our nickels and he held open the heavy metal top of the cooler.

My eyes swam lovingly around the choices: NuGrape, Nehi Strawberry, Coke-Cola, Dr Pepper, Royal Crown, peppery Orange Crush. The cold air off the floating ice felt wonderful and Bee-bee waited patiently. Most days, I chose NuGrape or Strawberry. With their long necks, the bottles looked taller. Mary Elizabeth and I climbed on stools. Bee-bee opened our drinks with a flourish, giving us each a cardboard coaster. We pretended the drinks were bourbon and I flicked an imaginary cigarette into the ashtray.

Bee-bee went along. "How are you ladies doing today?"

"Just fine." I took a swallow. The carbonated sting made my eyes water. Getting to this point in the day—chores over, clean, cool, and tired from the pool, with a grape drink sweating on a coaster— I felt like Mama with her first bourbon and water.

My cousin Doug ran around with older boys staying at the hotel, and when he invited me to do something, I was too flattered to say no, even if it was awful like jumping off the garage roof. One day that summer, I joined him and the big boys. We walked down a path past the guinea hens and the ruins of the old cockpit, where our grandfather used to fight roosters for money, through the woods and out into a field. The path wound deeper and the ground on either side was shoulder high. It was shady here, almost cool between the overhanging cliffs. I knew where we were. Doug and I had played Indians here last summer. We'd dug a shallow cave in the dirt wall and started a campfire that got out of control and burned almost an acre (*another* fire). When we couldn't put it out, we ran back to the hotel and never confessed, even when Uncle John sat us down for a talk. He said, "I think I know where to point the finger." Miss Hosford stood up for Doug, and I was too little to be blamed by myself.

Today's expedition turned out to be a snake hunt. We climbed uphill from the shade into a blindingly hot afternoon. The path was soft with powdered clay, and wild grass grew thick on either side. A good place for snakes and Doug found one, a five-foot rat snake sleeping peacefully on a rock.

The game began. We were the Allied forces. The snake was a booby trap set by the Japs. Doug grabbed it by the tail and swung it around his head. The rest of us backed away.

"Die, pig." The snake made a large arc against the white sky. We watched, mesmerized. Doug popped it like a whip against the rock. The sound made us jump. The snake went limp, its head crushed, eyes going milky, the body still wriggling as if trying to escape. The boys cheered. I got queasy. Doug dropped the snake and we watched it writhe in the dust at our feet until, finally, it was still. Draping it around his shoulders like a trophy, Doug led us back to the hotel, knocking enemy grass out of the way with a stick. Going home, we each had to take a turn carrying the dead snake. I shuddered when it was lowered around my neck, but kept quiet and avoided looking at the squashed head. The snake was surprisingly heavy, slickly smooth and cool as mud. I stroked it timidly.

When we got back, Doug said, "Let's think of something to do with it. Something fun."

I pretended to think.

He led us behind the Pump House to the woodshed where Ellis tied up his horse each morning. Carefully, he coiled the snake, half hiding it in dead leaves, looking like it was poised to strike. He stood back, satisfied. "Horses can smell snake. I bet Ellis will be scared white."

I felt uneasy about this game, but I didn't want to be called a yellow squealer either, so I punched my fist in the air with the rest of them.

We didn't see Ellis come to work the next day. He arrived at six when we were still asleep, but we heard about it. The horse reared, threw Ellis, and he hurt his back. Doug was taken under the house to Uncle John's shop and whipped—a first. Mary Elizabeth and I heard him hollering from the screen porch. He told Miss Hosford who'd been with him, and Mama came after me. It was the second time since we'd gotten to Allison's Wells that I made her cry. The first time was when Mary Elizabeth and I got caught entertaining guests by jitterbugging for a dime. Mama told us that little girls who started out selling themselves to strangers came to no good end. This was worse.

Tears ran down her face. "Ellis is your friend. What were you thinking?"

"Doug did it. It wasn't my idea."

That made her madder. "Don't tell me what Doug made you do. If he told you to jump off a cliff, would you do that, too?"

I thought of the paratrooper expedition where we had to jump off the garage roof. That scared me so bad, I almost wet my pants, but I'd done it, running from the very back of the flat roof and leaping into space. It jarred my neck so bad when I landed, I thought I'd swallowed my teeth, but it was over. I didn't have to do it again. Mother didn't know about that.

She was too upset to spank me. "Answer me when I speak to you." She meant about jumping off a cliff.

"No, ma'am."

"Here I am, working my fingers to the bone. There's a war on. Your father's on the other side of the world. I have to do everything myself and this is how you repay me?" She wiped her face. "What have you got to say for yourself?"

I stared at the green painted floor. I knew what she wanted to hear, an apology, acknowledgment of how much she did for us, a plea for forgiveness, and a promise to do better. None of those words lined up inside me.

She knew how to get me. "We'll see what happens when your

father hears about this." She wrote Daddy every week, and most weeks I put my letter in, too.

"Don't tell him, *please.*" I wanted to appear perfect for Daddy, the way he was for me.

"Of course I'm going to tell him. And you, young lady, are going to march straight to the kitchen and apologize to Ellis."

I went, taking slow steps. In the kitchen, everybody's eyes went down when they saw me. Ellis wouldn't look at me at all.

"I'm sorry." My voice came out in a whisper.

He nodded and kept folding napkins.

I went and lay down on the hot sleeping porch even though it wasn't naptime. Shame sat on my chest like a flatiron. This was the worst thing I'd done since Rosalie, and I hadn't gotten caught for that. Getting caught and apologizing was actually better. Ellis forgave me in a week, but I never got over Rosalie.

Not long after this, on a day when Doug didn't have any older boys to play with, he tapped with a stick on the screen of the sleeping porch where we were supposed to be napping, and whispered for me to meet him in the laundry room. It was the hottest part of the afternoon. The room was dim in the summer heat, light coming yellow through cracked shades and the window screens filled with lint. No one else was around. The help was done with housekeeping for the day. Both our mothers were lying down.

I touched the cold mangle, a square machine with huge rollers. I loved watching it run from a safe distance. The machine steamed and clanked while Parthenia or Savannah pushed damp, wrinkled sheets between the hot rollers. They came out the other side stiff and smooth as glass. You had to watch your fingers.

"Let's play Tarzan," Doug said. "You're Jane."

With my sister I got to be Tarzan, but with Doug I always had to be Jane. I let him tie my arms behind me with the cord from the ironing board cover.

"You've been captured by evil men."

I knew the Tarzan books. "Which ones."

"Natives. They're going to offer you as a sacrifice." He got a peculiar smile and showed his big front teeth.

Sweat ran under my shirt with a tickle that made me shiver. "What do I do?"

"Holler so Tarzan can save you."

I hollered, but not so loud that someone might hear and come check on us.

Doug went over to the far corner and put a hand to his ear like he could barely hear me through the thick jungle.

"Save me, Tarzan." I made my voice high.

Doug beat on his skinny chest and made Tarzan gorilla noises. He pretended to be swinging from vine to vine across the room, then felt around my ribs like he didn't know where the ropes were. "I'll save you, Jane. Let me get these knots undone."

His body pressed against mine. "You know what married people do, don't you?"

"That poking thing?"

His mouth was open and his breath hot. I turned my head so he had to breathe against my neck.

"You know how they do it?"

I could smell the hot dog he'd had for lunch. I didn't answer. He was going to tell me whether I wanted to hear or not.

"Your daddy takes his going-to-the-bathroom thing and puts it inside your mama down where she goes to the bathroom and lets seeds out."

I forgot about Tarzan. "He does *not*."

"That's how you make a baby. Why do you think they call your baby sister Little Miss Anaheim? That's where they made her." Doug moved his body against mine while I digested this information. They made my sister when Daddy was home on leave?

"Colored people do it a lot," Doug said. "That's why they have so many children."

"Where do they do it?" Curious in spite of myself

"In bed, stupid. You can only do it in bed."

I was aware of him, taller and pressed against me like a stranger. He had a funny look on his face, like he, Tarzan, wanted to do something to me, Jane.

I wiggled my arms. "Let me go. We'll miss swimming."

His eyes changed. He was Doug again, my mean cousin. He pinched me through my shirt and reached behind to untie my wrists. In seconds, I was free, and nothing had changed except the terrible thing he'd told me.

There was no one to ask if this new information was true. I knew, as soon as the words went in my ears, this was not something a child was supposed to know. Mama might get mad at Doug for telling, but she'd be even madder at me for listening.

That was the summer the mule died. Jake and Juno were the two old mules the hotel used to plow the garden and fields. I wasn't any fonder of Jake than he was of me. From an enormous height he seemed to regard me with dislike and invite me with a toss of his head to step behind so he could kick my brains out. But it was a shock to see him dead. The day before, he'd bared his long yellow teeth at me. Now he lay on the ground, flattened somehow, smelling worse than the slop barrel with a sweet stink of rot. Green bottle flies circled his open mouth.

Alan worked a sling around Jake and, using the other mule, he pulled Jake's dead weight up a sled into the bed of the wagon.

Mary Elizabeth tried to make me leave.

I shook her off. "You go on back. I need to watch."

Alan said, "Want to take a ride? Help me bury old Jake?"

Boy, did I.

"Go ask your mama."

"It'll be okay."

Alan said, "I'll wait behind the office. You go ask."

I found Mama in the office. I kept a calm voice and didn't bounce up and down. I'd noticed if you showed adults you wanted something too much, they were more inclined to say no. "Can I ride in the wagon with Alan?"

"May I. And where's your please?" She was busy with figures and hardly listening.

"He needs me to help take a load down the road. Please, ma'am." It wasn't exactly a lie. I looked bored. I looked as if it didn't matter whether she said yes or not. I tried not to even think about a dead mule.

"Be back before supper."

I forgot caution and flew out the door and around the building.

I heard her say, "Put on some shoes."

"Mama said yes."

"Climb in." Alan waited where the back road slanted downhill and bushes hid Jake from the guests.

Using the front wheel, I hoisted myself onto the seat board next to Alan and he clicked for Juno to start up.

"Pee-e-you. He *stinks*."

"Mules are its."

"Well, it stinks something horrible. Anyway, you never called him an it."

"Jake stinks because he's dead."

"See, you called him a he."

"Reckon Jake was a he if he was anything. Ornery as any man and hard working. Never complained about nothing, not even dying. Just fell over yesterday after I unhitched him."

"Where are we going?"

"To the river."

I'd heard about this river but never seen it. I looked back at the dead mule. Juno pulled the wagon creakingly out the bottom gate of the hotel toward the town of Way and the Big Black Swamp. The flies came with us, circling lazily over Jake's head, landing on his thick, yellowish tongue, buzzing around the one eyeball I could see, which was sunken and filmed.

I made a face. "Something green's dripping out of Jake's eye."

"Quit looking."

But I couldn't quit looking and wondering about being dead. The absolute finish of it, as if Jake had never lived or breathed. Could this happen to Daddy? My heart jumped with fear. If it did, I wouldn't be able to stand it.

The wagon made a turn. The trail to the swamp cut off at an angle from the gravel road, two dirt tracks vanishing into thick woods. Once under the trees, the air got cool and moist and smelled of something I couldn't put a name to.

"What's that?"

"What?"

"That smell."

"You smelling the swamp."

"But what's it smell like?"

"Smells like itself, smells like wet and dark. Smells like roots and mud, slime, snakes, and cooters. Smells like everything living and dying and rotting in water that never sees the sun."

That was exactly what it smelled like.

The wagon creaked and groaned down the dirt track. I rode with the bumps, shifting to keep my spine from jarring. I kept a watchful eye on Jake, expecting him to get bumped off the back on the uphill parts, or come sliding up against me when we tilted downhill.

Alan said, "He ain't going nowhere. Took me and Juno both to get him in there and he's in solid."

The forest grew darker. The trees were laced with vines and hung with moss. There wasn't land around us anymore except where the wagon tracks ran. Tangled roots grew out of an oozing mass of rotting leaves and mud. Slow, black mosquitoes sang and I slapped one whenever I could, leaving smears of blood on my legs. Except for the creaking of the wagon wheels, there was no sound. No birds here. Ahead, the road sloped sharply downward and I saw oily black water.

"Is that the river?"

"Yep, that's the Big Black." Alan pulled the wagon up. Maneuvering Juno with clicks and the reins, he began to turn us around. I watched nervously. If we got off the narrow track, the wagon would sink.

I sucked in my breath.

"Quit worrying," Alan said. "I'm the one doing the driving."

We backed slowly toward the dark river. The water gleamed like a black mirror in spots where the sky reached it. It was utterly still. Slime-covered logs and roots raised themselves along the bank. Full of snakes, I imagined, and the trees, too. The whole place was probably crawling with snakes.

Maneuvering Juno with quiet words, Alan levered the wagon's back end down to the edge of the water and pulled the mule to a stop. The back of the wagon was now much lower than the front. Blocking the wheels with stobs of wood, Alan climbed into the bed and began pushing at Jake with a flat rake. He grunted from the effort and slowly, reluctantly, the mule slipped toward the water, easing in almost soundlessly. The river accepted him with a low sucking gulp, first his head and forelegs, then quicker, the big-bellied middle, rump and hindquarters. The tail and hooves vanished last with a faint splash. The water rippled thickly where Jake had been. Oily bubbles broke the surface and then everything was still. Only the flies remained, buzzing angrily.

I stared, waiting. Was this all there was? You were alive, then gone. Nothing left, not a trace, as if you'd never been?

When we were headed back, I asked Alan. "Are you afraid to die?"

"What's to be afraid of?"

"Of disappearing, of being nothing."

Alan said, "Do you remember before you were born?"

"Of course not."

"Can't be no worse than that now, can it?"

I thought about that all the way home.

I got back in time for drinks in the Retreat. "I helped bury a mule today." I announced this as I passed the mint julep glasses filled with bourbon and soda.

Uncle John laughed, but Miss Hosford murmured, "Not now, dear."

Mama put a finger to her lips for me to be seen and not heard. This was her happy time. She had on a pretty dress and lipstick and had combed her short brown hair into waves. She'd screwed on her real pearl earrings and wore her diamond and emerald dinner ring. I smelled perfume. Laughing and drinking with people perked her right up.

The dinner bell rang. Miss Hosford separated the guests from their silver glasses, encouraging them with descriptions of something special Lena had cooked that day. She and Mama washed the glasses and locked up the whiskey. If the guests were very special, they ate with Mama and Miss Hosford at the family table, set with a lace cloth and the good silver. When Uncle John was here, as he was now, he and Miss Hosford ate last, alone in the back of the dining room at a table for two.

On this night, Mary Elizabeth and I raced by with the other children, up and down the dark porches, playing Ghost. We saw our uncle and aunt through the window, like people in a painting. They sat in shadow, the candlelight flickering on their faces, leaning toward each other.

I thought it was an odd, static thing to do with the night. I preferred playing Ghost, our game of hide and seek in the dark. Gathering the guests' children, we divided into two teams and ran full-speed around the porches, under the house, through the rose garden and coal cellar. I hid, waiting, listening for pursuers, heart pounding in my throat, as if it were death to be caught. When it was our turn to chase, we vengefully searched out the hidden ones, stealthily hunting down these children of guests as they crouched in the secret places that I, kind host, niece of the owner, had shown them on my tour, mentioning casually, "This is a good place to hide."

I sprang like a panther on their unwary backs, screaming as I leapt, feeling pleasure bubble like laughter at the fright on their faces. This was power. This was living, not the shadowy imitation grown-ups had.

When Mama called me to bed, I tried to stay awake on the sleeping porch until I saw a falling star to wish on. If I spotted one, I went to sleep happy and dreamed about Tarzan. I always wished for the same thing, that Daddy would come home safe. Tonight, I had to put all thoughts of Jake and the Big Black Swamp out of my mind. I pictured Daddy at the train station on the day he left in his white uniform. His face was fading. I needed to go in Mama's room and look at the man in the silver frame to remind myself.

Mama said Daddy had an operation on his sinuses and I thought it meant he'd been wounded. Mama said it was nothing like that and explained once again what Daddy did in the war. Every time she did this, my ears shut down. I didn't mean for them to, they just did. This happened a lot when I was being told important stuff. I knew he was in the South Pacific. We sent him letters and I had a box with his letters back, and the necklace made from polished cowry shells. I reread the letters trying to figure out things. He wasn't fighting. He didn't talk about battles or being on a ship. He sent me a tiny photograph of himself in a navy lieutenant's hat with khaki pants and no shirt. He leaned against the post of a thatched hut. There were coconut trees in the background. He looked tan and handsome and pleased. I missed him terribly. Without him, we weren't a real family. We were only relatives. Mama worked in the office and kitchen. Mary Elizabeth and I did whatever Miss Hosford told us to. We were like the help except for being white and we didn't get paid. In spite of the way I lorded it over visiting children, I was only a niece. I was better than a guest, but not as good as a son.

11

In the middle of August 1945, we celebrated V-J Day. The Japanese had finally surrendered. I heard talk of a terrible bomb, but our side won and everybody acted happy. My happiness felt purely selfish. The thing I'd been wishing for was finally going to happen: Daddy would come home. Life could resume its proper shape and I'd be free to go on with the business of growing up.

I waited. Mama said he might be home next week; then it was the next. He was sticking around for a buddy so they could travel together. I literally itched with impatience.

When the big day came, Mama said we couldn't go with her because this was her special time with Daddy. She left early in the morning driving to Jackson to meet his train at the Illinois Central Station. I counted the hours.

When the car pulled into a spot late in the afternoon, something was different. Mama's face through the windshield looked strained, as if she needed to use all her concentration to park. She usually drove like a maniac with her skirt hiked halfway up her legs and a burning cigarette in one hand. She liked for life to seem wild, as it once had been for her, with dances in the Delta and trips to New Orleans. Today, behind the steering wheel, she looked small and pale, the way she had after the operation for the baby.

Daddy got out of the car, handsome in his white uniform, exactly like his picture. The peaked officer's cap was cocked back on his blond hair. He held out his arms and I jumped into them.

Finally.

He held me and I waited for the sky to crack open like an Easter postcard. He smelled of starch and cigarettes.

"Look at you," he said. "Did you miss me?"

I wanted to say something enormous, to open my mouth and have the words come out like an opera singer's, but nothing happened. I was too choked with talking to him in my head to speak.

"I brought you a present all the way from Hawaii."

This was turning into ordinary conversation, the kind grownups had with children when they didn't know what to say.

I grinned my thanks. Over his shoulder I kept an eye on my mother. She hadn't gotten out of the car. She turned and spoke to someone in the backseat. I stretched around Daddy to see.

"What a big wiggle worm you've gotten to be." He put me down, looking disappointed, as if this meeting hadn't been all he'd expected either.

"Come and meet Helen."

Helen?

The lady who got out of the car looked like nobody I'd ever seen. I thought Momae was stylish in her silk dresses and perfectly waved hair, but this lady was a movie star. She had a big chest and wore a red suit with a slit up the side of the skirt. When she slid from the car, the skirt went halfway up her thighs with a shushing sound. She was darker than me after a summer of sun, and taller than Mama. She walked with a sort of strut and threw her head back to laugh, showing a long, brown throat. Her hair was black and shiny as patent leather. She parted it in the middle and pulled it back with combs. Behind one ear was a dark red flower. Her fingernails and lips were the same color.

When the red mouth opened, a voice like I'd never heard came out. "You darling thing. Give your Aunt Helen a kiss."

She smelled of cinnamon. She wasn't my aunt.

"You're a shy one." She rubbed my hair the wrong way and looked around at Allison's Wells as if it wasn't much. She put a red-

115

tipped finger under my chin. "Never mind. I've brought someone to keep you company." She motioned to the car and I watched a large boy climb out of the backseat wearing a flowered shirt outside his shorts. His mouth was stained red from something he'd eaten. He had black hair, short like fur, and skin so dark it looked bruised and purple at the knees.

"This is my son. Paul, say hello to your new little cousin."

He sneered and I sneered back, glancing at my mother to see if she noticed I was being rude, but she was watching Helen.

Daddy hugged Mary Elizabeth and made noises over the baby, Sydney, who was being held by Marie.

Mama said, "Come on, girls. Let's see if we can find Helen and her son a room."

Helen glanced at my father. "I hope in a place this large you have two rooms. Paul is such a restless sleeper."

Mama kept walking toward the office. "It's our busiest season."

I found out from listening to Marie and Parthenia that this was the wife of Daddy's friend Smitty. Smitty's discharge was delayed, so his wife and son came ahead with Daddy. There was something strange about it. I didn't know what, but things felt wrong. Daddy didn't act at all glad to see my mother, which, it seemed to me, a husband would if he hadn't seen his wife but once in two years. And here was this other lady with her curved body and sweet smell and that loud, throaty laugh.

She was everywhere. If Mama and Daddy had a drink in the Retreat, Helen had a drink. If they went swimming, she was swimming, wearing a bathing suit printed with purple orchids and cut so low I could see a line where her bosoms met in the middle. Daddy laughed at everything she said.

In the kitchen, Ora Dee said, "He's tuned into that woman like the radio."

Mama was upset. Not in front of Helen. I'd hear the two of them talking and think Helen was Mama's new best friend. Then I'd find Mama sitting at her dressing table crying and trying to cover it up with powder. When I asked what was wrong, she said nothing was wrong, and to go away. I overheard Parthenia saying Mama wanted that woman on the next train out of town. "And I didn't say lady because she's not one."

I wasn't sure how I felt. If I were Daddy and could choose, Helen looked pretty terrific. But he couldn't choose. He was married and he had us. Helen was married, too. There was proof of it in the awful Paul, who turned out to be a sneak and a bully. Doug was rough, pinching us, coming up and bumping the backs of our knees to make our legs collapse, but he did it because he liked us. Paul was mean because he didn't like us.

The weekend after Daddy got back, the whole family went to a party at the Lodge. The Lodge was Uncle Sam and Momae's fishing camp on a lake outside Canton. Nobody did much fishing; it was mostly a different place to drink. The grown-ups sat around in the knotty pine living room and on the deck, mixing each other drinks, playing gin rummy and bridge. The women brought food out of the knotty pine kitchen. They danced to the record player and the more they drank the louder things got.

We jumped off the dock and swam in the shallow lake. It was okay except when my feet accidentally touched the slimy bottom. I treaded water a lot. The lake was warm as a bath on top, with little cold spots underneath like warnings. I didn't really enjoy lake swimming. I couldn't relax. I was too busy watching for snakes. Doug told me water moccasins liked to drop out of the trees on people and could swim faster than any human. According to him, snakes would bite you underwater. He knew someone who swelled up and turned black from the poison before his friends could get him to shore.

After swimming, Helen asked if I wanted to show the family my hula. She'd been teaching me the steps. She liked to teach where Daddy could watch us, and did a lot of hula dancing herself to show me how. She dressed in a flowered bathing suit top and a grass skirt and could make her stomach go in circles like the clothes in the

Bendix. She sang in another language and her hands moved like little animals. The grass skirt rippled. I saw the way Daddy watched and how Mama looked at them both.

She was a good teacher and pretty soon I could do "Three Blind Mice" perfectly, singing the words in Hawaiian and making signs with my hands to tell the story. My hips didn't jiggle like Helen's but I looked pretty good.

Of course I wanted to hula for the family. We went upstairs to one of the knotty pine bedrooms to get ready. Daddy had brought me a little grass skirt and I pulled it on over my bathing suit.

Helen pointed to the bathing suit. "You don't need that, sugar."

"Yes, I do."

"No, you don't. In Hawaii little girls just wear grass skirts and leis. Wouldn't that be nice?"

"No. I wouldn't have a top on."

"You don't have to wear a top, or a bottom either for that matter, just a little grass skirt."

"People could see me."

She was getting irritated. "You don't have anything to see."

I started to cry. "I won't do it without my bathing suit."

"Oh, for heaven's sake, wear whatever you want." Helen stomped downstairs in her sarong and told on me. I heard them laughing.

I danced "Three Blind Mice" twice and the grown-ups clapped, but after that, I was on Mother's side: I hated Helen.

We were put to bed upstairs until time to go home. Doug and Paul were in one bed, Mary Elizabeth and I in another. I heard Doug sucking on his thumb, and the soft snuffle that meant my sister was asleep.

Paul leaned across the space between the beds and whispered, "You know what my mother and your father do?"

"Nothing, that's what."

"Not nothing." I felt his hot breath. "They're doing *it*."

I turned away. "They're just talking." But I was filled with a terrible dread. This must be what Doug told me about, and I didn't want to know, not if it had anything to do with my father and Helen. I put fingers in my ears and hummed.

The words came through like needles. I heard "pants" and "his thing" and "holler." I heard "tongue" and "suck" and "titties."

Without knowing anything, I knew.

He quit talking and I unstopped my ears.

He said, "She wants your daddy to run away and live with us. He'd do it, too."

I started screaming and didn't stop until the grown-ups ran upstairs and turned on the light. Uncle Sam said, "What's going on here?"

I wouldn't say, but that ended the party. We got in the cars and drove back to the hotel.

Something was going on. I didn't for a minute believe that weasel, Paul. Nothing could be that nasty, but things were definitely wrong.

On Monday, Daddy went back to the law firm and we stayed at the hotel. He said he'd see us on the weekend. The war was over and he was home, but we still weren't a family. Mama had bought us a new house in Jackson. She said we'd move when school started. In the meanwhile, Daddy lived in one room and we rented the rest to strangers.

Mama looked thinner. We'd been waiting for Daddy for so long. Now he was back and being together wasn't as great as I'd imagined. I never got to talk to him. We didn't have tickle time or stories the way we used to.

The next Saturday, at the pool, I said what was on my mind. "When is Helen's husband coming to get her?"

Daddy didn't look up from his magazine. "As soon as he can get here."

"Isn't it taking him an awful long time?"

He put the magazine down. He wasn't smiling. "It takes as long as it takes."

I got up my nerve. "I don't think Mama likes having her here."

"Your mother needs to grow up." His voice was sharp. "The lady is my friend. She and her son are all alone. She's been here for two weeks. I'd like to think my wife and daughters have enough hospitality to last two weeks."

I shut up.

I never saw him hug or kiss Mama and that worried me. Uncle John and Miss Hosford were a lot older, but Uncle John still acted like he loved her. They held hands in the rose garden and I'd seen them kissing. There was the business about skinny-dipping when everyone else was in bed. I wouldn't have believed old people could stand seeing each other naked, but Miss Hosford acted like it was nothing.

Daddy treated my mother like someone he'd asked out by mistake, but was too polite to take home. When one of her stories wandered, he'd close his eyes and say, "Could you get to the point?" My mother's face would turn red, then white. She'd drink about three bourbons and her voice would start to slur. I'd see Daddy's mouth pull down.

I blamed Mother. If Daddy didn't love her, there must be something wrong with her. Why couldn't she be smarter and say things to keep his interest? Put on more lipstick and a red dress? Why did she have to get drunk? And look how she moped when he talked to Helen. Who wouldn't rather have a glamorous Hawaiian lady wearing a red flower than my mother? I wanted to make it up to him, but Daddy didn't seem to like me much either.

"Your father says you've gotten sullen." Mama told me this on Sunday after he left.

"No, I haven't."

"He says every time he tries to talk to you, you run off. If he brings you a present, you just grab it and don't even say thank you. He's very disappointed."

"He's not the only one."

"What did you say?"

"Nothing."

The next weekend, I whined so much, Daddy let me come back to the city with him for a night. I wanted to be the perfect companion. I planned to be everything Mama wasn't. I'd be such a good pal, he'd stay with us just to keep me. We'd be a family again.

I couldn't believe how messy his room was. There was dust and dirty clothes everywhere. I spent the day cleaning. I wasn't very good at it, but I knew how things were supposed to be. While I cleaned, I played the same record over and over. Nat King Cole singing "Blue Moon." The first part was really sad, but in the song, things turned around and the moon turned to gold. I hoped they might do that for us.

Daddy came back after work and acted kind of surprised, like he'd forgotten I'd be there. "You've been a busy little girl. All that hard work deserves a reward."

He took me up the street to Brent's drugstore. We sat at the counter and ordered our favorite meal: cheeseburgers with lots of mustard and dill pickles and chocolate milkshakes.

He took me across the street and showed me my new school. We couldn't think of anything else to do so we went back home and put on our pajamas. It wasn't even dark when we got in bed. He read *Time* magazine and I lay there looking up at a spider web I'd missed.

It wasn't as wonderful being Daddy's companion as I'd hoped. It was okay, but it wasn't wonderful. He'd already started messing the room up again. I don't think he noticed I'd taken Mama's place.

In mid-September, we moved from the hotel to our new house. I couldn't believe it when Helen and Paul packed to come with us.

I went to Mama. "They're going to live in our house?"

"Shh," she said. "Not for long."

One day was too long for me. Mary Elizabeth, Sydney, and I crammed into the bedroom next to the kitchen. Helen and Paul slept across the hall from Mama and Daddy. I watched them through a crack in the door, Helen with her hair tied up in a scarf and Paul's fat stomach making a hill of the bedspread. My manners were used up. I couldn't stand the sight of either one of them. Everything Helen said sounded phony. My sister and I made Paul invisible.

When Daddy told stories at the dinner table—he told good stories—he watched Helen for a reaction instead of looking at us the way he used to. Helen laughed more than necessary. I'd look at them both and try not to think about the stuff Paul told me. They couldn't be doing anything now anyway, not with all of us squashed in here like the Old Lady Who Lived in a Shoe.

Finally, the week after school started, Mama said Helen and Paul were leaving on the train the next morning. Smitty, Helen's husband, was out of the navy. He would meet his family in New Orleans.

Mama told me I could drive to the station with Daddy. I figured she sent me along as a chaperone, to make sure Daddy didn't ride off on that train.

We waited in the station, with people hurrying by in that important way travelers have. Voices echoed. There was a wonderful lot of noise. Helen and Paul stood with their bags, looking lost.

I got caught up in the drama. The train whistle sounded down the track. I felt the steel wheels pounding through the floor and the roar of the engine shook the building. The big silver train pulled in, brakes screaming. Behind the windows I saw people sitting at tables with white tablecloths, drinking orange juice out of little fluted glasses. My stomach did a flip of excitement.

Daddy said, "Wish I could come along."

"Oh, Tom, would you? Ride with us as far as New Orleans." Helen looked like she was going to cry. She had on the red suit again, this time with a matching hat shaped like a pancake and a little black speckled veil. She held on tight to Daddy's arm. She didn't care a whit about me, but she'd take me and a gorilla too to get my daddy for a few more hours.

I turned traitor. "Can we, Daddy, can we?" I didn't think about

Mama's feelings or my job as chaperone. I wanted to get on that train and ride south. I tugged on his arm. "Let's do it."

"We can't, baby." He looked regretful. He looked like he might say yes. We could be on that train in two minutes following the Mississippi River to New Orleans.

"*We could.*" I jumped up and down in excitement. "We could ride as far as New Orleans and come right back. Please, *please?*" New Orleans was as exotic to me as Europe. I'd never even been to Memphis. "You could call Mama and explain."

My mother's name straightened him right up. "No, we can't. I wish we could, but we can't." He gave Helen a quick kiss on the cheek. He shook Paul's hand. He helped them onto the train, and he led me firmly away.

"I wish we could have, Daddy." We were riding home in the Chevrolet. "Wouldn't it have been fun?"

"Sure would, baby." He sounded sad. He gave my hand a squeeze. "Maybe we will do it one of these days."

He said "we." He meant him and me. I forgave him instantly. We were pals and someday we might do anything.

1945—1955

12

At Allison's Wells the summer I turned twelve, Parthenia, Ellis, and Ora Dee started calling me Miss Norma. I told them to stop. They smiled and went right on. I had crossed over or passed through some invisible boundary. I was no longer a child and the barrier between the races had been raised. More accurately, the barrier had always been there, but now I was allowed to see it and forced to acknowledge it.

The new formality killed me. It felt like a withdrawal of love. Miss Hosford said they were only doing what was proper. She even started. "Ora Dee, get Miss Norma to help you with those peaches." I wanted to scream. I wanted things back the way they had been, and still were for my baby sister, Sydney, who was three, and got carried everywhere, hugged, and fed bits of this and that until she grew round as a butterball. Mary Elizabeth, at nine, was spared. She was still Merlizbut to everyone I loved, the people who now ostracized me with a title.

We had settled into our new house in a suburb in Jackson. There were no problems in the parental marriage that I could see, but I wasn't looking much past my nose.

At my new school, I'd been brought down from my Canton Elementary success by a thing I'd never heard of: cliques. Ida, Gwen, Mary Jane, and Jackie were the popular girls. Mysteriously, the decision had been made before I arrived, and that circle was closed. I felt stung, but I found my own friends. I would be okay.

The baby part of my life was over. By twelve, I had graduated from Duling Elementary and finished seventh grade at Bailey Junior High, an imposing white pile on North State Street. In my own eyes I was practically grown, but Mama still made us go up to the hotel every summer. I loved the place and the people who worked there, but I was moving on to what I considered the real part of my life. Returning to Allison's Wells was like being pulled backward. Each year I went with greater reluctance.

In 1948, Miss Hosford started the Art Colony. I figured it was another one of her schemes like the Canyon Express or the Miss Allison's Wells contest, where girls from Canton teetered out to the end of the diving board in bathing suits and high heels. But this one took.

People gathered with easels, canvases, and paints. These were mostly women of a certain age, wearing slacks and comfortable shoes. They collected in the Pavilion, under the supervision of professional artists, to do still life or figure drawing in pastels and oil. Outdoors, they did watercolors of various picturesque locations—the rose garden with its tall wooden water tank, the well house, Parthenia's "cottage," as they called it, even the gullies.

I was too old for the gullies now, and too old for the Children's Porch, but I wasn't too old to pose. I hated it, but it was like weeding or picking beans. If Miss Hosford said do it, I did it. Sullen and squirming, I sat while people did bad portraits of me. During the Art Colony, everyone posed. Someone did a wonderful oil of Lena that captured her carved face and fierce character.

The teachers were artists from Memphis or New Orleans, often professors and mostly men. We didn't get many male students, except Uncle John, who had studied architecture. He did lovely watercolors of the hotel. The women students twittered under the eyes of the young male teachers, and the teachers were happy to drink with them at night, and to be fought over as seatmates at dinner.

These were ladies with a yen to express themselves, to make a splash with brush and color. They were women whose children were grown. Most had never worked outside the home.

One summer, I joined a landscape watercolor class, aiming my eye across a field at a row of trees. The teacher was Karl Wolfe, well known in Mississippi as a portraitist (he painted the picture of dead Aunt Thelma). His wife, Mildred, was a potter and they lived on what they earned from art and teaching. This meant, in the eyes of staid Jacksonians, they were practically bohemians. Their children were raised in a cottage on several acres of woods, where things were left as they grew. There was something about this disregard of convention that appealed to me.

Mr. Wolfe spoke to us about the discriminating eye, how we observed more than we could put on paper and must therefore select. That ability to select well, to discriminate, was what made an artist. He told me I had a good eye, and I packed that compliment away, a prize to be considered later. It was like being told by Aunt Leigh that I was special. I longed for qualities which might enable me to—not escape, I wasn't thinking of escape except into adulthood—to be different.

As much as I pooh-poohed the Art Colony when it started, it became Miss Hosford's great success. Two-color programs were printed up in the spring, with pictures of smiling ladies standing behind easels and photographs of the teachers. The hotel's suppliers were persuaded to buy advertisements in these programs, so they paid for themselves. Each summer, more were mailed out, attracting increasing numbers of students. Years later, I showed a couple of these brochures to a gay friend. Admiring the sultry photos of the teachers, he said, "Who *are* these men? *I* want to have dinner with them." I took another look and realized Miss Hosford may have turned a blind eye on more than I knew.

My aunt had her own artistic yearnings and jumped right in whenever the Art Colony was in session. She skipped the learning-to-draw part and moved straight to painting, producing small oils and watercolors with broad, bright strokes—two for the roof of a house, a yellow splotch for the sun. We received these as gifts for Christmas and birthdays, wrapped in recycled paper. I treasure them now, but at the time, we joked about Hosford and her art.

She began to dress in what I called gypsy clothes: long, full skirts, Mexican blouses that gathered with colored string at her neck, and multiple strands of beads (my favorite being an amber necklace, each stone as large as a bird's egg). I thought these clothes extremely peculiar, especially for an old person, unable to imagine that I might spend the late sixties and all of the seventies dressed just like her.

Under my aunt's veneer of southern gentility—the never- raise-your-voice, never-lose-your-temper—she was steel. One day when a pipe burst, she followed the plumber under the house, crawling right behind him through tunnels of coal-blackened spider webs. Scared the poor man to death when he looked back and realized she was at his heels. She told him to go right ahead and let her know if she could be of any assistance. We couldn't decide whether she'd gone to give him fortitude or to make sure he didn't turn back.

She never let up. Just when you thought you were safe, there was Miss Hosford to set you straight: respect your elders, do as you're told, don't talk back, answer when spoken to, look me in the eye, never tell a lie, don't forget your prayers, be thankful for what you have, don't whine, don't interrupt, stop running, don't shout, stop slumping. Remember, you're a child.

She had a family history done, which showed the Latimers were descended from Charlemagne. It was a little suspect, since Mother was dead and Aunt Thelma had given birth to us. Be that as it may, Miss Hosford made it clear that, however reduced our circumstances, money was not what mattered. We had noble blood. We must Remember Who We Were.

13

Marie started calling me Miss Norma and that was the last straw. I had been cast out of childhood and into the realm of master and servant. I'd wanted to grow up and have more power, but this was not what I meant.

More things were changing than I knew. I wasn't privy to the conversation Mama had with Marie, though I saw signs of trouble. At the dinner table one night, Mother mentioned she needed someone who knew how to cook. "Marie refuses to be taught," she said. Sliced, boiled carrots in butter was still the beginning and end of our nurse's culinary skills, or so she claimed.

In Maya Angelou's memoir (read years later), she wrote that part of African bush secretiveness was to never tell the whole truth. I figured refusing to cook saved Marie from becoming our chef as well as our housekeeper, laundress, and nanny.

Mary Elizabeth and I were growing up and getting messier. We had friends over, banged in and out of the house, put our feet on the furniture, dirtied the kitchen making sandwiches after school, and left our clothes on the floor. Marie followed behind us, punctuating our days with her low growls. I hardly heard the grumbling anymore: "Fast as I clean up around here—" We got the idea. We were getting worse, not better, and company was not welcome.

Our mother enjoyed having ladies over for lunch and bridge. When the grumbling got aimed at her company, "People coming in here—making more mess," she made a decision. She loved the way Marie cleaned. Marie could make a bed so tight and square, you'd swear no one had ever slept in it. When she finished with a room, it shone. But a successful social life was more important than a tight bed.

One night at supper, Mama announced she'd hired a new cook. From now on, Marie would come twice a week to clean and iron Daddy's shirts. Daddy made no comment other than a nod. Running the household was left entirely to our mother. As long as a change didn't involve more money, he didn't complain. Mary Elizabeth and I looked at each other. Once again, Marie was leaving us, and this time there was no Ellis to blame. Sydney started crying.

Which is how, in 1948, Annie Carter appeared, as different from Marie as two people could be. Annie was tall and broad with enormous breasts, scarcely contained by a gigantic brassiere, the top of which we spied above her uniform. She had what looked to our horrified eyes like a third breast growing out of the left one. We never dared ask and didn't want to stare—not out of politeness but for fear of what we might see, so we may have been wrong. Where Marie had been silent and grumbly, Annie was a thunderstorm. I'd see my father wincing at the breakfast table. She had a huge voice, a big laugh, and a mouthful of white teeth in a shining black face.

My favorite place after school was face down on the bed, propped on pillow and elbows, reading. Annie would come to the door and stand, not saying a word. I'd hear her plodding down the hall, the creak of the floor under her weight, and be filled with resentment at the space she occupied, the noise, and the intrusion on my privacy. She'd stand in the doorway, silent, and I wouldn't turn around. I made up this thing in my head: if I looked, she'd get me. By get, I meant murder. I didn't really think she'd kill me, but that's what I told myself. It was her or me, and I wouldn't be the first one to move. I couldn't let her win. We were stuck, Annie waiting, me pretending to read, until one of us gave in.

Me: "*What?*" Without looking.

Annie: "Where's your sister?"

Mama taught Annie to cook all the things we loved: fried chicken, roast beef that fell from the bone, crisp fried oysters and bream, fluffy white rice, spoon bread, rich gravies, corn cut off the cob and simmered in butter, turnip greens with cornbread sticks, lady peas, butterbeans. Every dessert: lemon meringue pie, chocolate meringue (my favorite—the pie I ate the top off of), chess pie, and Daddy's favorites, custard and sweet potato pie. In season, we had peach and blackberry cobblers. For special occasions, we had cake. Annie could make all the cakes we'd had at Allison's Wells, plus a three-layer chocolate concoction with a fudge-like icing that broke when you cut it with a fork. I would eat around the icing, getting rid of the moist cake first and leaving a ladder of fudge until last.

Chocolate cake made by a chocolate servant. I made no connection. Our world went along as it was meant to be.

No chocolate-colored person could be trusted with the family birthday cakes. Mama took over the kitchen on those special days to create chocolate angel food cake, which was chilled, cut into layers, and iced with a delicate cocoa-flavored whipped cream. It was truly the food of angels. The cake had to be baked in a pan in which nothing else had ever been cooked. All ingredients were sifted five times. Eleven eggs were separated with not a speck of yolk in the whites. The whites must be hand-beaten with a whisk. While it baked, we tiptoed through the kitchen and kept our voices low. The result was worth the trouble. Mama's chocolate angel food cake was so famous that the boy who taught me how to drive after my parents gave up was paid with one and felt amply rewarded.

I missed Marie. I never admitted that aloud, it would have seemed babyish, but I even missed the grumbling. With her gone, I stepped out of the safety of childhood. No more nights of carrots and radio programs. My sister Sydney was desolate. Marie had been her stand-in mother at the hotel and her constant companion back in Jackson. She was only three and wandered around every morning asking, "Where's Re-Re?" until Mama snapped and made her cry.

In place of Marie and the big radio, we got Annie and television. My father came home with a floor model as soon as Jackson acquired a station. We received only one channel and that for only a few hours in the evening, but my father considered it a marvel. When nothing was on, he sat and watched the test pattern. "Look at that," he'd say. "Pictures coming out of a plug in the wall. How do they do it?"

Mama persuaded Annie to move into our maid's quarters, a small, almost windowless room with a dark, scary bath behind the house on King's Highway. Annie put up with it, along with the enormous white and gray uniforms Mother bought her, the white orthopedic lace-up shoes, and the humiliation of being handed a bar of soap and a jar of deodorant with the suggestion she might want to use more of both.

I didn't see how Annie stood that room. Mildred, Ellis's oldest daughter, tried it for a while. She was supposed to be our babysitter and Sydney's nurse. She was far too young and progressive to work for Mama. First she dyed her hair red and then she disappeared. Turned up missing one morning when she was supposed to come to work, the room emptied of her stuff. We found out later she'd gone to Chicago.

"Ungrateful," Mama said. Smart, I thought.

Slavery might have been outlawed, but there was a sense in those days that the colored people who worked for you belonged to you. To leave as Mildred did, without permission or a word of explanation, was considered uppity and ill-mannered, not something you'd expect from a child of Ellis's. On the other hand, if you got dropped from five days a week to two, the way Marie had, you were owed nothing: no warning, no severance pay, no worries about how you'd make enough to live.

Marie found other work. Maybe Mama found it for her. She came to our house twice a week and went around like a dervish cleaning. She put up the ironing board in the sewing room and did up a week's worth of Daddy's white shirts. Light starch in the body, medium in the placket, heavy on the cuffs and collar, which ironed up stiff and shiny. She boiled the starch on the stove, and she and

Annie enjoyed a piece or two of the raw stuff out of the red and white Argo box. Colored people ate starch. When I asked why, they told me it tasted good.

With Annie on the premises and trained, Mama entertained more often. Daddy didn't mind, as long as all signs of company were erased by the time he got home. He wanted supper on the table at six sharp and then he was off to the office again. He worked all the time. I didn't wonder about this either. I thought all men did it. Along with not having to go to war, it was one of the few good reasons to be female.

For Mama's bridge luncheons, Annie made aspic with tomato juice, shrimp, scallions, and celery, mixed with gelatin and left to set in the refrigerator. Heavily seasoned with Worcestershire sauce and Tabasco, tomato aspic was served, quivering, on a piece of iceberg lettuce. Alongside were finger sandwiches, triangles of thin-sliced bread with the crusts cut off, spread with Mama's homemade mayonnaise and pimento cheese. Each plate got a deviled egg and a little pile of potato chips. The ladies drank iced tea with lunch, and switched to bourbon and scotch after.

Annie got a little sour on the days when there were three regular meals *and* a bridge luncheon. The ladies stuck their heads in the kitchen to thank her. One afternoon, the door shut behind one of these ladies and only I was left in the kitchen. Annie said, "Thank you don't buy shit." This was my first hint that things might not be as rosy as everyone pretended in the master-servant universe.

Annie loved a joke. One night Daddy told a funny story while she was passing a dish of string beans around the dining room table. She started laughing and couldn't stop. We laughed with her and she laughed harder. Mama managed to get the dish out of her hand before she collapsed. The dining room floor shuddered when she hit. From down there Annie kept on laughing, eyes rolling, tears running down her cheeks. We tried to get her up, Daddy on one side, me and Mama on the other. When we couldn't manage, Daddy got quiet, meaning he was upset. Annie tried to match the seriousness of the situation, but she kept busting out laughing, not at the joke anymore, but at her predicament.

We called the fire department, or rather, Mama called the fire department. Daddy would have left Annie to live on the dining room carpet. He hated asking for favors or making complaints. In a restaurant, if he were served a piece of bad fish, he'd push it aside and whisper for us not to make a fuss. Having men from the fire department arrive at six-thirty at night to lift a giant Negro off the floor was not his idea of a good use of public resources. After that incident, he wouldn't tell a joke anywhere near Annie. He'd get to the punch line of a good story and start to whisper. When we laughed, he'd roll his eyes toward the kitchen, and gesture for us to keep it down.

I liked Annie. I definitely liked her cooking, but I never felt she was my mother the way I did with Marie. I had gotten to the age of withdrawal. My world was the secret one inside me, and the world I shared with my friends. On Marie's days with us, I'd come in from school in the afternoon and greet her like some stranger I'd once known. Passing through the room where she had one of my father's white shirts splayed on the ironing board, I'd say, "Hey, Marie," and she'd say, "Hey, Miss Norma," in her high light voice, with a surprised lilt, like she thought I might have moved away, or on, which I was trying mightily to do. I was giving up the things of childhood and Marie was one of those things.

She and Annie both adored my sister Sydney, who adored them right back, and could be found most days in the kitchen being indulged by Annie—she wouldn't eat vegetables or fruits, and so got fed starches and sweets—or in the sewing room playing around Marie's feet while she ironed.

Mary Elizabeth was caught in the middle, a smart, quiet child, who wasn't the oldest or the darling baby. We kind of forgot about Mary Elizabeth.

14

It came on me like the Call of the Wild, except it was the Call of Sex. At nine going on ten, in fifth grade, too early for puberty, boys set up residence in my head and cleaned out what little sense I had. Which one did I like? Did he like me? Was there anything I could do to make him like me? That first year back in Jackson, I got caught carving John Lee Gainey's name on my desktop. What was I thinking, that the teacher wouldn't notice? A hopeless gesture as it turned out. He never gave me a glance, which was just as well. Daddy's sister, Emily, married his father, so it would have been practically incest.

These feelings, and I had no name for them, started earlier. When I was eight, during that first winter at Allison's Wells, a man came to visit. He arrived in the late afternoon of a cold, wet February. We had few visitors in the winter and fewer still with gas rationing. The man hugged Mama and reached down to scoop me into his arms. I didn't remember his name, but he knew me and I loved how he felt, muscles under a rough coat, a smell of damp wool and tobacco. He held me against him and smiled into my eyes.

"You're getting so big."

An eight-year-old can't say, "I love you. Hold me like this forever," but that's what I felt. I ached when that man hugged me. Later, in front of the fire, I sat on his lap. I liked that, too.

He bounced me on his knee. "You're the one for me, kid. Want to be my girl?"

"Sure."

"You hurry up and get grown and I'll wait. How's that for a deal?"

As far as I was concerned, we were engaged.

Mother laughed. He gave me a squeeze and put me down.

I kept the warm feeling, but forgot the man's name. He only came to the hotel that once, and when I asked about him, Mother claimed she couldn't remember which man I meant. My future husband was lost forever, taking with him the laughing brown eyes and delicious smell. I wondered later if Mother might have been fond of him herself, which brought on her amnesia. Children were not permitted to demand such information.

In sixth grade, I moved from helpless longing to strategy. Every Saturday, my two best friends and I walked around Council Circle and up North State Street to the Pix Theater. For twenty-five cents, we saw a cartoon, a serial, and a double feature. It took the entire afternoon. Boys from our class came. Each week, one of us got to sit on the end of the row with an empty seat beside her. If you were lucky, the boy you liked sat in that seat.

One Saturday when it was my turn, my current swoon, Jimmy Morrow, sat down beside me. We nodded. When the theater darkened and the cartoon came on, we chewed Necco Wafers and laughed. During the serial, I squealed at the scary parts and moved closer, leaving my arm on the armrest between us. When the first movie started, a western, I felt his arm, as if by accident, slide alongside mine. The hair on my forearm stood up with the shock of touching him, and I felt the tingling all the way to where I went to the bathroom. We sat silently like that, never looking at one another, until "The End" after the second movie. I hadn't felt anything like it since the man at the hotel. I still had no name for the feeling, but it was splendid and therefore probably forbidden. I never told anyone.

We girls walked home together after the show, picking candy out of our fillings.

Susan said, "Did he hold your hand?"

My grandfather,
Wm. H. Watkins,
admitted to the
Mississippi bar in 1899;
pen and ink sketch.
Courtesy of the author.

My grandmother,
Margaret Watkins, in
the house on North
State Street, 1910,
pregnant with my
father, the youngest
of their five children.
Courtesy of the author.

My maternal grandmother, Norma Wherry Latimer, 1927, the year before her death. Courtesy of John Fontaine III.

Aunt Thelma Latimer, age 31 in 1927, the year before she was killed. Courtesy of John Fontaine III.

My father, Thomas H. Watkins, the year he was admitted to the bar. Courtesy of the author.

My mother, Norma Elizabeth Latimer, age 25, 1933; her engagement picture. Courtesy of Leigh Roberge.

My father volunteers for the navy, 1943. Courtesy of Leigh Roberge.

Mary Elizabeth and me, 1943. Courtesy of Leigh Roberge.

Hotel when I lived there, 1943–1945. Courtesy of John Fontaine III.

Bird's-eye view of the hotel, drawn by Uncle John Fontaine. Drawing from *Allison's Wells: The Last Mississippi Spa, 1889–1963*, Hosford Latimer Fontaine.

Sketch of Lena Tucker, boss of the kitchen. Drawing from *Allison's Wells: The Last Mississippi Spa, 1889–1963*, Hosford Latimer Fontaine.

Miss Hosford, sketched by my Watkins cousin Babee Robinson. Drawing from *Allison's Wells: The Last Mississippi Spa, 1889–1963*, Hosford Latimer Fontaine.

Hosford: My friend and mentor since the summer of '44 at Allison's
Babee Robinson

Uncle Doug Latimer, in his navy uniform, 1943. Courtesy of Leigh Roberge.

Glamour shot of Aunt Leigh Latimer, taken around the time Doug met her. Note the ermine tails. Courtesy of the author.

15. Bee-Bee and Marie with us, 1944, on the steps to the Fishes Club. Courtesy of the author.

16. The Gullies, our playground at Allison's Wells. Courtesy of John Fontaine III.

Ora Dee Tucker, with us, 1943. Courtesy of the author.

At the Lodge: Uncle Sam, Momae, Mother (and two people I don't remember). Courtesy of the author.

My sister Sydney Thelma Watkins, one year old. Courtesy of Leigh Roberge.

Our new house on King's Highway in Jackson, 1945. Courtesy of the author.

Mother carving.

Daddy's secretary, Mildred Baker, 1945. Courtesy of Leigh Roberge.

I graduate from sixth grade, Duling Elementary, 1947. I'm the one on the front row with my leg cocked, wearing a giant gardenia corsage. Courtesy of the author.

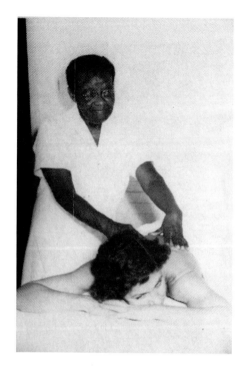

Parthenia Avery, housekeeper and hotel masseuse. That's me on the table, the unwilling model. Photo from *Allison's Wells: The Last Mississippi Spa, 1889–1963*, Hosford Latimer Fontaine.

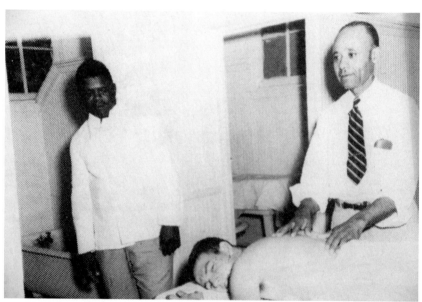

Preston Shelby and Ellis Lindsay, in the massage room of the men's bathhouse. Photo from *Allison's Wells: The Last Mississippi Spa, 1889–1963*, Hosford Latimer Fontaine.

Tea time in the Pavilion, early 1950s. Courtesy of John Fontaine III.

The wedding at Galloway Memorial United Methodist Church, November 1955. Courtesy of the author.

The wedding party: John Fontaine III is left, rear, Sam Latimer, Jr., is to my left in the picture, and my cousin, Doug Fontaine, is next to him. Courtesy of the author.

"The Help." Backstage at my sister Mary Elizabeth's wedding: on the left is Molly, who worked for Fred's parents; Marie holds Allison; Annie holds the veil; Evangeline, right, worked for the groom's parents. Courtesy of the author.

Mother and Miss
Hosford in the ruins
of Allison's Wells.
Courtesy of John
Fontaine III.

Left: Patricia Derian,
my fearless liberal
friend. Courtesy of the
author.

Above: The family, 1966. Fred holds Thomas and Linden; Allison stands at rear; Clay is on my right. Courtesy of Linden Craig.

Left: Bruce Rogow with his blue Triumph and Yossarian. Courtesy of Bruce Rogow.

"Of course not."

Judy said, "What happened?

"*Nothing.*"

The summer I was eleven, I slumped around, hating Allison's Wells. No telling what fun my friends were having back in Jackson. I was missing the movies and spend-the-night parties, not to mention arm-touching with Jimmy Morrow. It was really too unfair. Daddy only had to come up on the weekends, but I was stuck there every blessed day with nothing to do but show everybody how miserable I was.

Miss Hosford got sick of the whining and signed me up for summer camp across the road at Rose Hill. The place was called Bratton-Green, and the Episcopal Church ran it. I was not thrilled. The only thing I could think of worse than Allison's Wells was a church camp.

We were Methodists because my father, when he was anything, was a Methodist. His grandfather had been a circuit-riding Methodist minister in the small churches of southern Mississippi. I'd been raised in Galloway Memorial United Methodist Church, where we celebrated Holy Communion in our pews, drinking grape juice out of tiny glasses.

I didn't know anything about Episcopalians except Miss Hosford was one and they seemed snooty, or she did. Whenever she talked about the church, she got even more whispery, as if the whole business was too sanctified to speak about in a normal voice.

But if Miss Hosford said go, you went. I crossed the road with dread (a feeling I should learn to follow like white stones in a dark forest). I expected a whole camp full of whispery holy ghosters.

My first surprise was finding boys. Half the camp was male. The only other camp I'd gone to was all-girl, and I had been threatened with expulsion for pretending to be hypnotized and trying to kiss the owner's son.

My next happy discovery was dirty jokes. Nobody in my family told them, certainly not Miss Hosford. Every now and then Aunt

Leigh announced she was getting ready to tell a naughty story. My ears would prick up. She'd make us all promise not to say where we'd heard it, and then it would turn out to be some lame thing about having two glasses of wine. At camp, when the singing and storytelling around the campfire were over, the girls in my cabin sat around swapping dirty jokes. I didn't have any to swap, but I laughed enough to make up for it.

On the third night, after lights out, we sneaked away from the cabin and went down to the lake to meet boys. It was mostly whispers, giggles, and muted screams at the excitement of being outside running around in the dark, until a tall boy stepped out from behind a pine tree and kissed me on the mouth. I couldn't concentrate on how it felt, I was so busy being amazed. I was being kissed. This was my first kiss. Somebody actually *wanted* to kiss me.

That would have been more than enough for one week, but then it was Sunday, our last day at camp, and we went to church up at the big house, Rose Hill. I managed to follow along in the prayer book, and get down and up with the others. When the time came for communion, I went. Kneeling at the rail, I held out my hands for the host and popped it into my mouth. I watched the priest coming down the row with a silver chalice. You were supposed to help him by tilting the base of the cup with your hands so he'd know when you had a swallow. Then he wiped where your lips had been with a white napkin. I tilted the cup expecting grape juice and got a mouthful of delicious golden wine. It went burning straight down, converting me to Episcopalianism on the spot.

Was this a great church or what? Boys, dirty jokes, kissing, and now, *real wine*. I walked back across the road to the hotel with my duffle bag.

Miss Hosford said, "How was it?"

I shrugged. "Okay."

You really couldn't give grown-ups an inch.

My family was extremely modest, especially my father. I never even saw him in his underwear. Having only sisters, I had no idea what a man's privates looked like. I studied our set of *Encyclopedia Americana* and decided the fig-leaf-shaped thing on the naked statues must be it. But how, if what Doug said was true, did a man get that inside a woman, or, more important, how did he get it out? Wouldn't the pointy parts get stuck?

My next guess came from the telephone book. The green cover that year featured Mercury, the messenger god, naked except for his winged cap, carrying coils of thick—good grief, was that it? I realized later it was phone cable, but for a good long time I thought I'd found it, and wondered how men hid it inside their trousers.

Nobody explained and in seventh grade our sex education was limited to a film about the dreaded event, menstruation—shown to girls only—boys had to watch separately. The movie featured anatomical drawings and a cartoon girl shivering under a shower of ice cubes. You were not to take cold showers during your period. Nothing about the good stuff; no hint about doing it.

I got what my mother called the curse at the end of seventh grade. No celebration, no congratulations for becoming a woman, just a trip to Brent's drugstore, where everyone knew me and my mother sent me into a cringing fit by loudly asking for a box of sanitary napkins. Back at home, shut in the bathroom, she showed me how to use them, and how to wrap them in toilet paper afterwards so that none of the nasty blood showed. That was that. Except I knew what the real curse was: now I could get pregnant.

One month I missed my period and thought I was. I'd never slept with anybody, never let any boy close to down there, so how could it be? One possibility was the public pool. I'd heard if sperm got loose in the water, they could swim under a girl's bathing suit and make a baby. Could that have happened?

I knew my parents would never believe any story about a virgin birth. The only male in the house was my father, so my dark suspicions fell on him. He must have slipped down the hall while I was asleep and done it to me. How else was it possible? At the breakfast table, I glared at him until he lowered his newspaper and asked what was the matter. I said, "Nothing" in what I considered a meaningful tone, and he said to stop glowering and eat my cereal. Three weeks later, I got my period. I almost fainted with relief. I couldn't apologize to Daddy, since I'd never, thank heavens, actually accused him. It did occur to me that the warm feeling I got lying in bed picturing Daddy sneaking down the dark hall to do it to me was something I never need share with my friends.

In Latin class the next year, we learned about androgyny. The way Mrs. Johnson explained it, Zeus punished humans by splitting them in two. Alone, each was only half a person, searching the world for its other half. When you found it, you united and became a complete human being. Either the split up our behinds or our navel marked the place where we'd been divided. I got mixed up about that part, because, for me, the story had nothing to do with androgyny—Mrs. Johnson's point that we each had male and female characteristics. It was mythological evidence of my search for a prince. Somewhere out there was the perfect man and, when I found him, we would unite and find eternal bliss as a complete person. I spent a lot of time from twelve to eighteen looking for this man. When I brushed my teeth at night, staring into the mirror, I thrilled at the thought that, out there, he was brushing his teeth, ignorant of my existence but moving inexorably toward me in time.

By the end of ninth grade, I grew what Mama called a figure. I had a boyfriend and was smooching. Or that's what Mary Elizabeth claimed at the breakfast table one morning.

"I saw you smooching on the front porch last night."

"You did not."

"Did so."

"You're a liar and if you say one word, I'll kill you."

Smooching included body-to-body kissing, done standing (none of us was old enough to drive), awkward fumbling around the top of a girl's blouse, but no serious attempt to get under the clothes.

In the summer after ninth grade, I was fourteen and obsessed with sex. I thought about it, dreamed about it, and tried to find books that would give me some hard facts, like how exactly did you do it? Searching the drugstore racks for titles, I found most of the covers cruelly deceptive. A book called *Lust on the Cornish Coast* showed a dark-haired man leaning over a near-naked woman, but concluded all love scenes with "Softly he closed the bedroom door," or ". . . and then he took her."

The two best were *Forever Amber* and *The Chinese Room*. I read the good pages over and over in a fever of longing. In *The Chinese Room*, a woman sat in front of her mirror naked, preparing for her lover by rouging her nipples until they rose, bright red and hard as chocolate kisses. Reading this, I felt a weakening heat between my legs, a scalding longing for sex. Out there somewhere, waiting, was perfect lovemaking, and when you found that, when a boy put his thing inside you, bells rang, you fainted into ecstasy; you were fulfilled. Nothing was spelled out, there were no directions, but from the way I felt reading about it, if a boy got anywhere near me with his thing, it would probably work.

I stayed aroused all the time. I could walk down the street with my thighs rubbing together and get hot all over. Boys were filled with lust, too. I knew that. It was a girl's job to keep them from getting carried away and, if that didn't work, to stop them before they went too far. What if I couldn't? What if I lost my head and got pregnant?

One night, I heard my parents talking in low voices outside my closed bedroom door.

Mama said, "What if she's hot-blooded like Emily?"

Daddy's voice: "Let's hope not."

Emily was his older sister. She'd been married four times, three of them to the same man. I felt better. Passion ran in the family. I couldn't help myself. I had inherited hot blood.

In tenth grade, I met my first real boyfriend. He was two years older, a grade ahead, and played football. Actually, he rather resembled a football: short, round, and firm to the touch. His blond hair fell fetchingly over his forehead and he had a darling gap between his two top teeth. When we went out, he made sardonic remarks about his teachers and life. I found him brilliant.

One night we went to the Billy Graham Crusade. I went on a dare with myself, to prove I couldn't be moved by Baptist evangelism. But when the lights dimmed in the stadium behind our junior high and Billy Graham stood with a spotlight behind him, setting his yellow hair on fire like the pictures of Jesus, I weakened. His voice was low and soothing. "Let your heart be filled with love."

I felt myself fill with an enormous longing.

"Give yourself to the Lord Jesus Christ."

I longed to give myself to something. The choir of 150 voices sang, "I walk through the Garden alone, and the dew is wet on the roses."

Billy Graham whispered seductively. "Come on down. Come on down."

We looked at each other. Wordlessly, we stood and walked down the concrete steps toward the playing field.

"I see sweethearts coming hand-in-hand," Billy Graham said.

That was us, warmed by faith and by all those people watching.

Everyone being reborn stood together down front while the choir sang. I rededicated my life to Jesus Christ and swore that I would never tell another lie. Afterwards, in the tent, all the saved people were asked to make pledges to the Crusade for Christ, which sort of took the glow off, but when we parked later on the gravel street below my house, I kissed with renewed fervor. We were together now in our very souls.

Back at home, Mama asked where I'd been. Remembering my vow, I told the truth. "Parking."

The birthmark on her forehead lit up. "*Parking?*" She grabbed me, digging her fingernails into my shoulders.

"Ouch." I tried to pull away.

"Ouch yourself. Ouch nothing. Haven't I warned you about parking? You could be murdered by a pervert, or arrested, and no

boy respects a girl who lets him do that. You're going to be punished, young lady. No date next weekend. No going out at all."

I went to my room and wept in frustration. I hated my mother.
I lived for weekends and my date. He'd think I was a baby being
locked up this way. Telling the truth was stupid. I took back my
vow.

By now I was in love. We were going steady. His gold football
swung on a chain between my small breasts. After the Saturday
night movie, we went for a hamburger and an Orange Crush at the
Cherokee Inn. Then we parked on the gravel road below my house
and petted in the backseat of his father's car until we were both red-
faced and panting. I rubbed against him with my body and pulled
his hand away when he tried to reach under my skirt. If he wouldn't
stop, I raked his face with my long pointed fingernails, leaving red,
curved tracks. He yelped in pain, but he pulled away. I kissed the
hurt and told him we couldn't do it. I had to stay a virgin.

One Saturday night I carried petting one dangerous step further
and took off my underpants, or rather let him pull them down. "I
won't put it in," he whispered. "Just let me rub it against you." A rush
of air blew against my naked skin and I felt a dreadful need to be
filled. This is what those books had been hinting at.

"What are our bodies for?" He tickled my ear with his words.
"What are these feelings for? You know I love you. How can it be
wrong if we both want it so much?"

I moaned and twisted under him, but didn't answer. He had my
skirt and crinolines up around my waist. His thing was out, warm
and smooth against my leg. (Boys had "things"; girls had "down
there." We never used the p or the v word.) He rubbed it up and
down my thigh, feeling wetly through my pubic hair with his finger.
He had his finger up inside me. We ground our bodies together.

"Please baby, please baby, please baby, please." He moaned in my
ear, licking it, making the hair on the back of my neck stand up. I
wanted him. I wanted him to put it right in and lifted my hips to

meet him, keeping my eyes shut tight so I wouldn't see what I was doing. I felt it slide in.

Hot as I was, I couldn't do it. If I got pregnant, I'd have to kill myself. "No." I tried to lift him off. He held my arms. "I said, *no*." I shoved with both arms, pushing him onto the floor and slicing his face with my nails. I slid out the back door of the car and ran up the road toward home.

He roared. I heard his feet in the gravel behind me and felt his rough arms, no talk of love now, dragging me kicking and biting back to the car.

"That's enough, you cock-teaser."

"I can't." I was sobbing.

He was unmoved. "No more."

He threw me into the backseat and held me down with one arm, spreading my legs and forcing himself inside. I was thrilled and horrified at what I'd caused. I couldn't stop him; he was much stronger. This wasn't my fault. I kept my eyes closed. I was finally going to be fulfilled.

It hurt so bad I cried out at the pain. He didn't stop. He pushed harder, shoving his way until he tore through. He grunted twice, then let me go and sat up. Sticky stuff ran down my leg. I wept, wiping the inside of my thigh with my underpants. He drove me home without speaking. I leaned against my door watching him, worried that he might not still love me.

I went in the house, down the hall, away from my sleeping parents, not turning on a light until I was safely inside the bathroom with the door closed. My face in the mirror looked ruined. My hair was matted and kissing had left a red smear around my mouth. I felt dirty. Passion was fun; sex was awful. I licked the tears away as I washed the blood and gunk out of my underpants. "You're not a virgin anymore," I told the girl in the mirror, the one who had left home me and come back somebody else.

I could have called the police. I was only fourteen and he was sixteen, but that would have meant telling. It wasn't consensual sex, but I knew it was my fault. That's how things worked. I had let it happen. Good girls were supposed to be stronger. Miss Hosford was right: I would never be a lady.

I prayed not to be pregnant, I mean *prayed*. Got down on my knees next to the toilet and begged God.

15

I wasn't pregnant. Proof of divine intervention.

My personal problems made me miss the other signs of trouble in our house. Aside from being boy crazy, I considered myself a noticing kind of person. I noticed when Mother closed in the screened front porch, turning it into a sunroom like the one I admired at Momae's. The new porch had big glass windows, sisal carpet, and bamboo furniture covered in flamboyantly flowered cotton. We had built-in shelves for the record player, where I played my new favorite, *South Pacific*, on the new long-play record. I sang loudly along: "You've got to be taught to love and to hate." I was floored by that song. In the South, without the lesson being named, whites were taught to feel superior and colored people to serve. I sang the words fervently, hoping to make the point to anyone within earshot. Mama told me to either tone it down or close the door.

She'd moved on to her next project: turning the garage into a bedroom and bath for her and Daddy. I was for it. I would get their old room and furniture.

After work, Daddy went over the bills.

"What's this?" He sounded cross.

Mama leaned in behind him to explain.

He frowned and shook his head. "We can't go on this way."

"I got three bids and his was the best." I heard Mama's voice shake. She was frightened of Daddy's anger. We all were. Later I wondered if he'd meant something else entirely.

With the new room finished, the two of them began sleeping in

148

twin beds, hooked together under a single headboard. Those beds may have been one of the signs I missed, with their appearance of togetherness without the necessity of touching.

Mother seemed happy with her new card-playing porch and the garage-turned-bedroom. She was making plans to repaper the living room in dark green and the dining room in Chinese red. Daddy was Daddy, funny and teasing when he was home and not going over bills, but not home much.

I blamed my blindness on the times. This was 1950. People married and stayed married. Whether they loved one another wasn't a consideration. They were your parents and they were together, forever and ever, amen.

I'd put the exotic lady from Hawaii out of my head. She was a blip on the war screen, and that was long ago. Besides, for all I knew, nothing happened. If I had to guess now and Daddy was anything like me, he was grabbing Helen every chance he got, but back then, I didn't know the word adultery. I couldn't picture my parents doing it with each other, much less anybody else.

Daddy's true love, we were told, was the law. He loved it so much he went back to the office every night after dinner. He worked Saturday and Sunday mornings. He went to the office instead of church.

This was how a typical Sunday morning went in our house. We dressed up for church. My father dressed for the office. Galloway Memorial and his building were only two blocks apart. We dropped him off.

As he got out of the car, I said, "Are you sure you don't want to go to church?"

"Too much work to do."

I said (I can't believe this now), "Aren't you afraid of going to hell?"

He gave a snort. "I'm more afraid of getting hell from your grandpa if I don't have this brief done by tomorrow."

I was religious back then and genuinely worried. He was putting his soul in jeopardy for the law. Mama said we were lucky to have such a smart, hard-working father.

He and Mother went to bed in the same room every night. If we never heard sounds of passionate lovemaking (God forbid), we never heard raised voices either.

So it was a horrible surprise when Daddy called us out into the hall one afternoon. It was dark out there. The scene is all in gray.

"I have something to tell you." He took a breath. "I'm moving out."

Mary Elizabeth gasped and he put an arm on her shoulder. "Your mother and I are separating."

I felt tears prickling behind my eyes. He *couldn't* leave. He was the only thing that made this family okay.

His eyes filled, which really scared me. He was serious. "It has nothing to do with you girls. You know I love you."

Which meant it was Mama he didn't love, and loving us wasn't enough.

Mary Elizabeth began to cry, then Sydney.

"Why?" That's all I could say without bawling.

He shook his head and stood up. "It's something I have to do."

Mary Elizabeth wrapped her arms around his waist. "Don't go, Daddy. Please don't go.'"

We looked at Mama. Wasn't she going to stop him? She stood there with red eyes, her arms folded, lips pressed together.

Daddy pried Mary Elizabeth off, went to their bedroom, picked up his hat and a suitcase, and walked out the back door. "I'll be in touch." He didn't look back.

Mama was drained and gray. I realized they must have been talking about this for longer than I knew. The suitcase was packed before he told us.

Annie wiped her eyes on her apron. "What about this dinner?"

Mama said, "Let's eat in the kitchen tonight."

She didn't touch a bite, just smoked and drank while we pushed our food around.

After he left, the whole house felt like a funeral. It was one thing to have your father away at war, and entirely another to have him pick up and move to another place in the same town. I felt hollow, as if he'd taken away one of my body parts.

I kept asking Mother why? I thought she'd come up with an answer and I would understand. She said it was just something he was going through and not to worry, they weren't getting a divorce. That was not much comfort. It didn't make up for the silent dinners, for not hearing his stories, or only seeing him on the weekends, when he'd show up to take us to a baseball game. I didn't mention his disappearance to my friends. It was too shameful to talk about. Entering high school that fall, I filled out a form, which asked if my parents were living, dead, married, or divorced. In the blank provided, deeply humiliated, I wrote: *Separated*.

Mother had spies everywhere. Her friend Dimple called. Daddy had been spotted eating at Primos. Hilda saw him riding down South State. Frances heard he'd rented an apartment on Pinehurst. They were like her posse. The clues came in daily. I eavesdropped on these conversations and it wasn't hard to pick up the gist. Mother repeated everything. "He was at *Primos*? He doesn't even like foreign food." As if she could prove it wasn't him.

Mary Elizabeth and I didn't talk about it. She was too young and knew even less than I did. We tiptoed around, trying to stay under the radar, because Mama was either yelling, crying, or pretending everything was going to be okay in a way that was painful to watch.

One day Mama got a report that sent her over the top. I heard her on the phone in their bedroom. Her voice rose in a way it hadn't before.

"He was with *who?*"

Then it got flat and mean. "I know who Mildred is."

Daddy had been seen at a restaurant across town with his secretary. That did it. He could leave Mother, move out and get his own apartment, but he could not humiliate the family by being seen in public with a *secretary*. It was common, too trashy to believe. Mama, Dimple, Hilda, and Frances agreed about this on the phone and over cards. She would never give him a divorce. N-E-V-E-R. He could run around like some lowlife, but he would never be free to marry that woman, not while Mama had a breath left in her body.

Mary Elizabeth and I had never paid much attention to Mildred. She was pretty in a plain sort of way, tall and awkward, with light brown hair and blue eyes. At parties for the law firm, she hung back, smiling and silent. She had one of those smiles that showed a lot of gum. She was always dressed in something you couldn't remember five minutes later. That was Mildred in a nutshell: five minutes later, you forgot all about her.

Daddy worked a lot, so he saw Mildred more than he saw us. That's all we knew. It never occurred to us he might like her *that* way. She was a good secretary. He told us she'd won a contest as the fastest typist in the state of Mississippi. She came to work for Grandpa while Daddy was away in the navy, arriving straight out of high school from some little town in south Mississippi. She was always nice to us, bending her head to speak to us in her flat country accent, which, for educated Jacksonians, spelled *ignorant*.

How could our smart, sophisticated, cum laude father take up with a hick? We were entirely on Mother's side about this.

She was drinking her way through another dinner. "I'm not going to stand for it."

We said, "What?" because we weren't supposed to know.

She said, "Never mind. I've asked your uncle Doug to try to talk some sense into him."

Uncle Doug and Daddy played bridge together on Saturday afternoons. Mama must have figured her brother brought the more powerful male influence to the fight.

That didn't work. Uncle Doug went to Daddy's office and had a talk. From what I overheard, he was told to mind his own business. He'd hated doing it and said for Mama not to ask him again.

Mama went to Aunt Boo, Daddy's oldest sister. She was a partner in the law firm, the only woman lawyer they had. They met at Boo's house, so I don't know what happened, except Daddy called, really mad, and told Mama to keep his family out of this.

Mama even went to see Daddy's parents, Grandma and Grandpa, which must have been hard. Both were elderly and Grandpa had retired. They lived quietly in a big dark house on North State Street. Mama took a plate of her special divinity, but it didn't help. I heard her telling Hilda that they made it a policy not to interfere in their adult children's lives.

Mama's last resort was Miss Hosford. She hated asking. Her older sister was the kind who enjoyed pointing out your failings before she agreed to help. But Miss Hosford had big ammunition: she knew the bishop. She pulled strings the way she had with the school bus back when I was in third grade. She persuaded the Episcopal bishop and our Methodist minister, Dr. Selah, to go to Daddy's office. They reminded him of his duty, his place in the community, his vows, and of us, the children. They ground him down. I suspect it was the "place in the community" business that did it. Daddy was an ambitious man. Divorce was not acceptable. Dallying with secretaries in any kind of public way even less so.

He agreed to come home. We were overjoyed. Daddy and his suitcase returned and we had two parents again. I could go back to my self-involved normal.

But some sort of devil's bargain had been made to get him into that twin bed. We only knew what we saw. Daddy never touched Mother. No good-by pecks on the cheek, no hugs. With us, he was his old self. With Mama, it was as if he'd gotten stuck at her table on the ship of marriage. He was polite, even affable, but there was no affection. We must have had blinders on not to wonder what they'd agreed to, but we didn't want to know. No talk, please, about unhappy marriage or unrequited love. No more changes. In that respect, we were deeply conservative.

Was this what I was going to grow up and get myself into? Living inside the hollowness of that marriage, I pretended along with everyone else, but I swore it would never happen to me.

The damage showed up in another way. My sister Mary Elizabeth, though she'd been slow to walk, "lazy," Marie called it, never caused any other trouble. Around the time Daddy left home, she developed what the family called "a temper."

I got home from school one day to find Annie, Mama, and Marie in a circle around her in the kitchen. Mary Elizabeth was screaming mad. I don't know what about, some little nothing, but she was hollering loud enough to bring the police.

I said, "Stop it." Like she'd hear the voice of older sister authority and snap to.

She screeched louder.

Mama reached out to try and comfort her. Mary Elizabeth threw her arm off and bared her teeth.

We took a step away. Mary Elizabeth was that fierce. Her face went from red to blue. The noise was awful. Annie got a glass of cold water and threw it on her. She collapsed like a doll with her eyes rolling back. When she sat up, it was as if nothing had happened. She looked at us crowded around and asked what we were staring at.

Mama took her to the doctor. He said not to interfere. Some children were high-strung. Best to leave her alone. If she got too upset she might stop breathing.

We never knew when she might erupt; the smallest setback triggered tantrums so violent it was scary. We had to stand back and let her blow. I was more than a little put out. For one thing, it didn't seem fair. At her age, if I'd acted that way, I'd have been whipped. It felt like a trick, a way of showing off that you couldn't be punished for.

154

Mother said, "Try and understand, your sister is extremely sensitive."

After seventh grade, Mary Elizabeth got her period, and began having horrible pains. Every month, she skipped school and took to her bed, moaning and crying. Doctors were consulted. I felt bad about the hurting, but I also thought she was playing it like she did the tantrums, to get attention. I wanted to shout at my parents: can't you see she's pretending? But then there was an operation. Mary Elizabeth was opened up like a gutted fish and something called endometriosis was cut out. Menstrual tissue, I was told, wandering around her insides where it wasn't supposed to be. The surgery required a long recuperation, much special care, and missed school. Trust Mary Elizabeth to come up with something nobody ever heard of, a malady to turn the house upside down.

I'd come home from school and she'd be lying in bed, propped on pillows, looking pale and put-upon. She'd put down her novel, which she was free to read all day while I marched from one class to another, and speak in this tiny, sick voice. "Would you get me another glass of boiled custard?" Boiled custard was a special treat in our house. It was made only when one of us was ill. I loved it and hardly ever got it. Here was Mary Elizabeth drinking it every day.

In ninth grade, she took to fainting. I had never fainted and always wanted to. In books, it sounded romantic. You did it in the presence of a handsome man, and you collapsed gracefully, your skirt stayed down, maybe you made a little swooning sound. Mary Elizabeth fainted every day before math class, and she fainted in front of the coach, one of the few presentable men in junior high. It had to be a trick. Of course she was faking. Couldn't my parents see that? Once again, there were consultations with the doctor. It was a part of the turning blue thing. She had fainting reflex. Anything to get attention.

Because of her health and temperament, my sister could not be crossed. If she wanted something, she got it. I was filled with resentment. When I was little, illness was considered a weakness. You bucked up and didn't complain. You certainly weren't coddled. Here was Mary Elizabeth doing the opposite and being rewarded.

She loved shoes. I wasn't sure why. She didn't have Mama's small feet, though hers were smaller than my size eights. She got all the shoes she wanted. I counted the pairs in her closet once when I was home from college: fifty.

I tried to even things up the best I could. I told her that she wasn't the pretty one; I was (as if there could only be one). I said she'd never be the pretty one. She went crying to Mother and Daddy and I got punished. "Your sister is delicate," Mother said. "You need to be more considerate." Mary Elizabeth stole my diary and brought it to the dinner table one night. From her place across the table, she read aloud: "He kissed me and I felt it all the way to my toes." I got up from my place, walked around the table, and began to strangle her. My father slapped me hard across the face—twice— left, right. He'd never slapped me before. I blamed my sister for that, too.

One Saturday after seeing a Bette Davis movie, I discovered Mary Elizabeth had eaten the peach I had my eye on. We were alone and I chased her screaming into the backyard with a butcher knife, using my Bette Davis voice: "How dare you eat the lawst peach?" She told Mama and Daddy I tried to kill her, and I got punished for that, too.

I suspected she was as smart as I was, maybe a little smarter. And she was polite in a way that made teachers like her better. When it came time to go to college, my parents said they could only afford to send me to a state school, though I begged for Sophie Newcomb in New Orleans. Four years later, when Mary Elizabeth went, they sent her to Hollins, the most expensive girls' school in the South.

Even when swollen with resentment at the things my sister got, and got away with, I knew I was the lucky one. Something was wrong with Mary Elizabeth and it wasn't anything we knew how to fix.

◆ ◆ ◆

No matter how drunk on boys I got, I never ignored school. In our house, you made good grades or else. We got paid for them, but only for A's. Actually, when I wasn't swooning over some member of the male sex, I loved school. I worked hard and excelled in everything but math. Making A's was another way of showing off. Every afternoon, I raced through my homework to have time to read. After supper, I waited for a phone call from my latest true love. While we talked, I used my sharp fingernails to cut away tiny triangles of wallpaper. By the time I left home, a six-inch area around the phone alcove had been denuded.

I broke up with the deflowerer shortly after that horrible night. Too much violence. We pretended things were the same, but they weren't. In my junior year, I looked over the crop of available boys and chose a sophomore. Picking someone younger was considered a scandal, but youth did not dim the radiance of this boy's white-blonde curls, the length of his straight nose, or the ocean-blue marbles that were his eyes. The fact that he had trouble articulating a full sentence was offset by a perfect body and his grace when carrying a football down the field.

He came to pick me up the first night and was hauled before my parents for introductions. All my dates had to be put through this: Mother examining them with gimlet eyes, Daddy extending a hand and calling each one "son."

Mother approached after my first date. "Where does this boy live?" The question had never come up because all the boys I'd dated were from the neighborhood. I asked him and reported back. "West Jackson."

A tightening of the lips. "What does his father do?"

Further inquiries. I learned he had no father and his mother sewed for a living. Mother never said I couldn't go out with him, but I could see what she thought as plain as if it were written on her forehead.

In tenth grade, white students from all over Jackson poured into one big downtown school, appropriately called Central High. You couldn't tell by looking what part of town people went home to. We lived in northeast Jackson, the nice part. If you were nice, you lived there and if you didn't live there, you must not be nice. That was the message I got, though I don't think either of my parents ever said it out loud.

It wasn't enough to be white, you had to be the right kind of white, from the right part of town, with a father who did the right kind of work. Nice mothers didn't work. None of my mother's bridge-playing friends had jobs. If you had to work, it meant your husband was unable to take proper care of you. This seemed an odd bias, when, in our family alone, Miss Hosford ran a hotel, Aunt Boo practiced law, Aunt Leigh bought and sold oil leases, and Aunt Marguerite taught college English. The aunts were anomalies, I was led to understand. Those professions had found them; they didn't work because they had to. They weren't like Mama's friend who clerked at a clothing store. Nice women didn't have to work.

To be the right kind of white southerner, you must be educated and have the proper southern accent, not flat like Mildred's. You could be Jewish and nice, but I was told not to waste my time dating Jewish boys. They would never marry me. As for Catholics, who knew what they did over at St. Joseph's, the school we could see out Central High's second-floor windows: worshipping the pope, fish on Friday, incense? We had Catholic friends, but I was told not to waste time on those boys either. They only married their own.

Dating was a prelude to marriage. Girls took that in with their mother's milk. (If they were nursed, which I certainly wasn't. It was considered unhygienic and Mother did not wish to ruin her breasts.) All husband material should be prospected for in northeast Jackson. West Jackson was suspect, south Jackson more so. The boys should be Protestant: Methodist, Baptist, Presbyterian, or Episcopalian. We didn't know any Lutherans or Church of Christ people, but presumably they would be okay, too.

In my senior year, I dropped the sophomore as I had dropped the football player before him. I moved on. Eddie Dorgan played football and turned out to be Irish Catholic. This meant we could never marry, but that only lent poignancy to our gropings. Eddie introduced me to Dixieland jazz. We spent hours late at night, parked in some dark spot in his 1940 Ford, bent over the car radio trying to bring in station WWL from New Orleans. He brought records over to the house and I traded *South Pacific* for Al Hirt, Pete Fountain, and the Dukes of Dixieland.

I loved everything I heard about New Orleans. It was Sin City, where upright people from Jackson went to cut loose. I'd been dying to go since Daddy and I put the Hawaiian lady on the train. Sam Junior, Uncle Sam and Momae's son, promised to take me when I got old enough. The year I turned seventeen he and Mama decided I was ready.

The city looked as foreign and exotic as I'd hoped. People sounded different. We stayed in the French Quarter and walked down Bourbon Street listening to Dixieland pouring out of the open doors. Sam Junior and Julia took me to Pat O'Brien's and bought me a Hurricane, a pink and sweetly lethal drink made of rum and fruit juice. There didn't seem to be any rule about underage drinking in New Orleans. The Hurricane was served in a big curvy glass, which you got to keep. By the time I sipped my way to the bottom, I'd lost all inhibition. Sam Junior, with his huge voice, persuaded me up onto the bar, where I wriggled along as the band played "I Wish That I Could Shimmy Like My Sister Kate." The last time I'd done that was in fourth grade in the talent contest at Canton Elementary. My act hadn't gotten any better. The next morning, I could hardly look at myself in the mirror remembering. Through my first horrible hangover, I resolved to give up that song forever.

Mama was enthralled by my dating, and I was too carried away by popularity to realize I might be traveling a road that ended in her shoes. Any small doubts about my future were erased by the amazing dresses she conjured and created for me to wear to dances: aqua organza with layers of skirt and a gold beaded bodice; strapless black taffeta with a dropped waist and a silver sequin snake slithering down my front. Everything was fitted over a merry widow tight enough for Scarlett O'Hara, and worn with three-inch heels. I'd come home late and Mama would be waiting, sitting in bed beside my sleeping father. Had I been a success? How many boys danced with me? Those were the days where you went with one boy, but danced with as many as asked you. It was intoxicating swinging from one boy's arms to another. Mama's eyes glittered when I told her I'd been broken in on ten times a dance. She wanted her dresses to circle the floor in every man's arms. Listening, she forgot her troubles. It was as pleased with me as she ever got.

Dances were not enough to hide the distress in our house. When I came in the door from school, I was instructed to stop at Mama's card table and have a little conversation with each of the ladies. I gradually picked up that these afternoon games were as much about drinking as they were about card playing, especially where Mama was concerned.

One day, I made my greeting and Mama seemed all right. Maybe the smile was a little wide, the eyes a bit unfocused. By suppertime, she wasn't right at all. She served the plates okay, though her hands shook. In our family, she did the carving. My father had no manual skills. I'd never seen him so much as hang a picture. Mama sliced the roast, spooned out the rice and gravy, and called for Annie to bring in the vegetable.

She tried to tell a story. "Hilda bid four no-trump and I looked across the table at Frances. I knew from my hand Hilda didn't have the cards—" There was a silence. She looked confused. "Did I say, Hilda bid four no-trump?" She was slipping on the "s."

I stared at Mary Elizabeth and Sydney. We didn't have to say a word. We knew.

I glanced at Daddy. He sat chewing with his eyes shut. He had taken himself away to some other place.

Mary Elizabeth said, "Finish the story, Mama."

She gave a crazy laugh. "I guess I lost my drift."

These bridge games went on three afternoons a week, at our house or someone else's.

One day, I got her alone in their bedroom. "You're drinking too much."

The birthmark of South America lit up on her forehead. "No, I'm not."

"Yes, you *are*." I got ready to duck in case she threw one of her wedge-heeled bedroom slippers at my head, which she tended to do when words failed her. "It's almost every night. And it makes Daddy unhappy."

She made a derisive noise, as if I didn't know squat about being unhappy. "I'll tell you one thing, young lady, I manage this house. Three meals a day get put on the table. I make your clothes. If I ever get to a place where I can't do those things, then maybe I'm drinking too much. Until then, you can mind your own business."

She did manage the house. She was an amazing manager, and she did almost all of it by telephone. She ordered our groceries daily, standing in the kitchen, smoking a Lucky Strike, tapping her size 4½ foot as she checked her list: How did the lettuce look? Did he have any nice ripe avocados? Farm produce came to the back door from a man who walked our street hollering: "I got corn and butter beans; I got fresh lady peas and collard greens." Mama and Annie would study the day's offerings and buy a half a dozen ears of corn and a quart of lady peas, measured out with a tin can. I never took a moment to wonder how long it must have taken the man or his wife to shell that burlap sack of fresh peas.

We got pickup and delivery from Kolb's Cleaners. Brent's drugstore delivered cigarettes, soap, bath powder, and Bufferin. No cash involved: everything charged. We got milk, cream, butter, and even ice cream from the milkman. The Coca-Cola man stopped his big red truck at our house once a week to bring in a case of bottles. Once a month, Mother ordered liquor. Mississippi was a dry state, but that only confused the ill-informed. She'd phone our bootlegger over in Rankin County and order a mixed case of bourbon, scotch, and gin, which was delivered in broad daylight to our front door. The trunk of the yellow Cadillac carrying it was so heavy with illegal goods the bumper scraped. The bill at the end of the month read: "Merchandise."

Not that Mother didn't go out. She had her hair done once a week. She saw the chiropodist, who carved away at her yellow corns, and left her in a state of bliss Daddy no longer provided. She went to church and to play cards at Hilda's, Dimple's, or Frances's house. At night she went to drinking parties with the Vaugheys or Fitzhughs, friends with oil money. Daddy seldom went to these parties. He never went anywhere with her. It was as if they lived separate lives and met up at night in the twin beds.

Mama had gotten what she wanted. She was Mrs. Tom Watkins. She had a nice house, membership in the Junior League, well-brought-up daughters, and a prominent husband. But even a person as self-centered as I was in those days sensed the misery. She had a husband who didn't want to be there. She was married to a man who wouldn't touch her. In the mornings, she never admitted to a hangover, but her breakfast was a cup of black coffee, two Bufferin, and a Lucky Strike.

At seventeen, I decided to go to the heart of the matter. On the way home from school one day, alone in the car with my father, I got up my nerve. "Why don't you love Mama?"

I looked straight ahead. My father could go from warm to cold in about a second. Ask a question he found too personal and a wall came down behind his blue eyes. You knew not to say one more word on that subject. I'd seen him do it to grown men, so it wasn't just me. This time, he didn't get mad.

I was hoping he'd say, "Of course I love your mother." He didn't.

"Because of the operation."

"You mean the back operation?" Mother had recently had surgery for degenerative discs and worn a heavy brace under her clothes for weeks.

"The operation she had while I was in the navy. When your sister was born."

I thought he meant the Caesarean. "Why did that make you stop loving her?"

"The doctor said your mother shouldn't have any more children, that her heart wouldn't take it. She let them give her a hysterectomy without even asking me, wrote me a letter after it was done." His voice was bitter. "That was my last chance to have a son. There is no one to carry on the Watkins name."

The foundation of my world fell away. I sat there too shocked to speak. In one part of my brain, I felt flattered that Daddy talked to me like a real person and told me the truth. I'm ashamed to say, another part blamed Mother. I would have been happy to die trying to give him a son. But the truth behind his words sent me into despair. I thought they'd been joking about naming me Thomasina. What disappointments we must have been: me, Mary Elizabeth, and finally Sydney. There was nothing we could do to make up for the mistake of being female. I tried to be funny and smart. I wanted to be politically aware so Daddy would be glad he had me, but he didn't give a hill of beans about that. He didn't want smart, funny daughters. He wanted obedient women and a son to carry on the Watkins name.

We were quiet for a while. I didn't know what to say.

He said, "It doesn't mean I don't love you girls."

"I know."

I got up my nerve to ask the other hard question. "After we grow up, will you leave Mama?"

He didn't answer for so long, I glanced over at him.

"I don't know."

I sat silent for the rest of the ride, wrestling with this new information: the man I loved above all others had never wanted me. He never wanted any of us.

16

I kept what Daddy told me a secret and carried it around inside like a stone. I thought my father was the brightest, most handsome man in the entire world. Unlike my friends' fathers, he weighed exactly what he had in college as a cross-country runner. He had a full head of hair and flashing blue eyes. He could make anything funny. People said he was one of the best lawyers in the state of Mississippi.

If he didn't love Mother, it must be her fault. I observed her with a critical eye. She could do much better with herself. Stop drinking, for one thing. And how about that chin? She was getting the Latimer neck. I asked her why she didn't get a lift. We were in my bedroom.

"I thought about it," she said. "What good would it do?"

She looked so beaten I went ahead and asked the rest. "Why don't you leave Daddy? You could find somebody else. Somebody fun like Uncle Sam, a man who likes to drink and would take you on trips." Daddy had not only stopped going to parties, he'd quit going with us to Allison's Wells. We no longer took our lone vacation, a yearly trip to Biloxi for the bar convention.

Mama said, "Everything I do is for you girls. You're the reason I stay."

"Don't do it for us." I was being serious in the pretentious way of somebody about to escape that house. I didn't really want them to split up. We'd been miserable with him gone. I just wanted Mama to be happier. Daddy seemed to have made peace with a life spent working and eating with his eyes closed, but she hadn't.

"You don't understand." Mama shook her head in a way that let me know she'd chosen the sacrifice and I was ungrateful not to appreciate it.

Days would go by, months even, when I lived in cheerful oblivion. Annie, under Mother's direction, served us wonderful meals. At the supper table, we howled with laughter at Daddy's stories. I'd forget and decide we were a perfectly ordinary family. No one else's parents slept in separate beds, but sleeping that way must mean they didn't have sex, which was a relief not to contemplate. None of us ever asked why they didn't sleep together. A question like that was out of bounds.

Then something would happen. Mother would come to the table "tight." We said "tight" rather than "drunk." Drunk was how Uncle Doug got at the Petroleum Club, when Aunt Leigh had to call Hosford's older son, John Fontaine Three, to help get him home. Mother got silly and slurry. Daddy went silent in a way that made clear his revulsion. Or I'd watch him pull away from one of her small attempts at affection. It was like seeing the dark ropey backstage of a play. Ordinary life was a pretense. All I wanted was to escape, and I promised myself I would never be like my mother. I would never be trapped.

I got away by going to college. When I came home on vacation, everyone acted so happy to see me, it made me think we liked each other. They praised my high grades. Mother put a vase of flowers on top of the toilet in my bathroom as her special welcome. I told funny stories at the supper table about my professors and the boys I dated. I joked around with Annie. The noise I made served as cover and, by the time I ran out of energy and the weight of that house silenced me, vacation was over and I could leave.

Early in the summer of 1954, something big happened, big enough to make us forget our personal tribulations. The Supreme Court handed down *Brown v. Board of Education*, deciding unanimously that state laws establishing separate public schools for Negro and white students were inherently unequal and violated the Equal Protection Clause of the Fourteenth Amendment.

Just like in the Bible, the scales fell from my eyes.

Daddy and I were riding home from work when the news came over the radio. I had finished my freshman year and had a summer job as a deputy in the chancery clerk's office. I said, "Isn't that great? In a few hundred years we'll all have caramel-colored skin and no pimples."

He looked at me as if he'd given birth to a serpent. "You don't know what you're talking about."

But I did. Even at eighteen, I saw where we'd gone wrong. I should have seen it all along. If Negroes—that was my new word. I would never again, in my awakened state, say "colored." I still pronounced it wrong: "Nigras." I hadn't learned about the long "e." If Negroes went to school with us, the mixing would seem natural. All I had to do was convince Daddy, who in my mind represented the wrong-thinking people.

The local papers agreed with him, not me. "A Black Day of Tragedy," the *Clarion-Ledger* called it. "Blood Stains on the White Marble Steps," mourned an editorial in the *Jackson Daily News*. I did not change my mind. Here was our chance to right the sins of the past.

Daddy and I argued all that summer at the dinner table. I realize now he was hardening his ideas, gathering an army of "facts" for the battle ahead, working to convince not only me, but himself.

"It's not right that they only get to be cooks and maids and yardmen," I said.

Mama: "Lower your voice."

We were at the dinner table and Annie wasn't to hear.

Daddy said, "*Plessy v. Ferguson.* Separate but equal. It's been the law of the land since 1896."

"But things aren't equal and it's not fair."

He said, "Whoever told you life was going to be fair?"

"It could be." I felt as if I'd lived my entire existence in a tunnel, and now I was out and could see. Why couldn't anyone else? Parthenia, who was putting her nieces through college, shouldn't be living in a shack. Ellis and Alan, as hard working and kind as any white men I'd ever known, should be businessmen instead of waiting on tables and driving a mule at Allison's Wells.

Rosalie, the same Rosalie I did the bad thing to, showed me her diary one summer when I was about twelve. She had much better handwriting than mine. She'd read a Shakespeare play. She told me when she grew up she was going to write plays. She'd written one already. Would I like to read it? I did and it was good, but I knew—in the world where we lived—she wouldn't be able to grow up and write plays. Thanks to the Supreme Court, now she could. If white people would just open their eyes and see straight.

Negroes didn't have to have separate toilets and water fountains. They wouldn't be forced to work for us, and act grateful for our leftover food and cast-off clothes. The way things were now was so obviously wrong.

I even had a plan. We'd start with the first grade because, like the song from *South Pacific* said, you had to be taught to hate. Little children weren't so indoctrinated. We could integrate one grade per year. By the time people got to high school, they'd be over their prejudice.

I couldn't understand why my father didn't see the wisdom of this. He'd been Phi Beta Kappa in college. A man with that kind of brain ought to want to make things right.

Preparations for the battle to come were brewing out of my sight and knowledge. I thought the fight was between me and Daddy. If I could convince him of the error of his ways, opposition would tumble like a line of dominos.

A month after the *Brown* decision, the Citizens' Council formed. Daddy joined. The members were upstanding men, he told me. This was not riffraff like the Ku Klux Klan. These were doctors, lawyers, politicians, and businessmen. They were against violence, but they would stop any move toward integration.

The Mississippi legislature voted to close the public schools to prevent desegregation.

"You'd close the schools?" We were at the dinner table again. I couldn't believe it.

Daddy's mouth twisted. He set his jaw and made his hands into fists. "I'd man the barricades with a gun before I let my daughters go to school with niggers."

A shocked silence. We never used that word in our house. Things had changed. Sides had formed and for the first time, I wasn't on the same side with Daddy.

"You don't even own a gun." It was terrible to see the clay feet of someone you admired.

Mother loved it when we fought. It put her on his team. "Don't talk back to your father."

"It's not fair." This turned out to be my main argument.

Mother rang the bell for Annie to clear the dishes. "Let's talk about something else."

This was another thing I hated. The fight over segregation caused a silence between us and the kitchen. The unsaid things, the truths about white supremacy, the stuff you were supposed to absorb without thinking, were being said. You had to whisper.

In our town, if you were male and white and from a good family, and if you had ambitions for the law, you became an office boy at a firm like my father's. If you were diligent, you might be invited back to work as a clerk during law school summers, and, as your great reward, be hired as an associate after you graduated. A few of these boys chose Harvard instead of Ole Miss, or got Rhodes Scholarships after college.

"Lost," my father would say at the dinner table. "He'll get over-educated and be of no use to us."

Since Harvard and Rhodes Scholarships seemed like pretty big honors, it took me a while to figure out what he meant. If you went off to a fancy school outside the South, your world expanded. You got what my father referred to as "ideas." You forgot the two primary values that underlay our way of life: the sovereignty of the states over the federal government and separation of the races.

It was crushing to realize that almost nobody felt the way I did, not even Miss Hosford, who was always talking about God's love. God loved you, but he wanted you to go to *your* church, not ours. God loved for you to work at Allison's Wells and be content with the wages. God loved our southern ways, and God did not love change.

I had grown up in the middle of this huge family, and, until now, had been surrounded by love and embraced by approval. I realized, arguing with Daddy at the dinner table in 1954, I wasn't convincing him or anyone else. To him, my family, and in the eyes of the community, I was not only wrong, I was irrelevant. I was being "silly."

"She's always trying to be different," Mother said to her bridge-playing buddies, like integration was something I pretended to believe in.

"I was idealistic like you at eighteen," my father said at dinner. "You'll mature and see the world the way it really is."

"No, I won't." I got so frustrated, I started to cry.

He gave me a pitying look. "See. You could never be a lawyer. You're too emotional."

I was stung. Trying to make up for not being a son, I'd told him I wanted to be a lawyer like him.

His response was derisive. "No man would marry a woman lawyer. Too argumentative."

Everyone knew a girl's destiny was marriage; I had no comeback.

You could brush a female off like that in those days and there wasn't a thing to do about it but cry, which proved a man's point. We didn't have jobs. We had no money or power. Wives agreed with their husbands, spent their allowances, and kept the peace.

The peace was kept. *Brown v. Board of Education* might be the law of the land, but nothing changed. Mississippi—the entire South—went right on as if it had never happened. The schools stayed segregated. Annie kept cooking and Alan plowed the fields up at the hotel. The white people said, *"See?"* The South might have lost that other war, but we'd win this one. States were stronger than any federal government. We could continue to be as prejudiced and segregated as we liked here under the Mason-Dixon Line. Let them try to change things. We were safe and happy with our Jim Crow laws, states' rights, and our hallowed, tragic history.

By the time I went back to school that fall of 1954, the Citizens' Council had twenty-five thousand members.

During my sophomore year at Ole Miss, I met with a guidance counselor. What could I do with an English degree?

"You can be somebody's very fine secretary."

I thought about Mildred behind her Underwood, typing page after page of legal briefs. "I don't want to be a secretary."

"You can teach."

"I would hate that."

He shrugged. We had reached the end of the career path.

Two more years of college felt like a lot of drudgery for no good end. I lacked the imagination and the information to consider other possibilities. I could have left the South, maybe gone to New York and found a job in publishing, except I'd never heard of anyone doing that. I read a ton of books, but as far as I knew, they fell from the sky. New York might as well be the moon. Nice girls went to college to find a husband.

Why wait?

17

I went back to my quest: looking for the man who would make me whole. After my fling with sex in high school, I revirginalized myself. I went out with a lot of boys at Ole Miss and put out for none. As far as I knew, every girl in my sorority remained a virgin. Certainly, nobody admitted to anything else. Girls shook their heads in mock dismay after a night of drinking: "I can't remember a thing. I hope nothing happened." Voices rising with laughter. One girl in engineering school got pregnant and had to leave school. At the sorority house, they said that's what she got for wanting to be an engineer.

I met Fred Craig at a party in Jackson. I had just turned nineteen and was home from college on that January weekend in 1955. He was twenty-five, tall and lanky, a Korean war veteran and graduate of Georgia Tech. He was a member of Kappa Alpha, the same fraternity my father had been president of at the University of North Carolina. In my eyes, this fact alone raised his status. Fred was a grown-up and had settled parts of his life I couldn't see my way past. He said "ducats" instead of "tickets," which I found incredibly witty. He had a real job, as construction manager for a big residential builder.

Marriage was an approved way to leave home and I worked hard to make Fred love me. I caught a ride home from Ole Miss every weekend so that distance would be no barrier. I practically twinkled with charm and good humor. I won over his parents, Raymond and Fredibel (named for her parents, Fred and Belle; in my eyes, a most unfortunate combination). I won over Fred's frowning older brother, Raymond Junior. One Saturday, to demonstrate what a loyal mate I'd be, I waxed and polished every inch of Fred's pink and gray Chevrolet.

My efforts were not in vain.

At the end of March, we sat in his car in front of my parents' house. He pulled back from kissing and gave me a serious look. "I want you to be my wife."

I studied his intense, freckled face in the light from the street lamp and felt a twinge of doubt.

"Did you hear what I said?" He sounded amazed at what had come out of his mouth. "I asked you to marry me."

"I heard."

"Aren't you going to say anything?"

Was this the man who'd been approaching me in time, the way I imagined in Mrs. Johnson's Latin class, the person who would make me complete? I thought about two more years in gray-lidded Oxford, Mississippi. I thought about being a secretary or a teacher. He was close enough.

"Yes." *Maybe*, my mind said, *maybe*, but my mouth said yes.

He hugged me so hard my ribs hurt.

I was still in school. Fred had to ask my father's permission. It was after nine and my parents were in bed, Mama in a bed jacket leafing through *McCall's*, my father in his pajamas with *Time* magazine.

Usually when I stood in their doorway, the two of them looked like strangers who'd been assigned adjoining beds in a hospital ward. Tonight I was too nervous to be critical. "Fred has something he'd like to ask you."

They took off their reading glasses and waited. Fred looked scared.

"Mr. Watkins, sir, I'd like to marry your daughter."

Daddy looked him up and down without speaking. "You may marry her as soon as she finishes college."

"*Daddy.*" Graduation stretched further than my imagination could reach.

"Is this what you really want?" He stared at me hard. I was disappointing him by turning out to be exactly what he'd expected—a daughter.

Had I ever been shown an alternative? I nodded. Yes, this was what I wanted.

He put back on his reading glasses, washing his hands of the entire female business. "I guess that's settled."

Fred walked over to the bed and shook his hand. "Thank you, sir."

"You'll have to wait six months," Mama said. "She's never liked a boy longer than six months." She scooted over and patted the bed. I sat down and we began planning the wedding. Fred retreated to a chair in the corner and Daddy went back to his magazine.

This was not going to be just another wedding. This was a major event. It had to be perfect. I was the first daughter, the chief product of my mother's life. Every lawyer and judge from Tupelo to Biloxi would be invited. Old friends, forgotten cousins, plus whomever Fred's family knew. We weren't acquainted with Fred's people, and the unknown was assumed to be second-rate. I would be married in late fall, Mama decided, close to Thanksgiving. That was a safe seven months away in case I turned fickle, and fall colors were so lovely.

I was right there with her. I wanted spectacle. I wanted a *Gone With the Wind* wedding with the green velvet drapes from Tara torn down for the bridesmaids' dresses.

In May, I finished my sophomore year, packed my books and, without regret, parted with Oxford and higher education. My cousin, John Fontaine Three, worked with his father at Godwin Advertising. They got me a job as secretary to the radio-TV director. There I was, someone's very good secretary, exactly as the counselor predicted. I was glad to have the work.

Between typing copy:

CAMERA ZOOM IN:
MERCHANTS AND FARMERS BANK
OF KOSCIUSKO OFFERS YOU 3%
INTEREST ON YOUR SAVINGS.

I addressed wedding invitations on my knee. We sent out five hundred on heavy cream bond engraved in sepia script.

By August, the Citizens' Council, that highbrow KKK, had sixty thousand members.

"Nonviolent and nonpartisan," my father pronounced over his fried chicken one night at the dinner table.

Fred wasn't a member but he nodded in agreement.

"They have a committee that screens political candidates," I said. "Economic pressure is a kind of violence."

Daddy gave me a pitying look. "It only makes sense to try and get the very best people in office."

In August of that year Emmett Till was murdered. He was a fourteen-year-old boy. He'd come with a cousin from Chicago to visit a great-uncle in Money, Mississippi. He and his cousins went to a local store and, supposedly, Emmett whistled at the wife of the white owner. Four nights later, he was snatched from his bed by the store owner and his brother. Three days after he went missing, with the Jackson papers claiming he was in hiding with relatives or back home in Chicago, his mutilated body was pulled from the Tallahatchie River. Till's mother insisted the casket remain open and pictures of his beaten and broken body appeared in newspapers around the world. We were the shame of the nation.

I said, "They killed him for whistling."

Daddy said, "It may have been more than that."

"He was only fourteen years old." I was about to cry through another meal.

Daddy said, "A Chicago boy should never have been allowed to come down here. His mother should have known better."

Our mother said, "Hush."

Annie came through the swinging door with hot biscuits.

The two brothers who abducted Emmett Till were arrested. Mama went right on planning the wedding. Black people getting murdered were not our affair. I was riding two tidal waves: a southern wedding and southern racism.

Mama said, "They kill each other all the time." We were downtown on some bridal errand, driving home by way of Farish Street in the Negro section. "Life isn't as valuable to them."

I thought my head would explode. "That's the stupidest thing I ever heard. Emmett Till wasn't murdered by another Negro." I would never call my father stupid, but with Mama I didn't hold back. "Slow down. You'll hit those ladies."

Mama managed to get her foot on the brake. "Those are not ladies, they're women. Colored women can't be ladies."

"Listen to you: they can't be ladies, they can't have titles or last names. We're not supposed to shake hands." I could feel the blood rushing in my head. "Don't you see how wrong this is?"

Mama said, "I didn't make the rules. And don't get so upset. It makes you look ugly."

She hadn't made the rules and I didn't know how to change them.

I posed for my engagement picture in a poodle haircut and a dress Mama made for the occasion: ecru lace over brown taffeta with a square neck and dropped waist. "Smile," the man said. I obliged: lots of teeth, brown eyes gleaming. Send me your presents, the smile said, and they did.

Each day the trucks arrived from local jewelry stores. I could hardly wait to get home from work and tear into the shiny white paper. My values were completely overridden by greed. How bad could the people be who sent such lovely stuff?

The line of silver lengthened, the stack of dinner plates rose. There were crystal goblets, silver mint julep cups, epergnes and silver pitchers. "It's like a hundred Christmases," I said. Mama walked around the room touching things lightly, smiling to herself, as if each gift settled part of a score.

She decorated the sunporch like a little store. The display tables were hung with ruffled white skirts, tied at the corners with bells and lilies of the valley. China, crystal, and silver were tastefully arranged. I took Fred out there at night and we counted: ten dinner forks, sixteen salad forks, nine knives. I watched the loot mount up. The sewing room next to the kitchen became a hardware store, filled with the homelier items: the mixer, cookbooks, an electric percolator, toasters, steak knives, and finally, too late for fudge at boarding school, three chafing dishes.

Emily Post said the bride should furnish the marriage linen. Mother and I went shopping at the Emporium. We had everything monogrammed. When my father got the bill, he yelped in pain. "*Eighteen towels? Eighteen washcloths?*"

Mother said, " These linens will last her ten years."

"I'm not trying to outfit her for ten years. I'm just trying to get her married."

He offered me three thousand dollars to run away. Not because he couldn't afford a wedding, because he hated the fuss. I turned him down.

Fred and I got along great during these months. He was kind and considerate. Whatever I said, he appeared to agree. In September, Roy Bryant and J.W. Milam were tried for the kidnapping and murder of Emmett Till. An all-white, all-male jury acquitted them. Women weren't allowed to serve on juries. It would take them away from their real jobs, which was taking care of their husbands.

"Acquitted, can you believe it?" We sat in Fred's car, the one I'd waxed. "I don't think I can live in a place like this."

He took my hand. "Maybe I can get a job somewhere else."

He would do anything for me, which, inexplicably, made me feel better about Emmett Till.

Talk was all I was good for, and he let me talk as much as I liked. It never occurred to me that silence didn't mean assent. Besides, I didn't know what to do. I was only nineteen.

We became more chaste as the wedding approached. I had never made love to him, not all the way, but we had managed a lot of petting when I was home from Ole Miss. Now we sat in the car in front of my house, kissing and looking deep into each other's eyes, trying to see the future.

One night I said, "Remember our first date? We went to that café after the movie and I was whispering and you kept saying, 'What?' or 'I beg your pardon?' Finally I said in this really aggravated voice, 'Are you deaf or something?' and you said, 'Yes.' I could have died, I was that embarrassed. You must have thought I was the world's most insensitive person."

"You didn't know."

He was so kind. It made me wonder if I was a good enough person to be married to him. He *was* a little deaf. So was his father.

"Do you ever think we're doing the wrong thing? Do you get scared?"

Fred shook his head. "I think about going off to a justice of the peace somewhere and getting it over with."

"Not me. I love the ceremony. It's like starring in a play. I can't wait to get married. What I keep asking myself is, do I want to *be* married?"

He didn't like hearing that, and we had to kiss each other's worries away. I wasn't sure what I was afraid of, except I might end up like Mother, living with a man who didn't love me, and drinking too much. I reassured myself that my life would never turn out like hers, but something kept nagging at me.

Mama and I fought like two goats. After that first night of excited planning, there was nothing we agreed on. Every dress, phone call, and party escalated into a battle. She made fun of my opinions. I told her she didn't pay Annie enough: a hundred dollars a month for working five and a half twelve-hour days and every other Sunday. She said I might think I was smart, but I had no common sense and no idea of the things she did for Annie, like buy her those orthopedic shoes, which were not cheap. She said I was a selfish little know-it-all. I told her she claimed to love colored people—at least the ones who worked for her or at Allison's—but it was a lie. I told her this was my wedding, not hers. I went a little crazy, either from stress or fear over what I was getting myself into.

My father stayed out of it.

Fred was mystified. I complained to him for the umpteenth time during our nightly car sit.

"Why can't you two get along?"

"Because she drives me crazy."

"She's a perfectly nice lady."

"To you, she's a nice lady. To me, she's a monster."

"She's your mother."

"That's exactly it."

Three weeks before the wedding I got a permanent. The hairdresser undid the rollers, revealing red spots across my forehead.

"What's that?"

He looked worried. "The solution burned your skin."

"Do something."

He smoothed lotion over the angry blotches. "I'm afraid they're going to scab."

"I can't have *scabs*. I'm getting married."

"Let the permanent be my gift." He hurried me out of the shop.

The spots scabbed over, a dark brown. Mother was furious. I looked in the mirror and wept. This was definitely a sign I wasn't supposed to go through with it. Gradually the burns healed and by the week of the wedding, my face was my own.

I invited nine girls to be my bridesmaids. We ordered bolts of emerald green velvet. I would have those drapes from Tara. A seamstress made eight dresses with sweetheart necklines and long skirts, plus a small, wider one for my ten-year-old sister, Sydney, who was not outgrowing her baby fat.

On the night before the wedding, Aunt Leigh and Uncle Doug gave us a rehearsal dinner up at Allison's Wells. Ellis and Preston served. I went back to the kitchen to see Lena, Ora Dee, and Parthenia.

"Look at you," Ora Dee said. "Don't you look fine?"

Lena said, "Let me see that dress."

Mama had made me a beautiful dress of apricot *peau-de-soie*. I borrowed a pair of elaborate earrings she planned to wear at the wedding.

I moved into Lena's warm side, feeling seven years old again, halfway wanting to be back in this kitchen with the people I loved. "It feels like I'm leaving forever."

Parthenia gave me a sharp look. "You're doing what you're supposed to be doing. Growing up and getting married. Do the job right and you'll be bringing us some babies to pet."

My chest tightened, and I felt the sting of tears. They were pushing me away.

Parthenia wouldn't have it. There was no room for sentimentality, not after age twelve. "Get on out there and be with your company."

Fred and I sat at opposite ends of the King and Queen's table. We had artichoke and filet mignon. I got very drunk. The world shimmered. Someone drank champagne out of my size eight shoe. Life was hilarious.

Then I was on the end of the diving board in the dark, threatening to jump into a pool half filled with dead leaves. "I can't get married."

"You can't jump in there." It was my best friend's husband.

"Yes, I can."

His arm pulled me back.

Mysteriously, I was in the bathroom off the small parlor, staring mournfully down into the toilet bowl. Then I was lying on the sitting room floor, looking up at the ceiling. Fred tried to pick me up. Every time he let go, I slid horizontal again and lay there peacefully.

On the way home, I felt dreadfully sick.

"Why did you drink so much?" Fred drove looking straight ahead. I could tell he was angry, but I was too far gone to care.

"I don't know."

"Are you sure you want to get married?"

"I don't know." I had my head on my knees. The car moved sickeningly. I tried to throw up out the window on my side, but it was closed.

"*Christ.* Look what you've done."

I was too drunk to be sorry. Looking grim, he dragged me inside to my mother.

"I can't get married." I was staggering. "I'm drunk."

"Of course you'll get married," Mother said. "Take this red pill."

I tried to make her understand. "Drunk people don't get married."

She said, "It's too late for this foolishness. You should be ashamed of yourself. Look what you've done to that dress I worked so hard on." She pushed me into bed.

If the South had believed in psychology back in 1955, somebody might have picked up on the messages and told me not to do it. But we didn't. Mental disturbances were as taboo as liberal views.

I woke with a clanging hangover. What was I thinking? I was far too ill to marry. The earrings I borrowed from Mama were missing and I felt abominable. The November day was as gray as the inside of my head.

Mama was furious about the earrings. "How could you lose them?"

I tried to think. I remembered staring into the toilet. Maybe I'd flushed them.

"You can get out of that bed and go downtown and find me another pair."

I groaned.

"I hope you do feel bad. I hope you feel bad enough to teach you a lesson."

How awful could marriage be? It couldn't be worse than this. I spent a miserable morning hunting through stores for earrings to match the aqua silk taffeta evening dress Mother had made for herself. I found a pair that would do and paid for them with the last money in my account.

At one o'clock, there was a bridesmaids' luncheon at the Petroleum Club, hosted by Aunt Leigh. I gave each of my attendants a tiny silver basket with a blue velvet pincushion inside.

Betty Webb giggled. "We'll be thinking of you tonight."

They laughed. Knowing laughter.

They were thinking about me being poked. I remembered my cousin Doug doing the finger in his fist to show what would happen to Julia the night she married Sam Junior. That seemed like a century ago. I'd already been poked, though I would let myself be boiled in oil before I admitted it to anyone.

I acted the way they expected—embarrassed. Actually, I felt superior. I was the first in our crowd to get married. On Monday, they would be back in class and I'd be on my honeymoon.

"To honeymoons." I lifted my glass of sauternes, but didn't drink. The sight of wine made me want to throw up again.

I looked into their smiling faces: my sisters, two cousins, and five friends. Not one of them knew me. If I stood up and said, "I'm not sure I want to get married," they would howl with laughter. If I told them I didn't know what love meant and could not imagine staying with anyone "till death do us part," they would stop laughing and be mortified. And if I told them the truth, that I didn't know what else to do, that our whole way of life was a farce, they would look at me in stunned silence. Or worse, with pity. I kept quiet.

In the late afternoon I took a perfumed bath, studying my familiar body. These legs would be married tomorrow. I soaped them. My hands were as slippery as a stranger's. The bathroom was the only place I could get away from my mother, and privacy wasn't guaranteed unless I remembered to lock the door, which I hadn't.

Her head appeared. "Did you list those last presents?"

"Get out of here."

"I'm talking about the ones that came this morning." She stared as if my pubic hair might speak.

"I'll do them later. Get out and leave me alone."

She gave me a long last look.

I began the ritual. On went the silk underpants, the lace garter belt, white hose, white satin slippers, the white lace merry widow. Then, carefully: the makeup, thin and even, eyebrow pencil, a little rouge, clear red lipstick. I pulled on a borrowed blue garter and wore the family pearls. Mama, Momae, Aunt Leigh, and Miss Hosford came in to help get me into the dress. It was ivory satin with fitted sleeves ending in a point over my hand. The skirt had a lace train that would trail six feet behind me up the aisle. There was lace around the low neckline and down the front. Mother had beaded this with iridescent sequins and seed pearls, bending over her bedside lamp night after night, with her glasses slipping down her nose. "I hope you appreciate this," she would tell me when I came in to say good night. "I'm going blind." I did, but I felt a jab of guilt watching her. I could never appreciate it enough.

Mama buttoned the tiny satin-covered buttons down the back. I gave my short brown curls a final brush and put on the headdress, a circle of pearls and sequins attached to the long tulle veil. My aunts gave me a fluff here and a tuck there.

Mama said, "You've never looked better."

I squinted at the mirror. It was true. Miraculously, the sins of the night before had vanished. I glowed. I was everything a well-brought-up white southern woman was supposed to be, everything my father and those sixty thousand and counting Citizens' Council members vowed to protect.

Inside, I felt a thin twang of nerves, a strumming of anticipation mixed with fear. On the surface I stayed icily calm, telling myself not to be silly.

Mama said, "What are you thinking about?"

"Nothing." The veil covered my face and made a long filmy train in back. The two of us never had "the talk." She took me to a woman doctor for a humiliating premarital examination, my first. The doctor said I could have a seven-pound baby, and sent me home with a book on venereal diseases, which she said I wasn't to read before dates because I might become aroused.

I can't pretend I wasn't overcome by the glory of this wedding. When I was growing up, one of my fantasies—along with becoming drum majorette and wearing a pistol—was to be one of the royal princesses, Elizabeth or Margaret. This was as close as I was going to get.

Uncle Doug drove Daddy and me to the church in his big Buick. The two of us sat in the backseat, not touching. We left an off-duty policeman at the house guarding the presents. Annie and Marie, and the folks from Allison's Wells, had gone ahead to sit in the church balcony. Daddy was nervous. I could tell from the way he sat forward in his tailcoat with his back away from the seat.

I said, "Here we go."

He squeezed my hand. We were too dressed up to talk.

We pulled up to the church. Uncle Doug got out to open the door.

Daddy whispered in the dark car. "I love you, baby."

He would have let me call it off, right then, if I'd asked. I squeezed his hand hard, and we went inside.

The bridal march trumpeted. One by one, the bridesmaids walked down the two central aisles. The green velvet dresses looked fantastic. Fred, his father and brother and seven groomsmen waited in front with the minister. There were tall white candles and banked masses of greenery.

The organ gave a flourish and played louder. It was my turn. In stately steps, my father and I marched down. I looked over at him, but he stared straight ahead, cutting a stern path with his nose. Heads craned, people murmured. It was like a coronation. I wanted the aisle to be longer. I was too full of myself to glance up to the side balcony at the people I loved.

At the altar, Fred looked thin and scared in his tails. I felt confident as a queen. Everything was fine. I had it all in hand. I loved my speaking part. I used silver tones with only one crack in my voice when I said, "till death do us part." Everyone told me later how touching that was, but it was only a crack.

The veil was lifted. I wore the heavy gold wedding band proudly. Fred didn't get a ring. I thought men's wedding rings were demeaning. I allowed a chaste kiss. We turned and marched triumphantly up the aisle, smiling ecstatically.

Was I in love with him? I was in love with being loved. I was in love with the romance and pageantry of it all. I was in love with the idea of freedom, with leaving home, having my own stuff, and as much sex as I wanted. In all the ways I knew how at nineteen, I loved him madly.

My parents had reserved the double ballroom at the King Edward Hotel. Champagne punch flowed from a fountain. There were roasted pecans in silver dishes and white napkins that said *Norma and Fred* in gold. We had two wedding cakes, white for the bride, spice for the groom.

Our pictures were taken. We cut the cakes and fed each other. For two hours, people kissed and squeezed me and told me I was beautiful, which I believed. Mother stood next to Daddy in the receiving line, in her aqua silk taffeta. She kept her head high to hide the double chin. I could tell from the proud way she introduced each judge and lawyer how much this meant to her. She had produced a magnificent wedding. She was Mrs. Tom Watkins and no one could take that from her, certainly not Mildred, who came through the line in her cloth coat with the other secretaries.

Then it was over. Fred and I were flying to New Orleans for our honeymoon, but not until 1:00 a.m. I didn't want the marrying to end. It was the best part.

I stood on a gilt chair and threw the bouquet. In a lateral leap, my baby sister, Sydney, caught it. There was nothing left to do but go upstairs and change. I put on a new beige cashmere suit with a pheasant feather hat, another gift from Aunt Leigh. I hated to part with the white satin. I wanted to do it again, to be a white blossom floating endlessly down a dark aisle, hearing the voices sigh. I didn't want to be Queen for a Day.

We made the traditional escape. People threw rice, there were cowbells tied to the back of the gray and pink Chevrolet, and we raced away. No one followed and we had nowhere to go. We looked at each other. It felt anticlimactic. All that fuss and now it was just Fred and me in the Chevrolet where we'd been a hundred other nights. I could still see a little of where I'd thrown up on the window.

"We still have three hours, Mrs. Craig," Fred said. "What do you want to do?" He gave me a lascivious look.

I didn't like the sound of my new name. I certainly didn't want to do that. "Let's go to the Silver Slipper and find the others."

The wedding party had moved on to a nightclub on the edge of town, where Negro bands from the Delta played and you could drink if you brought your own bottle. Everyone looked surprised when we showed up. Newlyweds weren't supposed to be out clubbing on their first night. But we stayed, telling stories and drinking Jim Beam and water. Finally it was time for the plane. I hated to leave. I wanted to take off my green orchid corsage, put my wedding ring in my purse, and settle in for the night.

Instead we drove, rather silently, to the airport, climbed aboard a plane and flew through the dark night. In New Orleans, the first hint of gray showed on the horizon and the streets looked damp and forlorn. It was Thanksgiving morning and I was wrung of all feeling.

Fred had reserved the honeymoon room at the Hotel Monteleone in the French Quarter. It had crimson, flocked wallpaper and a huge four-poster with dusty red velvet curtains. A television on wheels peered over the end of the bed like a visitor. The room was filled with dark corners. I convinced myself the walls were riddled with peepholes. Outside, tittering bellboys and maids waited at five in the morning to watch the action.

We agreed that it was much too late and we were far too tired to make love, but I went off to the bathroom to put on my first night ensemble. It was cream satin with lace. I could pretend I was a virgin, but I didn't have the nerve to wear white to bed.

Fred came out in yellow nylon pajamas. I was horrified. I could see straight through them. He took his pajama pants off. I had never seen a man all the way naked. It was astounding they managed to get around with all that stuff between their legs. We went ahead and made love. We were married. It was legal. Fred pulled up my nightgown, nibbled on a breast, pushed inside me and came. It hurt like hell.

This was awful. After all those nights of panting inside parked cars, here I was with permission and room to move around, and—nothing—a little anticipation and a lot of hurting. This was the first time I'd ever made love in an actual bed. Fred thought I had never made love at all, and I let him think it. Once, when we were taking wedding presents to our new apartment, I tried to get him to do it. The bed was made up with our monogrammed sheets. Fred said it was only a few more weeks and he'd rather wait. I failed to see this as a warning.

After lovemaking—I did not mention my disappointment—we talked about the wedding. Rehashing was almost as good as getting married again. One of the groomsmen tried to leave the reception with a bottle of champagne under each arm. The look on his face when my mother waylaid him. My sister Sydney ending up with the bouquet. How weird was that? She'd managed to get completely drunk. We laughed. I don't know why we thought it was funny. She was only ten years old.

With dawn creeping in through the dusty velvet drapes, we settled down to sleep. My first night in bed with a man. Reality hit: I might live in an unjust state, but I was free. Being married meant I never had to spend another night under my mother's roof. I'd never become her either. My marriage was going to be completely different.

1955—1966

18

The honeymoon was brief—in more ways than one. We'd gotten married Wednesday night and both of us had to be at work by Monday morning. We flew from New Orleans back to our apartment—the first place I would call mine.

We had rented the top floor of a frame house near the Pearl River. The landlady, a small, bent woman, lived below and left us entirely alone. The railroad ran nearby and I couldn't sleep the first few nights for the freight trains. The house was old and slanted toward the river. A can dropped in the kitchen rolled without stopping through the dining and living rooms until it hit the front wall. The bathroom door stuck open. I was shy about using the bathroom in front of a man anyway, and the crack in the door paralyzed me. Fred took the door down and sawed off half an inch. How amazing. I had married a man who could use tools. When summer arrived, things dried up, and the bottom of the door developed a two-inch gap.

Arriving from New Orleans that first night, I realized we might be married, but we were not exactly on our own. As a surprise, the mothers had redecorated while we were gone. My first reaction was resentment—whose house was this? But the place looked grand. The hand-me-down sofa and side chair were slip-covered in beige linen. There was a gift TV on our gift bar. The secondhand refrigerator and stove both worked. Propped on a pillow in our bridal bed was a Marriage Prayer from Aunt Leigh, which said, in effect: pray unceasingly.

Miss Hosford had given me her advice in a hoarse whisper at the reception:

"Do you know what your Uncle John and I do after we do it?"

"What?" I was horrified someone might hear.

"We fall to our knees and thank the Lord."

I'd fall to my knees, too, if Fred and I ever did it right. My period started in New Orleans, which did nothing to slow him down. He wanted to make love all the time. By now, I was sore and mad. Since age twelve I'd been waiting for fulfillment, reading novels like *Forever Amber*, where Amber goes to the king's ball in a transparent gown, gets seduced by a nobleman, and finds fulfillment. Making love, according to the novels, meant transformation. I was supposed to fly off on a passionate journey—maybe fainting and howling. I was due. Where was it?

"When's it going to get better?" We were in bed after another one of Fred's speedy entry and exits.

"Sometimes it takes awhile."

"What's awhile?"

"Maybe three or five years."

"You've got to be kidding. I can't wait *three years*."

Fred was supposed to be experienced. He'd slept with girls when he was at Georgia Tech. He claimed to have had a mistress in Korea. He was supposed to know about this stuff. Now that we were married, he wanted sex all the time, at least once a night and more on weekends. He didn't have any trouble with fulfillment. I lay there looking up at him dispassionately, while he hung above me with his eyes closed, ecstatic. It wasn't fair.

"We're just beginning," he said. "Be patient. We'll work it out."

Some days I forgot my sexual problems in the pure joy of having my own space. I loved opening a cabinet and finding china I had selected, the matching crystal lined up beside it, shiny pots and pans below. I liked opening the refrigerator and seeing food I'd gone to the store and bought.

I couldn't figure out how working people had time to cook. Fred told me if he didn't eat supper by six, he got a stomachache. I didn't get off work until five. Fred picked me up and the soonest I could get anything on the stove was five-thirty.

I asked Annie how long it took to bake sweet potatoes. She said at least an hour. I had this brilliant idea. I'd leave the stove on real low and put the potatoes in before I left for work. Annie told me how to fry pork chops, and I bought canned string beans. At five-thirty, the baked sweet potatoes looked just right, skins tight and crisp. I cooked the pork chops in bacon grease, letting them fry for a long time so we wouldn't get trichinosis. I heated the beans. I served our plates and poured us each a glass of milk in our new brown crystal, which turned things an odd color. I hadn't thought about that when I picked it out. We sat down. Fred said the blessing. I cut into my potato, ready to slather it with butter. The top collapsed. There was nothing inside. The potato part had cooked entirely away. We ate dried pork chops and beans that tasted of the can. Fred said it didn't matter, but for me every swallow went down like failure.

You would think, during all those years at Allison's Wells with Lena, and hanging around the kitchen with Annie, I'd have learned how to cook. I was too busy eavesdropping or disappearing into my bedroom to read about seduction. Now that I needed the skills, I couldn't believe how stupid I'd been. I had to learn every step like a baby, stumbling and falling.

At our first dinner party, I served champagne out of our gift champagne glasses. They looked clean enough. After all, they were new. My tidiest friend, Susan, the one who'd drawn a line down our dormitory room in college because I was such a slob, reached into her glass and pulled out a piece of tape, the tape that had held the gift card. She gave me a look I could read from across the room: I might be married but I hadn't changed.

I was still working at the advertising agency, except now I wrote thank you notes on my knee instead of invitations. All my life I'd been waiting to grow up and get away and here I was, nineteen years old—a certified adult—and it wasn't what I expected. I'd pictured perfect freedom: I'd know life's answers, nobody could tell me what to do, and I could eat sweets before dinner. Instead, I appeared to have volunteered for the Marriage Army. We got up, showered, choked down breakfast, went to work, came home, cooked, washed up, watched a little TV, went to bed, read, I let Fred do his thing, we slept, got up and started over again. On weekends, we cleaned the house and ran errands. On Saturday nights, we went to movies with other young married couples. We were too broke to take trips.

I had married to get away from home, but managed to trade one family for two. We were expected at Fred's house on Thursday nights and Saturdays at noon, and at mine on Wednesday nights and Sundays. Without saying so, my mother and mother-in-law strove to outdo each other. We were served meals so heavy we had to take naps after. I saw the months and years stretching ahead, meals to cook, meals to eat, endless beds to make. I couldn't blame Fred except for the sex part. He was loving, considerate, and funny.

It was me I blamed. I'd gotten exactly what I asked for. I wondered if that was how life went. You wanted something, you worked hard to get it, and sort of forgot yourself in the fun of trying. Then you got whatever it was—a new dress, the job, the man—and it wasn't so wonderful after all. In college, my sorority turned out that way. I thought I'd die if I didn't get in. Then I did and thought I'd die of boredom if I didn't find a way out.

The next thing to want was children. Procreation was expected, the sooner the better. I was stymied at work where, no matter how smart I thought I was, I would never be more than a secretary. A husband-wife team ran the agency, but that didn't make it any easier for a woman to rise. They already had one female account executive and they didn't plan on making that mistake again.

Pregnancy got you out of the office. No matter how little money you made, in Jackson, Mississippi, in the midfifties, if you were white and your husband had a job, you didn't work after you had a baby. I would be free.

We'd been married not quite a year when I got pregnant. I kept working. Fred's salary was small. We'd gotten a deal on a house in one of the subdivisions his company was developing. We needed the extra cash. Our baby would not be born in an apartment. The house was in northwest Jackson—not quite as good as northeast, but acceptable for young couples. It had two bedrooms, a paneled den, two baths, a living-dining room, a separate kitchen, and a carport. In 1957, it cost six thousand dollars, an enormous sum, which we would eke out in monthly payments.

I hid the pregnancy for four months before moving into those skirts with stomach holes and the huge tops. I swelled like a pumpkin. By the time I quit at the end of June, I'd gained forty pounds. People at the office gave me worried looks, like I might drop the thing at my desk. The secretaries threw me a good-by party and wished me well, but I wasn't fooled. I'd been in a stall in the bathroom one day and heard them talking.

"Who does she think she is?"

"Miss I'm-So-Much-Better-Than-You."

I lifted my feet and held my breath in horror.

"She was only hired because of who she knows."

"You mean, who she's kin to."

They were talking about Uncle John and my cousin, John Fontaine Three, who both worked as account executives. I thought the other women liked me. I didn't think I was better, exactly, but I knew I wouldn't be a secretary forever. I pretended there were no class distinctions. We were all in this work thing together. It probably hadn't helped when two Junior League ladies showed up one day asking for me, and, in front of the receptionist, invited me to join. I got all tittery and flattered and went, red-faced, back to my desk, acting like it was nothing.

As a young married person—young married *woman*—you were

expected to do good. Since I was working, the Junior League gave me night and weekend duties. At night, I was part of the Civil Air Patrol. This was during the cold war. We watched the skies for Russian planes. I had a laminated sheet of airplane shapes, and we were to call headquarters if we spotted one. I was such a dunce about technical stuff, the entire Russian air force could have flown over and I'd still be trying to figure out which shape fit.

My Saturday volunteer job was at the University Hospital. The Junior League gave away medical equipment if you were poor enough. These pitiful white families came in (I had no idea where Negroes went), people with nothing and one of them crippled. I sat behind a desk with my forms and asked nosy questions about their income. Did they actually deserve crutches or a brace or, God forbid, a wheelchair, or were they faking? It was horribly condescending. I wanted to hand them whatever they needed—the walls were hung with used crutches and braces—but I had to turn in paperwork on every case. I couldn't wait to have this baby and be a daytime league member. They got to put on the Carnival Ball, which sounded like a lot more fun.

If I hadn't liked being "Miss Norma," I liked even less becoming Mrs. Fred Craig. My photograph appeared in the newspaper doing some league thing and there I was: Mrs. Fred Craig. I'd lost my first and my last names. Married women belonged to their husbands. They needed no names of their own. The only way to keep your name was to stay an old maid.

The integration question hadn't gone away. In 1956, the Mississippi legislature formed the Sovereignty Commission, an organization authorized to collect information on race agitators and subversives. First the Citizens' Council and now this.

"No wonder we're such a backward state," I said at Sunday dinner.

Daddy said, "Maybe people who don't know what they're talking about should keep quiet."

My sisters snickered. They loved seeing me put in my place.

My life and the way I was figuring it out would have been funny if it weren't so pathetic. Everything I did to get free bound me tighter. Like the baby. It was due on July Fourth, which I thought appropriate. I would have a male child on Independence Day and declare my superiority to my mother, who could only produce girls. Doing this would make it up to Daddy for having the three of us. I didn't know if the baby was a boy. They couldn't tell back in 1957, but I *wanted* a boy, and I suffered under the delusion that, within the limits of being a female, whatever I wanted badly enough I could get.

July Fourth came and went. No baby. We were in the new house. I kept swelling. Mother called every day asking if I was still there until I screamed at her to stop. I decided to make it come. I would jump off something high and jolt it out. Balancing twenty pounds of stomach wasn't easy, so the tallest thing I had the nerve to climb on was the toilet. I pulled off my gown. If the baby fell out I could catch it. I stood there, trying to get up the nerve to jump, and heard a noise on the roof. It was eleven at night, Fred was long asleep and I would have been, too, except for the pregnancy insomnia that kept me up into the early morning painting the baby's room unisex yellow.

I waited on top of the closed toilet, listening. There it was again. Climbing clumsily down, pulling on my gown, I shook Fred awake. "There's somebody on the roof."

"No, there isn't."

"You have to go see."

"I'm not getting out of bed in the middle of the night to climb on a roof."

"Then I will."

"Come to bed."

"Fine." I pulled on a robe and started out of the room. "Imagine how it's going to sound when people find out you let your giant pregnant wife fall off a ladder in the middle of the night."

I heard him coming after me. "Anything to keep you happy."

That was pretty much Fred's motto.

He got the ladder and I waited in the dark backyard while he climbed up and out of sight. I heard a startled cry and some muttering. Two figures came down.

I couldn't believe my eyes.

Fred said, "It's the boy from next door."

The pimply-faced fourteen-year-old who would never look me in the eye. He stood there, head down, snuffling.

"He says he's been lying on his stomach, leaning over to look in our bathroom window. He's very sorry."

Fred gave the boy a talking-to and let him go.

I went back in the house feeling both vindicated and horrified. I imagined what the boy had seen. The pale swollen globe of my stretch-marked belly, the breasts which had grown enormous chocolate brown nipples, the navel turned into a fried egg, pubic hair lost somewhere underneath, never to be seen again. Me, standing morosely on the closed toilet lid trying to get up the nerve to jump.

I read somewhere that you could make a baby come by drinking gin. I tried that, too. It tasted vile and did not bring forth a baby. I had nightmares where I gave birth to tiny dark brown creatures no bigger than my thumb. In the dreams, I kept trying to explain that something had gone terribly wrong, but it wasn't my fault. During the day, I dragged my heavy body from bed to kitchen and back. I had never been in such a foul and hopeless state. Plus, I was sure I would die in childbirth.

At one in the morning on July 20, when I finally felt what I hoped was labor, I leapt out of bed like a gazelle. The baby was here.

Little did I know what humiliations lay ahead. At the hospital, they stretched me out, painted me orange, and shaved off my germy pubic hair. Roughly, pulling at it.

"That hurts."

"Hold still."

Then they gave me an enema. I couldn't believe it. I'm in labor and I'm getting an enema? Not satisfied, they gave me another. Serve them right if I dropped this baby in the toilet.

I got a "spinal," anesthetic injected into the spinal fluid. When the needle went in, I heard a crunching sound. Oh, great, now I would be paralyzed. The pains stopped and we waited. My mother showed up, high heels clacking down the hall. She started bossing everyone around, asking the nurses this, telling the doctor that. I let her. Day came, but no baby. They wheeled the whale—me—down to x-ray. The waiting room had filled with relatives: Fred's parents, Daddy, Aunt Leigh, and Uncle Doug. I waved wanly as I was rolled down and back. I needed a second spinal. There was talk of a Caesarean. At 12:30, right before Daddy departed—baby or no baby—for his regular Saturday afternoon bridge game, Clay arrived. Eight pounds, two ounces of boy, exactly the way I'd planned. I'd won the birthing contest. The doctor gave me a big cut to help Clay's giant head out, and lots of stitches after. When the anesthesia wore off, I felt like somebody had plowed me with razor blades.

Fred bent over the bed. "We should thank God for what he's done." He accidentally bumped the rail and it hurt so bad I screamed.

"God had nothing to do with it. You'd better thank me."

On his first visit to my room after Clay's birth, the doctor climbed into the bed and gave me a big hug—a didn't-we-do-a-great-job hug. I thought it a bit odd, but this was my first baby. I wasn't sure about the rules.

I wanted to nurse. Nobody nursed in 1957. Nobody nice.

"You don't look like the kind of person who would choose to nurse." The nun scrubbed my nipples with alcohol, so the baby wouldn't get contaminated.

"It will ruin your breasts," my mother said.

I ignored them. I loved holding my baby and looking into those swimming eyes. I loved the way we fit, and how, when he fastened on, it was as if a wire tautened between breast and uterus. We were perfectly satisfied with one another. It was the happiest I'd been since the wedding.

"Whatever you do, don't fall asleep with that baby," the nurse said.

But I was so tired. The baby drifted off and so did I. I couldn't help it. Sleep pulled me under. When I woke, the baby was gone. I looked over the side of the bed, sure he'd fallen on the floor. Nothing. He'd vanished. I started crying. They'd taken him away and probably wouldn't give him back. I was already an unfit mother.

Having a baby and taking care of a baby turned out to be two different things. Once I got out of the hospital with its twenty-four-hour meal service and baby bathing and changing, I realized what I was in for. It wasn't freedom, that's for sure. It was full-time service to a tiny being with no communication skills. I went into what I now know to be postpartum depression, although nobody called it that back then, and I would never have admitted to it. Admission would have sounded like a cry for help, like I shouldn't have gotten married and didn't know what I was doing.

Fred left for work every morning and I crawled back into bed. I got out only to see to the baby, then headed back under the covers. Forty-five minutes before Fred got home, I got up, made the bed, dressed, and pretended to have been up all day.

I was interrupted in my misery by the sight of Governor Faubus on television keeping the Negro children out of high school in Little Rock, and then of U.S. paratroopers escorting them in. The newspaper called it "The darkest day in Southern history since Reconstruction." I did a little jig through the pea-green shag carpet of our paneled den.

One day, Clay lay in his crib in the yellow room, screaming in that high-pitched, maddening way infants have. I couldn't figure out how he did it without taking a breath. I was in the kitchen screaming back: "I can cry louder than you." I'd read stories about mothers who held their babies by the ankles and popped their skulls against concrete walls. I'd never understood before, but now I did. I promised God if he'd let me sleep through one night, I would never ask for another thing.

I got over it. I had to. Clay grew and slept like a normal person. I forgot my promise to God. Clay was a happy baby when I let him be. I was one of those system mothers. Everything had to be done according to a schedule I'd read about in a book. If the baby cried, let him cry unless the schedule said it was time to feed him. This was supposed to build character in both of us. When he wouldn't eat his vegetables, I told him he could sit in that high chair until he was twenty-one. Everything you could do wrong, I did. It was a miracle we both made it through, and a testament to Clay's sunny temperament and forgiving nature.

I got my figure back along with my sense of humor, only to discover I was pregnant again. I told the doctor I couldn't stand a repeat of that first birth. We agreed to try self-hypnosis. He'd never done it, but he was a new doctor with plenty of time and I was willing to be the experiment. He gave me a book on the subject, and every week for seven months, I went to his office to practice going under. At home, for an hour a day while Clay napped, I lay in bed and practiced putting myself into a deep enough state to make an arm go cold or hot, to make it rise off the bed like a helium balloon or grow so heavy I couldn't lift it. As a side benefit, I learned how to hypnotize away a headache. I could go down, and tell myself when I opened my eyes in fifteen minutes I'd be completely refreshed, and it worked.

Fred was building us a new house, this time in proper northeast Jackson. It was long and low, with lots of glass. On the exterior, he used slave-made bricks left over from the remodeling of the Old Capitol (slave-made bricks: weren't we lucky?). Inside, there was a fireplace, brick floors, and exposed beams. I chose pumpkin-colored carpeting and countertops. We had a sitting area and television in the master bedroom. Our first house sold for nine thousand dollars, more than we'd paid for it, and we'd gotten to live there. We felt shrewd.

When the time came for the birth, I told the doctor I'd give myself the enema at home this time, thank you. I waited past the due date and had the baby induced. At the hospital, I couldn't avoid the shaving part, but managed to skip the humiliating squat on the toilet.

"You don't look like the kind of person that would give herself an enema," the nurse said. I ignored her. I was in charge of this birth.

I crawled up on the bed, my water was broken, the IV did its work, and labor began. I put myself under. Hypnosis must have been incredibly boring for Fred. I lay there looking asleep. It took intense concentration. Down where I was, I rode the contractions like waves.

I heard my mother clicking down the hall. Her sharp voice, asking questions and giving orders, brought me right out of the trance. I told the doctor not to let her in. He explained that I couldn't be disturbed. She left, but I could tell from the way her heels sounded, she went away mad.

I was right. She never came back to the hospital, not once during the week I was there.

After she left, I put myself back under. When the contractions grew intense I floated above the bed, watching. They rolled me into the delivery room. I heard the doctor from a distance, pushed when I was told, and felt the baby emerge.

"It's a beautiful girl."

I'm ashamed to say my first response was disappointment. I'd been as indoctrinated as any Chinese peasant to the value of boy babies. I opened my eyes, ready for the birthing to be over. I'd forgotten the fourth stage of labor, delivery of the placenta. I got agitated and so did the doctor. "You're contaminating the drapes," he said, but I heard, "grapes," and wondered what wine had to do with it. "If you don't stop thrashing, I'll have to put you under." He'd thrash too if someone were sewing up his bottom with black thread.

We'd named Clay, Frederick Claiborne Craig Jr. after his father, a southern custom. We named our second Norma Allison, after me and the hotel. She was the fourth Norma.

When I found out I was pregnant that second time, I reassured myself that two babies couldn't possibly be more trouble than one, since one took all the time I had. I was wrong. I managed to compound the chaos. Clay at two was a logical and placid child. If you told him the stove was hot, he didn't put his hand on it. Allison came wriggling into the world. If you tried to reason with her, she stomped her foot and screamed.

Marie, our old nurse, worked for me now. She mumbled under her breath in exactly the way she had when I was a child, but I kept out of her path. We'd come to an unspoken agreement: she would pretend I was an adult and I would not question her methods. I was in awe of the way she cleaned my house, the tautly made beds, the sparkling floors, and how she loved my babies. They returned the favor. For two days a week she set me free, a favor I couldn't return.

Fred and I, after much discussion, decided he would quit his job and go to work for himself building custom homes. I had made friends with lots of well-off women in the Junior League. His first house was built for the daughter of one of the richest men in town. The profit from that house was more than Fred earned in a year at the old job. We were jubilant.

In my ongoing search for autonomy, or at least something creative and worthwhile to do, I became his office manager. It made me feel a part of things and for a while that was enough. I answered the telephone, paid suppliers, figured up tax deductions, and wrote his workers' checks. Once I learned the skills, the job grew tedious. Fred built a spec house and let me pick all the colors and materials, which sounds like more fun than it turned out to be. I didn't get a salary. He said everything was ours anyway. His CPA told him it wasn't worth the money he'd have to contribute to my Social Security. I got a weekly allowance instead, a generous allowance, but an allowance just like my mother.

I had my figure back, so of course I got pregnant again. I consoled myself. People must think we had a fabulous sex life. We must be insatiable. We didn't; we weren't. Five years had gone by and sex was not one bit better.

Our third, Linden, was named for a tree and because I thought the word had a beautiful sound. Her middle name was Elizabeth for my sister, my mother, and my father's sister, Aunt Boo. Turns out that was too many Elizabeths. Instead of being complimented, they all felt insulted.

I had her by self-hypnosis, too. I remembered to stay under for the last stage and it was a breeze. Three children weren't more trouble than two and she was a calm baby like Clay. Marie worked for us three days a week now. She became the children's surrogate mother, exactly as she'd been for my sisters and me. Clay was in preschool, Fred's business was doing well. I should have been happy. A good person would have been satisfied. Instead, I felt my brain turning to mush.

I decided to go back to school. Fred didn't mind. I would only take one course each term. The main college in our town was Millsaps. I'd disdained it when I was younger. It was a Methodist liberal arts college, but all I heard was the Methodist part. They trained ministers. Rumor was, they didn't allow dancing or makeup. At seventeen, I wouldn't have gone there on a bet.

Millsaps had changed and so had I. College turned out to be everything that life at home with three small children wasn't. I found myself part of a real learning community. One English professor invited us home to sit by the fire, sip sherry, and talk about great books. Another introduced us to Emily Dickinson and I wrote so many bad Dickinson-like poems, he begged me to desist. Dressed in black, several of us artistic types climbed onto tall stools and read our work aloud to whatever audience we could persuade to show up. My brain exploded. I took the required year of Bible and lost my religion. I became an honors student and studied the nature of time with a group that included a physics professor and Eudora Welty.

I wrote a long story for that honors course. In it, a large, plain woman longed to be seduced. I based her on a secretary I'd been in awe of at the advertising agency. The character finally met a man. On the night the deed was to happen, she put on her best dress and her good-luck red underpants, then had an awful time. The man was crude and forced her. Sex wasn't romantic, nothing like her fantasies, and she felt terribly hurt. It was actually a lot like my experience with the football player in the back of that car. I skipped the actual sex scene and had the character think about it in retrospect. This was the time part—the character's inner time running alongside ordinary time. I was trying to write like Henry James, talking in circles around events. My English professor said it wouldn't do. "You can't lead the reader on for seventy-five pages and then skip the sex." So, I wrote about panting and clothes being ripped off and the guy getting it inside her and groaning, and the woman's humiliation.

I wrote about bad sex because bad sex was the only kind I knew. I'd never had an orgasm and couldn't describe one except in the vaguest plagiarized terms. I was afraid someone who actually had them might read my story and say, "This is no orgasm," and I would be exposed. Like my Catholic friend Isabel, who when I asked many years later if she masturbated, said, "If I do, I don't know it." Not having an orgasm was a big shame. I didn't admit it to anyone. I decided never to be anesthetized, in case I blurted it out in the operating room.

I went to a gynecologist looking for a solution. I didn't choose my regular doctor. I knew him too well by now. His wife was in the Junior League, and his nurse might gossip. Silence was my only protection. I was too proud to ask any of my friends about their sex lives. As far as I knew, everyone but me had orgasms, and I couldn't bear to find out. I picked a doctor at University Hospital, someone I'd never have to see again. It took me months to get up the nerve to make the appointment and I thought I'd faint sitting at his desk before I got the words out.

"I don't like making love to my husband."

The doctor twisted a pen between his fingers and stared at my forehead instead of my eyes. "Have you been examined by your regular doctor? Are you sure there's nothing organically wrong?"

"It's not physical—I don't think." I was blushing so bad I could feel the roots of my hair burning.

"Then what seems to be the trouble?" He studied his pad and I saw his eyelashes beating nervously behind his glasses.

"I don't know. I get all worked up and then nothing happens. He, my husband, comes—has an orgasm—and falls asleep. I lie there feeling frustrated. After a few years of that, I've gotten where I don't want him to touch me."

The doctor stopped blinking, but didn't look up. He seemed to be deep in thought. He cleared his throat. I leaned forward. There *was* an answer and I was about to get it.

"Sex is like turnip greens."

I was dumbfounded. I'd never thought to connect the two.

"If you don't like turnip greens, you eat some every day. After a while you get to like them."

He was from the north. Maybe turnip greens had been an issue for him down here. "You mean if I have sex every day, I'll get to like it?"

He nodded, blinking furiously again. This was obviously embarrassing him to death. "It worked for us."

I didn't know if he meant it worked with sex or with turnip greens. His wife's photograph stared at me from his desk. She had a face like a pudding. It didn't seem fair that these two were having great sex while I wasn't. "We made love every day in the beginning and it didn't get any better."

He shrugged, tapping his pen and foot together now, looking at the closed door behind me. I'd gotten all he wanted to say on the subject.

Fred said I was frigid. I didn't believe him. If I was frigid, how did I get so worked up back when I was dating? It was only him I couldn't stand to touch. I decided to try other men. I had to be very careful and the opportunity didn't present itself often. I chose men passing through town, no one who might stick around to rat on me, or remind me of my guilt. I was hoping to stumble onto good sex. It hadn't worked yet, but illicit sex was plenty scary and therefore exciting. The excitement always fooled me for a little while. Sometimes I learned something new and took it home to Fred. I told him I read it in a book.

I felt lower than a snake. One day a week I taught Sunday school. I cochaired the church bazaar and volunteered for the Junior League. I kept house, took care of my husband and children, and went to school. In the cracks in between, I sneaked around, cheating on my wedding vows. I wrote a forty-page paper on sin for my religion class, trying to see to the bottom of my black soul. The question, as I remember, was original sin. Were we all born bad or was it just me?

Somebody must have watching out for me. I never got pregnant or caught anything worse than poison ivy on my butt from sneaking off to the woods. I did get pregnant a fourth time, but, thank God, with Fred. In December 1963, I had Thomas, who turned out to be practically Fred's duplicate. I named him for my father: Thomas Henry Watkins Craig. My sister named her adopted second son Thomas Henry Watkins McLaurin. My father was singularly unimpressed by both our attempts to carry on his name.

The self-hypnosis worked like a charm with Thomas. It was a forceps delivery, because his head faced the wrong way. I managed to stay under for that part, too. He came out with yellow curls and cauliflower ears from the forceps. I was twenty-seven. In eight years, I had given birth to two boys and two girls, a baby every two years. You would have thought I planned it.

The baby factory had shut down as far as I was concerned. Birth control pills were approved in 1960. I asked for a prescription. My doctor said they hadn't been properly tested and why didn't I have a hysterectomy instead. Nobody was going to take out my organs. I would not turn into my mother. I found a new doctor and got the pills.

I called my old doctor and told him that from now on I was in charge of my body. I wouldn't be coming back. He wept on the phone. I thought that was odd, but then we'd been through a lot together.

19

While I ran the baby farm, my family was falling apart. I could lie and say I was too busy to notice, but every single thing broke my heart.

Uncle Sam and Momae were still up in Canton. I only saw them at Christmas or for family weddings. I loved them exactly the way I had as a child; but I had drifted from their small world into what I considered my much larger one. I hardly thought of them, but I knew I could go back if I chose. They would always be there in the dark, cool house, waited on by Mateel and happy to see me. I just didn't choose.

That's why, when the terrible thing happened, I blamed myself.

Uncle Sam married Momae when she was sixteen. He called her Baby. "What you need, Baby? What you want me to bring you?" He treated her like a porcelain doll, leaving Momae with nothing to decide each day but which outfit to put on. Mateel, their maid, did the shopping, cooking, and cleaning. Uncle Sam's secretary took care of the bills. Momae was free to call the big department stores in New Orleans and order all the silk dresses, loose pants, and crepe de chine jackets she wanted. She never had to leave the house except to get her hair and nails done or go to church.

She appeared to accept the life she'd been given with languorous grace. She drifted through the days from bed to shady back porch. From her dressing table, filled with jars and tubes and heavy cut-glass bottles of perfume, to the luncheon table and the subsequent nap. Momae had sick headaches. That's why she had to rest in a room with the shades drawn and a cloth sprinkled in eau de cologne over her eyes. That's why she needed the teaspoon of spirits of ammonia in her morning Coke-Cola. She also had a bad back. She would lie in her special back-relief chair in the late afternoons, smoking and waiting for Uncle Sam to get home. When he arrived, he'd say, "What can I fix for you, Baby?" He'd make them drinks on a mirrored cart that rolled from room to room. Mae never ate much. I admired her disdain for food and the way she kept herself so pale and lean.

One Saturday, with Uncle Sam off at the farm and Mateel gone for the day, Momae shot herself. Took the pistol that Uncle Sam kept in the house to protect Baby and aimed for what she thought was her heart. She hit her stomach instead and took three horrible days to die.

"In agony," Miss Hosford informed us.

We weren't allowed to go to the hospital. Uncle Sam wouldn't let anyone else in the room. I didn't want to see her, and couldn't bear to think of her suffering. I dwelled on it, especially the agony part, and decided it was my fault. I had been careless and disloyal. I had forgotten those days when the two of them made my life rich with love, and this was my punishment. If I'd let Momae know how much I loved her, she wouldn't have done it.

Back at the house after the burial in the Latimer plot, the dining table groaned with ham, biscuits, casseroles, pies, and cakes. Liquor flowed. Everyone in town came. Sam Junior, their only son, backed himself into a corner with his head down like a cornered bull and wept. Uncle Sam refused to come out of his room. Mateel forked through us like a dark silence, eyes red and swollen, clearing, replenishing, blaming. I went around fervently telling my other aunts and uncles how much I loved them, that I didn't want something terrible to happen where it would be too late and they might die not knowing. That we didn't tell each other often enough how we felt and it was the only important thing. By this time in my declaration, I would be bawling, while my victim shifted from foot to foot, staring at the floor, desperate to get away, saying, "Fine, fine."

In 1962, Doris Lessing published *The Golden Notebook*. I was swept up into the idea of feminism. A woman had a right to a life rich with politics, love, work, and motherhood. I decided Momae killed herself because she didn't *have* a self. Uncle Sam, in his quest to take care of her, left her with nothing useful to do. No one expected anything of her. She had no purpose and nothing she wanted to accomplish. She looked for a way out of an empty life and found the pistol.

I resolved not to let this happen. I would find what I loved and do it, and it wasn't going to be simply keeping house for some man who went out and did what he loved. I didn't speak of this; it was a private resolve. I didn't know what I loved except going to school and, though I'd pretty much made a career of it, I would eventually have to graduate.

The next thing we heard, Uncle Sam had started seeing a divorced teller at the Canton bank. None of us approved. His worship of Baby was supposed to extend beyond the grave. When he gave the woman Momae's diamond solitaire, Sam Junior went to his father's office and socked him in the face. The two of them never spoke again, even though they must have passed a dozen times a week in that small town.

Uncle Sam married the woman at the bank and I decided he'd been fooling around before Mae died. He'd made Momae into a baby-wife, then grown tired of the bad back and sick headaches. He'd gone out and found someone more independent and interesting. Momae discovered this betrayal and shot herself. I nursed this theory for a good long time, making further resolve to keep myself so interesting and occupied no man would ever want to leave me.

Hosford's older son, my cousin John Fontaine Three, told me the truth. The one thing in the world Momae truly cared about was Sam Junior. She'd raised him with unconditional love and no restraints. He grew up bigger and louder than his daddy, drinking, gambling, cursing, wrecking cars and jobs. Mae despaired. With her own money, she set him up in several businesses, which inevitably failed due to the above. Finally, Sam Junior reformed. He swore off liquor. He quit betting hundreds of dollars on Ole Miss football games and found Jesus. Momae had him in that Baptist church every time the doors opened. She'd gotten what she prayed for—her baby was saved. Then she found out his new job was running the gambling concession at the Canton Country Club. That's when she shot herself.

I found this explanation totally unsatisfactory. It wasn't about me, or lack of purpose, or Uncle Sam's betrayal. What a waste to kill yourself over Sam Junior, who any fool could see was born to drink, gamble, and generally raise hell.

My sister Mary Elizabeth squashed any fantasies I had left. She said Momae always loved her best, and presented me with the evidence to prove it. Momae had started a savings account for her at the Canton bank when she was born, adding to it little by little, so that by the time my sister was in high school, there was enough money for a week in New York with a friend.

You never got so mature that a secret couldn't knock you off your illusions.

Bad news arrived by telephone. It got to be, if the phone rang at an odd hour, I knew. The next summer, it was Mama's voice again. "Your uncle John has died."

People died. I was resigned to that. Daddy's parents, Grandma and Grandpa Watkins had, first him, then her. But they'd been old when I was born, and I never got over my awe of them enough to feel close. I wasn't ready for *my* people to die, the ones I'd depended on growing up. I'd already lost Momae. Nobody else was supposed to go.

Uncle John wasn't perfect. At twelve, when my body betrayed me by poking out breasts, he'd put an arm a little too far around me and connect with a nipple. When I complained to Mama, she said I shouldn't mind; he was an affectionate man. Despite this failing, Uncle John was unfailingly kind and patient. He and Miss Hosford, unlike my own parents, seemed to actually love one another. He'd worked hard, at the job in Jackson and, in his every spare moment, to keep Allison's Wells going. His death was completely unfair, and how was Miss Hosford supposed to run that crumbling monster of a hotel without him?

Mama, Mary Elizabeth, and I drove up. Miss Hosford looked smaller, but she didn't cry. She said the evening was like many others. She and Uncle John had dinner, as they did most nights, alone together in the big dining room after the guests were done. They went to their rooms at the back of the family wing and Uncle John complained of indigestion. Miss Hosford went to unlock the office and get him a bicarbonate of soda. By the time she got back, he was unconscious and never woke up. Not indigestion, but a massive heart attack.

We buried him in the same family plot at the Canton cemetery, next to Momae and long-dead Aunt Thelma. I cried along with the help, but Miss Hosford didn't. She stood, small and dignified in her dark suit and hat, thanking people for coming. She viewed tears as a sort of wet sentimentality. Life was filled with suffering; you had to expect that and carry on. If you needed strength, the Episcopal Church was there. Any grieving she did, she did in private.

She continued to run the hotel, plugging away one day at a time. The Art Colony went on. I took my children up for a few days in late summer. I didn't want them to grow up not knowing the place.

I was the only one in our crowd with a hotel. One year, Fred and I invited all our friends to celebrate New Year's up there. Anybody who wanted to could rent a room in the Warm Part and spend the night. Miss Hosford and Uncle John, who was still alive, applauded the idea. We paid for food and set-ups. Renting that many rooms in the middle of the winter helped the cash flow.

I decorated the Pavilion with pine boughs. We put checked tablecloths on the small tables, and candles in wax-dripped bottles. A fire burned in the round fireplace.

Before the party, we served drinks in our room. Ellis and Preston brought up water and ice and kept the fire going. One of the men said, "Last place on earth you can buy yourself a boy for a dollar." I almost choked. Was he calling Ellis and Preston boys? I didn't say a word. The man was my guest, and he hadn't said it in front of Ellis or Preston. But I thought less of him and never forgot it.

We lit the candles and danced to the jukebox. It was a costume party—dress as your wildest fantasy. I came as a can-can girl in lacy stockings, a short skirt, and lots of mascara. I loved dressing up and hiding behind a secret face. At midnight, when we'd counted down to the new year, I kissed Fred and let other men kiss me. It was the one tingling moment of the year when open kissing was allowed. We drank as much as we liked because nobody had to drive home. The next morning, we served Bloody Marys, and ate a huge breakfast of turkey hash, grits, and biscuits. Lena was dead, but her son, Johnny Tucker, had taken her place at the big wood-burning stove.

Except for that crack about buying a boy, it was the best New Year's I ever had.

At my parents' house, Mother was still drinking. Daddy chewed with his eyes shut and left for the office as soon as he put his napkin down. Mary Elizabeth, wearing my wedding dress, married her high school sweetheart, an elfin man, who matched her so well in size and soft-spoken gentility they could have been siblings. Poor Sydney was left to sit through those family dinners alone. She told me there were many nights when not one word was spoken.

20

Misfortunes aside, in 1960 the family received a promotion. Daddy became Governor Ross Barnett's personal lawyer. The glory trickled down to Mother, to my sister Mary Elizabeth, who appreciated status, and to me, though I pretended to disdain it.

Daddy got me a job working for the governor for a few weeks the summer after he was elected. A staunch segregationist, Barnett had been handpicked to run by the Citizens' Council. He was a tall, hawk-faced man, who dressed in black suits and went around bowing and nodding like a courtly undertaker. Along with many southern men, he claimed to put the lesser sex on a pedestal, but at the office he treated us with preacherly condescension. Women weren't allowed to smoke in the governor's presence. Every female in that office smoked, but if we heard his door open, we balanced our burning cigarettes on one of the Capitol's wide stone window ledges, and he pretended not to notice. The governor never corrected us himself. He had a snaky male assistant who came around and chewed us out. Years later, the man blew away trying to outrun a tornado in his car. I remembered how he'd made me squirm and felt secretly avenged.

Barnett took Negro murderers out of the Mississippi State Penitentiary at Parchman to be his personal servants. All Mississippi governors did this, but it seemed particularly heinous for a man so convinced of white supremacy. If the white-coated, bowing and scraping murderers didn't slit the family's throats in their sleep, at the end of the governor's term they received pardons.

The governor bragged that his door was always open. Poor white women came to the office, often with several wet-nosed children, and sat all day waiting to see him and beg him to pardon their husbands. A few of them came out crying and blessing his name. The rest just came out crying. It felt like justice on a whim.

Daddy said Barnett was a wonderful man and I should be grateful to be working where I could learn from him. He said when Barnett was a lawyer, he represented so many poor Negroes that once, when a colored man got hurt on the job and was asked if he wanted a doctor, he said, "Yes, get me Dr. Ross Barnett."

Everyone at the dinner table that night laughed. I kept my mouth shut. I worked there. I knew what he was like.

Daddy invited to dinner the man who'd written a book that proved the South's case. Carleton Putnam was the author; the book was *Race and Reason*. I was presented with an autographed copy. I lost the book, but I remember it being filled with statistics about Negro skulls being thicker and their brains smaller. There were photographs of the results of racial mixing: people with light-colored skin and misshapen heads. Putnam argued that only science, not the Constitution, would protect the South from miscegenation and chaos. Mongrelization had caused the fall of every great civilization. According to him, Egypt had been a glorious white empire until the Nubians came rowing down the Nile. Now look at it.

His philosophy lost some of its punch when we sat down to dinner. If you ate at our house, you'd better rave about my mother's cooking.

"Roast beef and potatoes," Putnam said. "Dangerous combination, but I know what to do when I get back to the hotel."

"Apple pie with cheese." He frowned at his dessert plate. "Terrible combination. Luckily I know what to do when I get back to the hotel."

I couldn't stand it. "What do you do when you get back to the hotel?"

Mother gave me the look. Personal questions were forbidden.

He winked. "Baking soda."

Yet another dinner. Daddy scooped up a forkful of butter beans. "There is no need for integration."

"How else are things going to be fair?" I said.

Mother interrupted. "Colored people don't want to mix with us. They'd rather be with—" she hesitated "—their own kind."

I turned on her. "They'd rather be in shacks instead of a house like this? Is that what you're saying?"

She gave me a warning look. "Lower your voice." Nice people weren't supposed to talk about integration.

"Before all this mess started, things were changing," Daddy said. "The people of Mississippi were ready to make separate-but-equal mean equal." (He meant the white people were ready, the people with power.) "There was a bill in the legislature that would have done that. Built wonderful new colored schools. Then Nigras made the mistake of demanding things."

"Maybe they got tired of waiting."

He shook his head at my ignorance. "You can't force people." (He meant us, the white people again.) "It just gets their backs up."

"So what happened to the bill to make us equal?"

He looked at his plate. "Defeated."

"And instead we got the Citizens' Council. We passed laws making it harder for colored people to vote."

He put down his fork and fixed me with the blue-eyed gaze that froze us all. "Do you really want people voting who can't read?"

I didn't have an answer. Mother made a be-quiet sound. Annie was coming through the swinging door to clear the plates. There was custard pie for dessert.

I fought most of my civil rights battles at this dinner table. I never won and I often wept out of frustration. I was filled with feelings and empty of facts. To this day, if I begin to argue with someone who disagrees, I am thrown back to those years of being faced down by my father. My throat closes, my chest constricts, and I feel the tears behind my eyes. I retreat before I begin, undone by anger and helplessness. I've learned to avoid touchy subjects. People's beliefs, especially the illogical ones, cannot be dislodged by reason.

In the summer of 1961, Freedom Riders began to ride buses through the South, testing the Supreme Court's ban on segregation in interstate travel. To avoid the bloodshed the riders encountered in Alabama, the governor worked out a deal with President Kennedy. The highway patrol would protect the travelers from white mobs, and the local police could arrest them when they arrived. When the jails in Jackson filled, the protestors were shipped to Parchman State Prison. I watched on TV as busload after busload of polite well-dressed young people, black and white, let themselves be led away. I was a mother; I couldn't do that, but I recognized my cowardice. I'd never have the guts to do that.

In 1962, James Meredith, a Negro, applied to Ole Miss, and the whole state geared up to fight. The university tried to turn him down in every way they could: he was late registering; he had transferred from an unaccredited college; he registered to vote in a county where he didn't live (this one a crime). Meredith, backed by the NAACP, sued, and the courts overrode every excuse. Finally there were no more barriers, and the university was ordered to admit him.

Three times, Meredith showed up with federal marshals to register. Each attempt ended the same way. Governor Barnett presented him with a fancy sealed proclamation and turned him away. The governor argued a theory called "interposition." The state interposed their sovereignty over the federal court's decision.

There was much legal skirmishing, court orders and injunctions flying back and forth, but when the Fifth Circuit Court of Appeals in New Orleans cited Barnett for contempt, and the personal fine was ten thousand dollars per day, he gave up. Not publicly, he didn't dare. He'd aroused too much passion with his rantings: "We will not surrender to the evil and illegal forces of tyranny. We must either submit to the unlawful dictates of the federal government or stand up like men and tell them NEVER!" He couldn't be seen to back down. His political career would be over.

Daddy negotiated with Bobby Kennedy on how to have the governor give in without it looking like capitulation. Like most southern conservatives, my parents despised the Kennedys, but there was Daddy on the phone next to our red Formica kitchen table, talking to the Justice Department and the White House. Whatever their politics, they couldn't help but be a little awed. I was, too, and for once my father seemed to be on the side of sanity.

They came up with a plan. Daddy said there needed to be a show of force. All the marshals must draw their guns. Kennedy said that was too dangerous. Crowds were gathering in Oxford. Too easy for someone to start shooting. Finally, Kennedy agreed that the marshals would put their hands on their holsters, one would draw, and the governor, helpless in the face of federal might, would give way and let Meredith into the Lyceum to register.

The plan failed. The governor didn't even get to Oxford. The lieutenant governor turned Meredith away once again and Kennedy lost patience. He told Daddy he was slipping Meredith onto the campus that Sunday afternoon. He would be registered Monday morning. No more dawdling. Kennedy needed Barnett's guarantee that the Mississippi Highway Patrol would be there to maintain order.

Daddy got Barnett to agree, and then the governor wavered. Bobby Kennedy made a threat. The president was speaking on national television that night. If Barnett didn't stick to the agreement, J.F.K. would reveal to the entire country the private pact Barnett had made with Washington. Barnett was stunned. "You wouldn't do that." This would ruin him.

On that Sunday, events in Oxford got ahead of anyone's agreement. We were at my parents' for dinner as usual, except nothing was usual. In the kitchen, Annie and Marie grumbled to each other and got quiet when we came in. Taking them home after lunch, we had to change stations on the radio. They kept playing "Dixie" and a new song: "Ross Is Standin' Like Gibraltar, He Will Never Falter."

The night before, the governor had gotten up in front of the microphones at a packed Ole Miss game in Jackson and roared: "*I love our state. I love her people. I love her customs.*" That doesn't sound like much, but I was there. It was enough to send the crowd into a frenzy. Everybody knew what he meant: be prepared to fight to the death to defend these customs.

Edwin Walker, the retired general turned John Bircher, went on the radio and told people to bring their tents and their skillets and come help Governor Barnett defend Oxford. It was 1863 all over again and this time we planned to win.

In Oxford that Sunday, the crowd around the Lyceum swelled as dusk fell, and went from curious to angry. Kennedy posted hundreds of marshals around the Lyceum building. A full-blown riot developed. The Mississippi Highway Patrol was supposed to guard the roads onto campus and into town to keep away outsiders. In the midst of the riot, someone ordered the highway patrol to pull out. Daddy was on the phone with Washington and with Barnett.

We were all at the house. Things were too tense to leave.

Daddy hung up. "The trouble with the governor is he listens to the last person he talks to. I persuade him we can't win this thing and we don't want violence, then the radicals get to him and he goes back to thinking he can stare down the entire federal government."

"Can't you stop him?" I was so nervous, I was shaking.

"Kennedy's asking what I'm doing about it, and I'm doing all I can. The governor's not a bad man. He's just being pushed and shoved in too many directions."

I was tired of hearing about Ross Barnett being a good man. "If ignorance is no excuse under the law, neither is being pushed around. He should never have let this mess get started."

"Things happen one at a time. Sometimes you can't see the end." Daddy looked exhausted. He sent us home. Everything else I found out later.

The highway patrol came back, but as the night wore on, the crowd got meaner. Gunfire joined the rock throwing and the Molotov cocktails. The marshals were unarmed and under siege. They began firing tear gas. Two people died by gunfire that night, a French reporter and an Oxford bystander. Hundreds were wounded. Kennedy federalized the Mississippi National Guard and sent in U.S. troops. On Monday morning, Meredith registered and, escorted by federal marshals, began attending classes. Thirty-one thousand troops moved in. Oxford was occupied.

The governor ordered flags flown at half-mast to mourn the invasion of his state.

I was horrified. I couldn't believe that once again, we'd managed to make ourselves the shame of the nation.

"It could have been much worse," Daddy said. "It could have been the second Civil War."

21

In the coldest part of January 1963, the winter after Uncle John died, Mother called, practically screaming into the phone. "*Allison's Wells is on fire. I have to get Hosford off the train.*"

That morning, Ellis had taken my aunt to catch the train to New Orleans. When the hotel closed for the season, she liked to take a break and go visit friends. We used to joke that she spent the winter staying free with people who paid to stay with her during the summer.

I sincerely believe if she had been at the hotel, things would have turned out differently. She was so skilled at smoothing over the daily emergencies at Allison's Wells, she actually might have been able to talk out a fire.

When Ellis drove back from putting her on the train, he saw flames coming from a lower bathroom window. We were never sure of the cause. The place was so old, it could have been any failing, from the furnace to the wiring. John Fontaine thinks it was a towel or curtain, left too near a bathroom space heater.

Johnny Tucker was in the kitchen. He knew nothing about the fire until Ellis ran in shouting. Ellis grabbed Miss Hosford's silver service and pistol. He moved the cars around front. He and the rest of the help tried using fire extinguishers. When those weren't enough, they unrolled the fire hose. I pictured their panic, and the agony of stretching the ancient, cracking canvas hose, only to discover it wouldn't reach. I thought of how awful it must have been to watch the fire grow, jumping from roof to roof, while they shouted, ran, and tried one fruitless thing after another. Garden hoses waited under the house, but there had been three days of subfreezing weather and the pipes were frozen. What despair when they realized they had waited too late. Not only was the hotel destroyed; none of the other contents could be saved.

The place was enveloped, and burned as it had been built, from the oldest wing—the Warm Part—down the Cold Part, to the Annex, and on to the Fishes Club and Bath House.

The Warm Part had been built in the 1870s. The dry wood went up like kindling. In an hour, it was gone. Nothing was saved: the family furniture, pictures, and jewelry, Uncle John's architectural paintings, the grand piano in the entry hall, Aunt Thelma's portrait, art by all the well-known people who'd taught at the Art Colony, the King and Queen's table, and, my favorite, a crazy quilt on the wall next to the dining room.

It was a clear day. They said you could see the smoke for over thirty miles—all the way to Jackson.

Miss Hosford had hired a man from Biloxi to help her manage the place during the winter months. Struggling to put the fire out, he had a heart attack and died on the lawn. No one else was injured. By the time the Canton Fire Department arrived, there was nothing left but the Pavilion and office. The firemen filled their tanks from the pond below the rose garden and sprayed that building.

Mother got Miss Hosford off the train in Brookhaven and they rushed back. The next day, photographs on the front pages of both Jackson papers showed them standing in the ruins. Nothing remained but the tall chimneys of the Warm Part. My sisters and I drove up and picked through the wreckage. We found bits of the thick white hotel china.

John Fontaine Three said he was glad his father was no longer alive. It would have been too much for him to bear.

"What a shame," people said to my aunt's face, but privately they said it was better for Hosford, that she couldn't continue running that place alone. It was an accident waiting to happen.

I wasn't sure how Miss Hosford felt. She maintained the same maddening calm she had when her husband died. She had no place to live and almost no clothes. The endeavor she'd devoted her life to was destroyed. She said it was just stuff. You could always do without stuff. She seemed more heartbroken over the manager's death than the loss of the hotel. I wanted to shake her. Couldn't anyone but me see our impoverishment? This was where Mama, Miss Hosford, Uncle Sam, Uncle Doug, and dead Aunt Thelma were born and raised. Their entire history was in ashes. I wanted wailing and rending of garments.

I had fought going to Allison's Wells as a child, and ended up loving it more than any spot on earth. It formed the cornerstone of my best memories. The people I cared most for had been there. After the fire, the buildings were gone and the help left without jobs. They had always worked for cash, as needed. No one talked about how they would live now, or what our responsibility to them might be.

Johnny and Ora Dee moved to Jackson. Johnny was hired as cook at the small private school our son Clay attended. Ora Dee worked for Mama a couple of days a week, helping with the sewing and arranging flowers. Ellis and Preston stayed put. There was no money for pensions, no settlements. Ellis owned the acreage left him by Grandpa Latimer. He could farm. The rest managed the best they could. The money from insurance and sale of the land was barely enough for Miss Hosford to live in modest comfort. Allison's Wells would not be rebuilt. The place had held us together, black and white. Without it, we scattered.

My aunt found a small apartment in Jackson's Belhaven district. Ora Dee cleaned for her one day a week. Miss Hosford served tea and drinks in the late afternoon, just as she'd done in the Retreat. She stayed active in arts organizations, took classes at the local college, and made friends with the students. She managed to continue her daily swims, using borrowed pools.

What I learned from her was not to give up. If one thing didn't work, the next might. You didn't stop trying. You didn't waste ener-

224

gy crying over things that couldn't be changed. From Miss Hosford and not my mother—who was inclined to give in to her temperament and to drink—I learned the power of optimism. For most of the war, Uncle John held a job in a city far away. She was left to run the hotel alone. Even after the war, Uncle John worked in advertising in Jackson, thirty-three miles south. He left the hotel early and returned late. The daily crises were left for my aunt to manage.

Everything I absorbed from her must have come from osmosis, since I spent most of those years at Allison's Wells trying to keep out of her way, desperate to dodge the lethal lectures that began—"I am quite disappointed," "I expected more," "A lady never." These were much harder to take than Mother's yelling and spankings.

I made fun of Miss Hosford, but I was impressed with how much she managed to accomplish, powered not by money, but with soft-voiced determination and an unbeatable will.

When she was settled into her new place, furnished much like the old Retreat with piles of pillows, pictures, and art magazines, she sat down and wrote a book about Allison's Wells and had it privately published. She cajoled Eudora Welty into doing a brief foreword, and included a sentimental poem I wrote after the place burned, a poem so bad I still can't stand seeing it in print. She was an enthusiastic promoter, and had to be dissuaded from peddling copies of the book in the vestibule of St. Andrew's, or out of her car during a reading given her by the bookstore at McRae's department store.

Looking through Miss Hosford's book (which now goes for 130 British pounds on eBay), I was reminded of that conversation I overheard on the kitchen porch long ago. She described the help by the shade of their skin: Preston was "caramel colored," Savannah "a light summer tan," Ellis "very light colored." Jimmie Lee was "rather light" with "such rhythm." Haymore, a head waiter who terrified me as a young child, was "small, rather chocolate colored, a mustache, always immaculate and distinguished looking." Ora Dee was "pretty, beautiful skin, a warm tan." Lena was "light colored with a very strong face . . . a mixture of Negro, Spanish, and Indian blood." Her son Johnny was "coal black." Parthenia was "ebony black, her skin looking polished."

Maybe it was Hosford's artistic eye; I suspected worse. Invariably, the help were described as "happy go lucky," "filled with joy and laughter." They had "pleasing, smiling" personalities. They were forever "in a good humor." Johnny Tucker had "a happy smile, always bowing and taking off his hat." At Allison's Wells, we lived, according to my aunt, in a world filled with cheerful workers. Never out of sorts, never resentful. I would love to read a book about the hotel written by the servants.

Skin-color designations were a leftover from slavery. An owner's slaves were listed by color, often not by name, and never by last name. When everyone who worked at the hotel was gone, I realized how much I'd never known and never thought to ask. Where did the help go to the bathroom? Except for Ellis and Parthenia, I didn't know where anyone lived. I didn't know the names of their children unless those children worked for us. I didn't know who took care of these children while the parents worked, or where they went to school. I never asked how they made it through the long winters when the hotel closed.

These questions came later. At the time, all I felt was loss. The best part of my past had been erased. I felt the way I did when Momae died. I regretted all the things I had neglected and now could never do again. I wanted to sit in the cool early morning dining room, with my bare feet not quite touching the floor, and pour sorghum syrup out of the hinge-lidded silver pitcher onto a stack of crisp-edged corn cakes. I wanted to plunge into the dark green swimming pool, the water heart-stoppingly cold, and swim underwater, eyes open in the mineral murk, to the shallow end and back again without coming up. I wanted to be able to run barefoot over the gravel drive without pain, and to feel the powdery dust of the path to the gullies between my toes.

There was only one person to blame. The hotel had been there. I could have taken my children more often and done all those things. Ellis was fifty-eight when the place burned. He would have waited on us, bending over the table with a slight smile, dignified in his starched jacket. I hadn't gone, just like I hadn't gone to see Momae, because I thought life would wait.

The day after the fire, as I shuffled through the cold, wet ashes, I wondered what future the hotel would have had without a fire. Miss Hosford would carry on, she wasn't a quitter, but she was no longer young. My cousin Doug went into the business, but he had a hotel of his own in Pass Christian. His older brother, John Three, worked in advertising. Uncle Doug and Aunt Leigh had no children. Uncle Sam had Sam Junior, but, lord knows, he wouldn't have wanted to run the place and would never have been trusted with it.

That left the three of us. In January 1963, I was deep in academia. By the end of the year, I would have four children. My sister Mary Elizabeth had married and moved to New Orleans. Sydney was eighteen, just starting college. If the place hadn't burned, she might have one day run it. Growing up, she spent her summers there and loved it as much as I did. She had a glad, easy way with people. In another universe, she could have taken over Allison Wells and her life might have turned out entirely different.

But maybe the time had come and gone for Mississippi's last spa. In 1909, when my grandfather ran the hotel, a horse-drawn bus met four trains a day down the road at Way, bringing back guests. Wagons followed, carrying five-gallon jugs of the medicinal well water to be shipped all over the country, and returned with the guests' trunks. People came for a month from the Delta, New Orleans, and Memphis. Days were filled with simpler pleasures: horseback riding, buggy rides, moonlit hayrides, walks to the gullies, tennis, croquet, euchre and auction bridge. Bud Scott's orchestra played in the Pavilion from ten to eleven each morning, and in the dining room for luncheon and dinner. There was a dance every night and on Thursday nights, a ball.

By 1963, people could afford to vacation in more exotic places—New York City or Europe. A fusty country hotel no longer seemed interesting. The rooms, which had once been everything a room needed to be, looked plain and dumpy. The food stayed amazing and plenty of people drove up on the weekends to eat, but fewer and fewer people stayed for a week or a month in the summer. Maybe it was better to burn than go bankrupt, better to go up in flames than crumble into obscurity.

It didn't seem better to me, and surely not for Miss Hosford, in spite of her stoicism. Keeping the place going gave purpose to her life. Surely she longed for the beautiful things she lost. I mourned those amber beads. She was the family historian, and the record of their lives burned with that place. I never heard a word of regret.

They say you are alive as long as one person remembers you, but with Allison's Wells, it was the buildings themselves, the echoing halls, the sun-warmed porches, and the loud, sweet-smelling kitchen. These held my memories as much as I held theirs. Nothing you love stays because you love it. Like the universe, we race away from each other, love be damned.

There was another matter, one which Miss Hosford and the rest of the family appeared to ignore. The entire enterprise had depended on the labor of poorly paid people whose ancestors had been slaves. The fire brought the end of an era we white people got nostalgic over, but it was the beginning of a far better time, if not for them, for their children.

22

Braver people than I took to the streets in 1963. Black college students held sit-ins at the all-white lunch counters of Woolworth's and McLellan's. A crowd gathered. People poured coffee on them and put cigarettes out on their backs. I read the papers and shuddered.

The Junior League called off our planned project to teach literacy when they realized that most of the people who needed to learn to read and write were colored. I hated my town, my state, and the entire South. I longed to do something to make things better, but I felt helpless. Plus, I was terrified. Menace hung in the air.

I had a small group of friends, women who felt the way I did. We gathered to talk about how awful the situation was, how wrong and backward. But we had no solutions. Nor did we pause in our philosophizing to recognize the irony of leaving Negro maids to watch our children while we met. We were inextricably tangled in the system and we were afraid. The Citizens' Council and the state-sanctioned Sovereignty Commission operated like secret police. We were white women, married to respectable men from north Jackson. They probably wouldn't physically hurt us, but word would spread. A person with views was shunned, punished by indirection.

If I had managed to come up with a plan, and possessed the fortitude to stand up and shout what was right and decent, we would have suffered the consequences. People wanting the expensive homes Fred built would find themselves another, less controversial builder. The bank would call in his construction loans; the state would find a reason to cancel his contractor's license. All but our closest friends would shun us. Few liberals felt free to speak out, and the wrath that fell on them discouraged the rest of us. Even the word "moderate" became an anathema. No one with any sense wanted to be called a moderate. I was a coward. I'm ashamed of it now, but this was the only life I knew. These were my people. I wasn't strong or brave enough to push my way out.

In June of 1963, Medgar Evers was shot down like an animal in his own driveway. He was field secretary for Mississippi's NAACP, a man who refused to bow to the pervasive fear. His fight for the integration of Ole Miss and his investigation into Emmett Till's death made him a hated target of white supremacists. A Molotov cocktail had been thrown into his home; he'd been almost run down leaving work. On June 12, a rifle shot in the back felled him.

"It's all part of the Communist conspiracy," my father said.

A Klansman named Byron De La Beckwith was arrested for Evers's killing. Former governor Ross Barnett and one-time Major General Edwin Walker visited him in jail.

In November that year, I was hugely pregnant with Thomas. We were adding a bedroom to the house and the workmen were there. When the horrible news came on the television, I ran crying into the hall.

"They've shot President Kennedy."

The head carpenter looked up with a grin. "Got what he deserved."

His assistant nodded, shifting a wad of tobacco to the other cheek.

I retreated, slamming my door. That was it. I had to get out of this place.

Paul Johnson became governor in 1964. Campaigning, he'd gotten big laughs with lines like: "You know what the NAACP stands for? Niggers, alligators, apes, coons, and possums."

President Lyndon Johnson signed the landmark Civil Rights

Act, saying that "those who are equal before God shall now also be equal in the polling booths, in the classrooms, in the factories, and in hotels, restaurants, movie theaters, and other places that provide service to the public." Mississippians were outraged, but the "White Only" signs began to come down.

This was Freedom Summer. SNCC recruited hundreds of young college students to come to Mississippi and register Negro voters. Freedom Schools were set up in black communities to educate potential voters about their rights. Civics was not taught in Negro schools, so the Freedom Schools reached out to students of all ages, teaching literacy, black history, and black literature and encouraging social activism. Mass meetings were held in churches.

At the time, less than 3 percent of the nonwhite population in Mississippi voted. The state had many ways of keeping the unwanted from the polls, from outright intimidation—several Negro men were shot after registering—to more devious techniques.

One day I asked Mother if she let Annie vote. She said, "I have no objection, but I don't know when she would since she comes to work before seven in the morning and leaves after seven at night." She gave me a sly smile. This was the way a southern lady operated, not with ugly words, but by moving the undesirable action out of reach.

I went to the kitchen and asked Annie if she was registered.

"I don't fool with that stuff."

I made a promise to myself that she would vote one day when things weren't so scary. I didn't know how, but I would see to it.

Aunt Leigh, whom I adored among my aunts, second only to Momae, told me a story one day when I dropped by her sandalwood-scented house. There had been a storm the day before and, when her maid left to catch the bus, she had no umbrella. "I loaned her my raincoat," Aunt Leigh said, "but of course I'll never be able to put it on again."

Here was the truth I was supposed to absorb under cover of the rhetoric about our way of life: people of color were genetically inferior. They weren't as smart as we were, and this ignorance caused them to be dirty, which meant they smelled. Their dark skin was a curse sent by God. There was a lot of talk in the South about Ham, and how the curse of black skin, once used to justify slavery, now meant Negroes were supposed to be servants, stay servants, and be happy with their lot.

The dark color supposedly sullied anything Negroes touched. They could shop in white stores, but weren't allowed to try anything on, because if the clothes touched black skin, no white person would buy them. These were the same people cooking every bite we put in our mouths, so the logic didn't quite carry. Logic didn't matter. If you were being operated on and got transfused with one drop of Negro blood, you became a Negro.

When I was small, riding in the back of the bus with Marie, or sitting in the balcony at the movie theater, I thought we were special. Now I realized this was where we had to sit—above in church and at the movies, behind on the buses. When Marie told me to stay still and not make a fuss, she was protecting herself. No colored person wanted to attract attention, not even one in the company of a small white child.

The "Miss Norma" business that startled me at twelve was the work of Jim Crow. I had been too blind to see. Between one birthday and the next, I was shown the deference that must be given by Negroes to white adults. They, on the other hand, were never allowed a title. They were Lena, Parthenia, Savannah, Ellis, and Alan, never Mr., Miss, or Mrs. They had no last names. You couldn't invite them in the front door or sit down and eat together.

When you rode through the Delta in those days, old black men stepped off the road and doffed their hats to any car with white people in it. Fred's father was from Sunflower in the heart of the Mississippi Delta. He grew up running a plantation. When the depression hit, and the banks took his land and his livelihood, he brought his planter ways to Jackson. He got a job with the government grading cotton. One of those planter habits was ignoring all bills until fall when you sold your crop. The Jackson utilities were not familiar with this way of doing business. After the lights went off that first year, his wife, Fredibel, took over the bill paying.

The other habit he brought was a rougher attitude toward the race issue. In my family, we were polite. We were taught to respect everyone. The same benighted racial mores governed our lives, but we were too civilized to acknowledge them until forced by the threat of integration. In polite society, such things were understood. There was no need to say them out loud.

Raymond, Fred's father, suffered from no such inhibitions. "Niggers want this," he would say at the dinner table. "Niggers better watch out." While his dignified graying cook, Molly, passed the vegetables. He took my son Clay along one night when he drove Molly home. Clay, who was five, asked Molly why all the houses in her neighborhood were so small.

Raymond answered for her. "Cause white people got brains the size of a grapefruit and niggers got brains the size of a cherry."

He reported this story proudly when the two of them returned.

Anger blew me right out of my chair. "You have no right to fill my son's head with your prejudice." I stood over him, shaking my finger in his face. "You may have done it to your children, but you won't do it to mine."

He sat there and grinned, unperturbed. It was the kind of grin southern men gave women in those days, the way you'd smile at a child in a temper, a grin that could (and probably did) provoke murder.

Growing up, I sensed the inequality around me, but I didn't know why it was, or what to do about it, so I tried not to see. When I got old enough to realize the pages torn out of magazines on the walls of Parthenia's cabin weren't a colorful and interesting way to decorate, but an attempt to keep the cold from seeping through cracks in the dried boards, or that the funny smell inside might come from not having access to anything but a wash tub and scrub board, I averted my eyes. When Annie finally moved out of the dark room behind our house and got a place of her own, my sisters drove her home without a qualm. It killed me to see where she lived. My easy life depended on the service of these people. I was as much a part of the system as any racist. Guilt was painful. I didn't want to see.

Marie was the exception. Her house was a tiny replica of middle-class decorum and twice as clean as most white people's. We gave her an engraved silver tray when she'd worked for the family fifty years. She hid it in a drawer, considering it tasteless to call attention to one's age (and probably to the length of one's servitude).

A man from Irish television came to town to report on our troubles. Visiting liberals were often sent to me. I was always good for a hot meal. I offered to introduce him to my father, the segregationist. When I did, the Irishman came right to the point. "Why do you people hate the Negro?"

I saw anger flash in my father's eyes, but his voice remained courteous. "We don't hate Negroes, but we haven't forgotten Reconstruction."

Lord, so that was it. We were still pushing that hundred-year-old rock up the mountain. White southerners had been tossed out of office after losing what we called the War of Northern Aggression. Negroes were put in their place. Some were educated ministers, but a few could not read or write. The South never got over the humiliation, or the memory of the poverty that followed. In our school, it was Jefferson Davis's and Robert E. Lee's birthdays we memorized; Confederate Memorial Day was sacred, not the country's. In the minds of conservative southerners, any Negro gain meant a white loss. Outside agitators like CORE, SNCC, and the NAACP, busybodies like the Supreme Court and the federal government, had returned a hundred years later to forcibly violate our sovereign state's rights, including the most sacred: the right to separation of the races. It was part of a Communist conspiracy to overthrow the country. It was the second Reconstruction.

In small towns throughout Mississippi, Freedom Summer volunteers were greeted by whites with threats, beatings, and bombs. This was a "nigger-Communist invasion" overrunning our Christian way of life. Even my cousin Sam Junior turned brutal. We were talking up in Canton one evening.

"Let them try and get out of line up here," Sam Junior said. "A bunch of us drive around nights and shoot niggers off their front porches."

His wife, Julia, said, "*Sam.*"

I said, "You're joking."

He gave me a smirk.

I'd read about the night riders. They were the terror of rural communities actively working for civil rights. Was Sam Junior a night rider? This was a man I'd grown up loving, the person I envied for being the family rebel. Now I saw the dark side of that rebellion. I stared at him, red-eyed, laughing, half-soused, a man who, without a shred of shame, bragged about shooting people because their skin was a different color. I hoped he was lying, but how could anyone joke about that?

Losing the battle over Meredith didn't make our father any less determined to fight on every other front. Arguing for the city, which was under an order to integrate public facilities, he succeeded in closing our pools. Colored bodies and white in the same water? It couldn't be tolerated. Daddy argued that swimming (for either color) was a privilege, not a right, and the city of Jackson was not required to provide that privilege.

At supper, Daddy claimed the Negroes were burning their own churches. The troubles were caused by "outside agitators." When the civil rights workers Goodman, Schwerner, and Chaney disappeared in Neshoba County, he said it was a hoax. They were hiding in Cuba and the Communists were behind it.

After their bodies were found, murdered and buried in a landfill, I confronted him. "Did they kill themselves, too?"

He said I was too blinded by idealism to see the big picture. "Laws never change people's hearts."

I sincerely believed they could. And if they couldn't, I wanted to live in a different place.

My relatives were solidly behind preserving our heritage. In their eyes I was a subversive. The entire South was blind to its own behavior. It was like a form of collective insanity.

What did I do? I took a vacation from the troubles. I left my children in the care of Marie, Fred, and his parents, and went to New York with my friend Kay. It was my first trip to the big city. Two other friends were already there, one studying acting and the other at NYU. The World's Fair was in town. Our husbands would join us to see it, but we had two glorious weeks on our own.

Everyone told us not to go. A month in New York in the heat of Freedom Summer, were we crazy? Violence had broken out in Harlem, and Mississippians were bitterly pleased. Our families said we'd be murdered in the streets. We promised our husbands, for the sake of the children, never to venture inside Central Park at night. We settled in a sublet brownstone on West Fourth Street, where the husbands expected us to wait, cautiously, for their arrival by car.

We did not wait, nor were we cautious. I was twenty-eight and had four children. I had been out of the South once—to Aspen— not exactly a slice of life. Manhattan was an even greater bite of freedom than higher education. I had never met a black person who was not a maid, cook, or gardener. I walked the streets of Greenwich Village astounded. There were black people and mixed couples, shopping in stores, buying flowers, pushing their children in strollers. I saw a couple in a sidewalk café, he black, she white, having a drink. She pushed a maraschino cherry between his lips. I watched, mesmerized. Nothing bad happened; no one else noticed.

Each day we went to see our friend Jane do scenes at the Herbert Berghof Studio. The black students were tough and funny. They scared me. We gave a party at the brownstone, and they came. Sitting on the stoop outside our house, they passed around a pipe of marijuana, the first dope I'd ever seen. How deliciously evil. They told jokes I did not understand and laughed cynically. Jane danced with one. How deliciously forbidden. A lawyer from Mississippi somehow found us. "I'm going to tell," he said.

It wasn't a joke. He would. We laughed, but I remember the dread.

Kay and I went everywhere. We talked to anyone we met in the White Horse or Chumley's. We ate little, slept less, and I could not look hard enough. I had found a world that no one of my acquaintance knew existed. Or maybe they did know, people like my father, and that's why they tried to keep us from leaving home. People who went away to school often never returned. We felt sorry for them. It was dangerous to go away, dangerously eye-opening to see what lay outside.

We went to wonderful plays: *The Subject Was Roses, Dylan, Three Sisters, Funny Girl, High Spirits*. One night we went to the Cherry Lane to see Albee's *The American Dream* and LeRoi Jones's *Dutchman*. I sat through the Albee play thinking that Millsaps College in Jackson, Mississippi, had done a better job with this play, and wasn't that weird? At intermission an old black man with wine on his breath stumbled against me on the street and tried to bum a cigarette. I refused, insulted. In Mississippi we never let drunk people wander the streets with their hands out.

Dutchman began. The play might have been a snake uncoiling in my lap. I had never seen such naked boiling hate. On a subway car, black Clay lashed out at white Lula, telling her his suit and polite demeanor were an act, devices, and she'd never know his heart. He said it was all he could do not to cut white people's throats. I cringed. Was this how Ellis, Preston, and Alan felt at the hotel when they were calling me "Miss Norma"?

Yes, I thought, I'm finally hearing the truth. Lula stabbed Clay. My stomach lurched and I cried. She made the other passengers throw his body off the train. She ordered them off at the next stop.

She reached into her bag and pulled out a small tablet and wrote something. As she was about to leave the train, another middle-class black man entered the car. She took an apple from her bag and began her murderous seduction.

Curtain.

I couldn't move. If the black wino had come down the aisle, I would have given him a whole pack of cigarettes for permission to get out of my chair. Singing "We Shall Overcome" suddenly felt like sentimental claptrap, a whitewashing of hatred and fear. What would become of us?

We went next door for a drink and tried to sort out how we felt. Robert Hooks, who played Clay, came in. We invited him to our table for a drink and told him what his performance had done to us—for us. He was handsome and gracious and did not laugh at our southern accents.

He leaned across the table. "Do you know what Lula writes in that little book of hers?"

We waited.

"One less nigger."

In New York, for the first time in my life, I felt free. I wanted to stay. If someone had assured me my children were okay—Marie would care for them—if I'd had money or a job, I might never have gone home. I failed to see the irony in this fantasy—I would earn my freedom to be a liberal on Marie's back.

Fred and Kay's husband arrived. The sheriff in Hinds County, Mississippi, had given them a New Jersey license plate, so they could switch plates in Virginia. Whites were as afraid to drive through northern territory as blacks were to drive through the South. The men found this hilarious, part of an accustomed privilege. They had been done a surely illegal favor by an officer of the law. I watched them laughing, wondering, who was this person I'd married?

"You've lost weight," Fred said. "Where did you get those clothes?"

I'd found them on sale. These were my New York clothes, part of my new self.

When the month was over, I went home. What choice did I have?

In Mississippi, the movement boiled over in a way no one could ignore. Daddy and I renewed our old arguments. I was stuck with "it isn't fair." He preferred eugenics. "Miscegenation caused the fall of the Roman Empire." When he had federal judge Sidney Mize over for dinner, he introduced me: "My daughter, Norma. She's a little pink." I was different, therefore I must be a Communist.

As I remember, I grinned, hapless in the face of opposition. I felt sick and tired of arguing, sick of the South, sick of saying hello to smiling people every time I went into a grocery store, people who would turn their backs on me in an instant if they knew I supported integration. The movement was going on all around me and I wasn't doing anything. Every night on television, we watched the protests. Colored and white people, well dressed and polite, letting themselves be arrested.

Fred never took part, but he never forbade my making small gestures. There was something called "Wednesdays in Mississippi." Prominent women from the North flew down on Tuesday night. On Wednesday, they were taken around to see the way things were: the shantytown houses, the inferior colored schools, the Jim Crow laws, and then they flew home, experts in bigotry, to work for change from a safer distance.

I volunteered to be a host. My first visitor was a terrifyingly chic woman from Chicago, the sister of Senator Evan Bayh. In her nasal voice, she said the bed was "excellent," refused our offer of a drink, and headed out to investigate "the problem." After she flew back north, I stared critically at the empty guest room—actually Thomas's room with the baby bed moved out. I felt disappointed. This wasn't doing anything.

One night after dinner, with the children bathed and in their beds, Fred and I settled, as we did every night, into the two easy chairs in our bedroom for the news. These were the chairs we'd bought instead of an engagement ring.

239

I was mentally going over the next day's errands when I heard President Kennedy's voice. He said something about church burnings.

"Bunch of Communists," Fred said.

"So you agree with Daddy? They're burning down their own churches?" I was being sarcastic. I motioned for him to be quiet so I could hear.

Kennedy said, ". . . cowardly as well as outrageous." He was talking about the shootings in Ruleville. He was talking about *us*, right here in Mississippi. "I commend those who are making the effort to register every citizen. They deserve the protection of the United States government, the protection of the states . . . and if it requires extra legislation, and extra force, we shall do that."

Extra force. Those were the words I wanted to hear. Send in that extra force and make us obedient. I hit the arm of my chair. "We shall do it." A commercial came on.

"Bullshit," Fred said.

"It's not bullshit. That's what's got to happen."

He grunted.

"I wish I could do something."

No response. He was too kind to say so, but he would have been happier if I'd shut up about the race issue.

I asked him to pay his colored workers the same as he did the whites. He said they didn't deserve the same pay. I asked him to stop talking about them as if they were animals. He said they acted like animals.

Fred, his family, my family, and most of my relatives and friends had lined up on one side, convinced they were right and the South was right. I was on the other side with three or four other misfits.

We joined the Episcopal Church soon after we married. In these fraught times, it was considered moderate. Negroes were holding kneel-ins, going around to various churches to see if they would be admitted, and kneeling on the church steps if they weren't. At my former church, Galloway Methodist, the minister who had

240

baptized and married me had been sent packing for not agreeing to keep Negroes out. Every Sunday, all over town, stern deacons and ushers stood on the steps of white churches, ready to prevent a dark invasion. They were called "The Color Guard." Anne Moody, author of *Coming of Age in Mississippi*, said that Sunday morning at eleven was the most segregated hour in the South.

One night at a church meeting we talked about whether to let Negroes come to services. A heavy man spoke. "If I thought they were coming to pray, I'd have no objection. But they have their own churches to pray in. They're coming here to agitate, to make trouble. They aren't *our* Negroes, they're outside agitators."

I found myself arguing against several middle-aged business-men. "This is a Christian church." My throat closed up, my voice squeaked in fear. "No one can be barred whatever their motives."

The heavy man put his red and pulsing face close to mine. "You're a tool of Communism, a nigger-lover."

My eyes burned. I could not cry. "I'm only stating our church's belief. If you do not agree, perhaps you should join another church."

Wonder of wonders, they voted my way. Negroes came. All the people who said they'd lie down in the street before they let this happen, went and joined another church.

This was my single small victory.

The arrival of civil rights lawyers galvanized us jittery liberals. Here were strangers doing the very things we were terrified of—speaking up, defending the organizers, getting quoted in the newspaper. We fought for the chance to have them over for dinner. After drinking our scotch, eating our good cooking, and sipping brandy, they told us how awful we were. We knelt at their feet (literally—gathered around them on the floor of my living room) soaking it in.

Everyone but Fred. My husband sat on a far couch, resolutely silent. He could go hours in company without speaking. When he was small, his mother told him if he didn't stop talking, he'd use up his words. It had happened.

The civil rights lawyers said, "People are dying because of your cowardice."

We shivered, knowing we were hearing the truth.

"When good people like you do nothing, evil triumphs. You're pseudoliberals, all talk and no action."

Yes, yes, we were worms. Beat us into bravery.

They were young and fierce and unafraid. These young men had gone to Harvard and Yale and had accents I marveled over. I felt as if I were in one of those sci-fi movies where higher beings arrive from another galaxy to show humans how to live in peace. But they were not from our planet and could not fathom the pressure we were under to conform, a pressure so great it made speaking one word of opposition difficult, and taking the smallest action impossible. I knew I would roast in hell for my craven ways, but the bare truth was—I was terrified.

Daddy said the outside lawyers worked for Communist-front organizations, and the only reason they came here was to sleep with Negro women. He was enthusiastically behind keeping an eye on them. The Sovereignty Commission functioned as our local FBI. They watched people with "views" and took names.

One night, I went to hear Joan Baez sing at Tougaloo, a black college founded during Reconstruction. The crowd sang "We Shall Overcome." Arm in arm, rows of black people and white people swayed in the darkened auditorium. Joan Baez, with dark hair framing her pure face, looked like truth with a guitar. I felt my heart swell with happiness. We could, we *would* overcome.

The next morning I got a call. My mother's job was passing on my father's disapproval. He spoke and she dished out the punishment, with some relish.

"You were seen."

I felt like a twelve-year-old. "So what?"

"They say you refused to leave the auditorium when the photographers came during intermission because you wanted your picture in *Life* magazine."

The invisible but omnipresent "they" who ruled our lives and kept us in our places. I never saw a photographer, but I didn't argue. I was still using the philosophy I'd developed as a child: never admit to anything. With Mother, the best defense was silence.

In our neighborhood bookstore one day, I made a new friend. Patricia Derian was a doctor's wife from Virginia. She was tall with commanding blue eyes, liberal views, a strong voice, and she was not afraid of anybody. I was in awe of her. I was afraid of everyone.

Fred built them a house. She disdained the Greek Revival mansions preferred by most well-off people. Her rooms were large and spare. There was a small, dark pond in the entry hall, a trap for the unwary. She had an office, a room of her own, filled with masses of papers. She and a few other women were working to peacefully integrate the public schools, holding coffees with women of good will all over the state. She made me dizzy with admiration. I couldn't believe she liked me.

The powers-that-be couldn't do much to her husband. Mike Derian was Armenian, an orthopedic surgeon, and a professor at University Hospital. A foreigner and a professor—beyond reach of threat or persuasion.

I told Patricia how brave I thought she was.

She gave one of her great ringing laughs. "Why should I be afraid?"

"You can't know because you're not from here."

She took me with her to the Negro business section to meet the brother of slain civil rights activist Medgar Evers. Charles Evers sat behind a desk in an upstairs office, bulky in a suit and tie, his dark face shiny and hostile. Next to his right hand was a large black pistol. I couldn't hear what he was saying for watching it.

He was the first I met of the other kind of Negro. It was as if I'd been living in a cocoon. There were Annie, Marie, and Ora Dee, who, I thought, loved me, but refused to talk about the troubles. You couldn't blame them. Maids with views were being fired all over town. Outside my cushion of comfort, there were these new people like Charles Evers, who didn't like or trust me. I couldn't figure out how to be around them. I went to a party one night, without Fred, my first mixed party except for the acting students in New York. I wanted to show how open and friendly and liberal I was. I went around shaking hands with all the dark faces, introducing myself. One said, "What are you—running for office or something?" I felt crushed. I hated the old world and couldn't find a way into the new.

When I haltingly tried to explain to Patricia what exactly I was afraid of, she said she gave people until age thirty to find the courage of their convictions.

I was twenty-nine.

23

In the spring of 1966, we'd been married for almost ten years. Every working day of that time Fred lived his life by a precise schedule. Up and out to check the construction jobs by seven. Home at nine for a breakfast of orange juice, cereal, two fried eggs, bacon, toast, and coffee. The same breakfast every morning. Home for a sandwich at twelve-thirty. Dinner by six or he got a stomachache, and into bed and asleep by nine. His ideas were just as fixed. He knew exactly how he felt about everything from integration—he was against it—to children's spend-the-night parties—he was against those, too. I hadn't seen this quality when I married him. I assumed he was like me, not absolutely finally sure of anything.

Some days I got a clear view of my life. I would march into oblivion on a road of breakfasts, lunches, and dinners for six. Like the story in the Bible about the ten talents, I would dig up mine and they'd be shriveled. God would say, what did you accomplish? I'd say, I cooked. He'd say, And? I'd say, I never managed to fix one meal that all six of us liked.

Clay tapped me on the arm. Linden's ride to Miss Jo's nursery school was here. I buttoned her into her coat. She stood on tiptoe to kiss me. "Tell me to learn a lot." That's what I said to Clay each morning and, at four, she wanted to be just like him.

"Learn a lot, sweetie."

She grinned and headed out the door, fire in her eyes.

Clay and Allison's ride came. Allison stomped outside, too mad about having to wear her uniform to say good-by. I kissed Clay, noticing he had already managed to pull his shirt out. It hung like a tail from under his coat.

"Tuck your shirt in."

"I love you, Mama."

"I love you, too. Learn a lot."

"I will." I never saw a child go to school so happy. As far as Clay was concerned, the world was filled with interesting things to know and every day he got a chance to find out a few more. When he learned to read at four, I couldn't have given him six bicycles and made him as happy, which turned out to be a good thing.

Three years before, at five, he rolled off the couch and fell a few inches onto the living room carpet. It didn't hurt and he laughed. But there was a lump on his thigh, not a bruise, but a raised place like a little egg under the skin. When I noticed him limping, I took him in to the pediatrician, who sent us to a bone doctor.

I sat in the small white room giggling with Clay while we waited for the x-rays, with not a thought in my mind that this could be anything serious.

"Is he limping because of his flat feet?" I said to the doctor.

"Not flat feet, no." He clipped the x-rays to a lighted panel. "See this spot?"

I stared, but Clay's bones look like white moths against a dark window, dream bones. I couldn't see a thing.

"I don't like the look of that."

"Where?"

"Upper femur there."

"What is it?"

"Could be several things, a tumor, a weak spot in the bone." He paused and spoke in a voice too low for Clay to hear. "Could be cancer."

"It's not cancer." The word hammered in my head. I would stop the possibility by saying no.

The doctor cleared his throat. "We can't discount anything, I'm afraid."

My head rang. I could hardly hear him.

"We'll need to go in and take a look."

In? That meant surgery. I left the doctor's in a hurry, trying not to let Clay see my panic. I dropped him at school and drove to Fred's office where, out of sight of the secretary, I sobbed against his chest.

After the operation, I bent over Clay's bed. He lay there, tiny and pale inside an enormous cast, a mummy suit of plaster from his chest to his calves, with a wooden stick across the knees to pick him up by.

He cried, hurting.

"I'm here, baby. Everything is okay."

He opened his eyes and looked at me with perfect trust. I wanted to take him in my arms and absorb the pain. I put my cheek next to his.

"It really hurts."

"I know it does. They'll give you some medicine to make the hurt go away."

The doctors said he had fibrous dysplasia. His femur was like soapstone instead of solid bone. They set the fracture and filled the cavity with calf's bone. If it took, new bone would grow around the implant. *It's not cancer,* I sang in my head.

My mother-in-law came to visit, limping into the room with her high hip and twisted spine. "You took him off the bottle too soon. He didn't get enough milk."

Resentment rose in my throat, followed by guilt. Had I? One day when Clay was eight months old, I handed him a cup and took away the bottle. He hadn't seemed to mind. Was this my fault?

The Episcopal priest arrived. I had been standing beside Clay's bed for almost twenty-four hours. I was feeding him little slippery pieces of ice. We pretended they were silver fish.

"Don't overdo it," he cautioned. "You have to be here for the long haul."

What was the long haul?

Clay was almost nine now. He'd broken the leg again and had a second operation. Patricia Derian's orthopedist husband did the second one. The calf bone implant hadn't worked, and this time he got a steel rod. He limped a little, and he could never ride a bike or play contact sports, but he would never have to go away to war either. I held that thought triumphantly. For now, he was in one piece, always cheerful, and seemingly unembittered by those months in bed.

At the stove, I spooned hot bacon grease over two eggs. Fred sat at the table with a cup of coffee reading the morning paper. It was exactly nine o'clock.

I watched the eggs idly. I liked the moment when the yellow yolk first skimmed over with white. I liked making perfect eggs with the yellow runny but not slimy. I liked making them, but I wouldn't consider eating one. Runny egg yolk made me gag. I'd as soon drink blood. I corrected the exaggeration. Blood made me sicker than egg yolk unless it was my own, oozing out of a cut. I didn't mind the metallic taste of that.

I remembered a pool of blood one summer at Allison's Wells, more blood than I had ever seen, sinking into green grass. The Coca-Cola man unloaded a week's supply of drinks. When he tried to drive away, the truck got stuck in the muddy lawn. He got out and pushed with one hand against the window. The window broke and glass sliced his wrist. Blood arced out, red as the truck, pumping into the grass. The man fell to his knees as if to pull it back. He gripped his muscular black arm and bellowed. The grass filled with blood. Uncle John came running. He made a tourniquet from his handkerchief and he and Preston carried the driver off in the hotel station wagon. I stayed there staring, watching the thick, red stuff seep into the ground, watching it coagulate and turn black at the edges. It was Negro blood and it looked exactly like mine. On a blade of grass I saw a fly bend over the pool and drink.

Fred said, "Am I going to get any eggs this morning?"

I jumped. In the skillet, the two yolks were pale and hard. "They've cooked too long. Do you want me to fix you two more?"

"That's okay."

He was the least troublesome husband a woman could wish for. At nine-thirty, after he left for the office, Marie arrived. The children called her "Re-Re," the name my sister Sydney gave her. Thomas came running and grabbed her around the knees. She patted his blond curls and began cleaning the kitchen. He chattered at her. My children loved Marie exactly the way I had. I used to think she was my real mother and Daddy was just too embarrassed to admit it. I hoped she loved us back but after the age of twelve, I never asked. She was stern, like Mary Poppins. There were boundaries.

As I retreated to the bedroom, I heard her mumble. "Don't know why I bother. Fast as I clean, someone comes along behind me messing."

The unmade bed looked tempting, but I couldn't let myself climb back in, not with Marie in the kitchen. I sat in a straight-backed chair at my desk and began reading Dostoevsky. On Friday, I had an exam in my Novel class. The test covered ten books and I had two more to read. I could read a book a day when I had to. Doing that, bent over the pages, concentrating, marking significant passages as the chapters flew by, filled me with a fierce joy. This is what the brain could do when you weren't wasting it.

The best part of being back in school was this head-swelling joy. There was so much to know. I had taken American Poetry, the Greek tragedies, and the Philosophy of Physics. This term it was the Novel and Shakespeare. The years I'd spent having children and keeping house were like a desert. School was the oasis. If I drank deeply enough, I might figure life out. Sometimes, for five or ten minutes, I thought I had. I was drunk on education. I didn't want to finish and had already started talking to Fred about graduate school. He was not enthusiastic. There were no English graduate programs in Jackson. I would have to go away and come home on weekends. Fred gave a reluctant "maybe" to the University of Mississippi at Oxford, and a definite "no" to the University of Arkansas, where one of my favorite professors from Millsaps had gone to teach.

The phone rang. It was Carmen, a Venezuelan friend I knew from the tennis club, the first woman I'd heard say the word "shit" out loud, in public.

"I have a surprise."

"What?"

"Not what, a who. A very good-looking man I want you to meet."

"What makes you think I want to meet a good-looking man?"

"I know you. I know your darkest heart."

I hoped not.

"Wait until you see him. His name is Bruce and he's a civil rights lawyer."

My first thought was: Fred won't like him. Positions had hardened since passage of the Voting Rights Act, and Fred toughened his stance along with the rest. He started referring to his Negro workers as "niggers." When I objected, he claimed that's what they acted like. He was only calling a spade a spade.

"He's here working for one of those groups," Carmen said. "SNCC, CORE, one of them."

"An outside agitator, as my father would say."

"Precisely. Can you and Fred come to dinner Friday? I want him to meet some interesting people."

"Love to."

"Want to play tennis today? We could take a lesson and stare at the pro's *cojones*."

"I'm studying for an exam."

"Dull woman. Never mind. Friday. Eight o'clock."

I hung up and smiled. The trouble with my life was I wanted to do both: read *Crime and Punishment* and stare at *cojones*. In class later that day, I looked around. Being older made a difference and I tried to pinpoint what it was. I was both more and less serious than the other students, more serious about learning and less serious about authority.

I made myself listen. Marguerite Goodman, my father's older sister, the professor who'd given me the only B to mar my A average, prepared us for senior examinations. We would have one day of written exams and a second day of oral testing in front of the entire English faculty. Two by two, we would be called in and expected to answer any question on grammar or literature from *Beowulf* to Faulkner. Aunt Marguerite was going over the seven uses of the nominative absolute. I sincerely believed I would never need one of them, but I dutifully wrote down all seven.

When I first went back to school, I fell in love with every subject. In philosophy, I wanted to be a philosopher, a geologist in geology, an astronomer in that class. I felt like a lighted sparkler, shooting off in every direction, but I had settled on literature. I would be like my favorite professor, a meek, ugly man who smelled of stale sherry and lectured brilliantly. I wanted to stand in front of a class the way he did, gently cynical, heavy with knowledge, and talk about literature and the meaning of life. My friend Jane said he was a homosexual, but I didn't care. I wanted to *be* him, not sleep with him.

Five forty-five. I fried six pork chops and dished out six servings of mashed potatoes, six spoons of peas, six pie-shaped pieces of cornbread. Milk all around. At six sharp, we sat down at the trestle table off the kitchen. Fred asked the blessing.

Clay said, "I hate this meat."

Fred said, "Take your elbows off the table and eat your dinner."

"It's white," Clay said.

"It's pork. It's supposed to be white. Eat it. Allison, sit up. You're not in bed." I issued the same instructions every night. I had turned into Miss Hosford.

Allison rolled her eyes. "I can't eat peas. They make me sick."

"They do not make you sick."

She nodded solemnly. "Yes, they do. If I eat peas, I vomit."

Linden giggled, which made Thomas start. He banged his spoon on the tray of his high chair.

I frowned to quiet the uproar. "Don't say that word at the table."

I cut Thomas's meat into tiny pieces. He ate with his hands, smearing grease on his mouth and chin.

"How was your day?" I asked Fred.

"Fine. Are you coming to the office tomorrow?"

I tried to look sorry. "I have class."

When I started taking classes, I told Fred to hire someone to take my place as office manager. She was working out fine, but he kept asking when I planned on coming back.

"Carmen invited us to dinner on Friday. She has a civil rights lawyer she wants us to meet."

Fred's twisted mouth let me know how much he didn't care to meet yet another liberal-spouting lawyer.

There was a gagging noise from Allison. She stiffened, rolled her eyes up and opened her mouth. A glob of chewed peas dropped on her plate.

"Yuck, that's disgusting," Clay said.

Linden went into hysterics laughing.

Thomas roared.

"Allison, that's enough." From me.

She opened her eyes and smiled at her father. "I told you." She turned her plate so that the chewed peas were on the far side and ate tiny bites of her mashed potatoes. Thomas methodically crumbled his cornbread. Clay reached for the salt and turned over his milk.

I screamed. "I can't stand it."

He went brick red with misery.

Fred mopped at the milk with his napkin. I went to get the sponge.

Dinner was over.

We loaded the dishwasher, wiped the table and the floor around Thomas's chair and went to our bedroom for black coffee. We sat silently watching the evening news. The children got to watch a half hour of television in Clay's room. Fred helped me bathe and put them to bed. He put on his pajamas and climbed in bed with *Time* magazine.

I washed my face and climbed in beside him with *Crime and Punishment*.

I felt him looking at me and didn't look back. Looking meant he wanted to make love. His pale, freckled hand reached for my breast. I managed to avoid this twenty-nine nights out of thirty. The look on his face was warm and pleading, but he didn't ask. I would rather be asked, but when I told him that once, he started asking and I hated that, too. Nothing about sex felt spontaneous.

I turned away from the hand. "Not tonight."

"Why not tonight?"

I couldn't stand the way his face changed when he was disappointed. "I read too much today and my eyes hurt. I guess I'm not in the mood."

"I'll put you in the mood."

I felt a twinge of desire, but it was no good getting excited. I'd only lie there in the dark afterwards, resenting him.

"Just let me put it in for a minute."

"Okay." The word came out as a sigh. There was a moment, when it slipped in like a key in a lock, that I felt a sure jolt of sex. Something, almost, if I could just get it right.

He fell heavily to the side. "That was great, sweetheart, really great. Thank you."

I hated being thanked. It underlined the one-sidedness of our lovemaking.

"Don't thank me," I muttered, but he was already asleep, his breath heavy and even.

I lay in the dark and tried to imagine the man Carmen had invited to dinner.

253

I dreamed of boats. There was a marina with slips in the blue water. A sailboat, white and glistening, slid into one, fitting perfectly, rocking the water.

24

On Friday night I found myself dressing with special care for the stranger. I imagined his eyes examining the red silk as I smoothed it over my hips. He watched me brush my hair into brown waves, and smiled knowingly at the places I stroked with perfume. I dismissed him and looked at myself critically as I put on rouge. I was almost pretty when I got it right. I had moments when my eyes looked big and I didn't have circles under them. I could tilt my head and smile and be twenty again, well, twenty-five. At other times, when I forgot to concentrate on looking pleasant, I caught my reflection in shop windows and cringed, wondering who that unhappy woman could be.

I was aware of Fred getting ready quietly around me. He would be sad if he knew I was secretly dressing for another man. He looked sad a lot these days. Once back in February, as we walked hand in hand across a street in New Orleans, a truth I hadn't spoken to myself came unbidden from my mouth. "I'm not going to spend the rest of my life with you."

"What do you mean?" He bent and looked worriedly into my face. I stared straight ahead. I didn't know what I meant, and saying even that much scared me into silence.

I spotted Bruce Rogow from across the room. He was beautiful. When I studied photographs of him later, he wasn't. He was tall and thin with wide shoulders and dark curling hair that fell over his forehead. He had hooded eyes and a formidable nose.

"He's Jewish," Carmen whispered.

Bruce leaned over, laughing out loud at something my friend Ellen was saying. I felt a twinge of jealousy. He was the most intriguing-looking man I'd ever seen. He didn't resemble anyone I knew.

When Carmen introduced us, he looked at me, a thing few southern men did. Southern men appeared to look at you, even pretended to listen, but if you said anything out of the ordinary, anything serious, they were startled, as if their dog had spoken. Bruce actually saw me. After I went through the buffet line for Carmen's Spanish spaghetti, I found a place next to him at the table. Up close he had brown eyes that twinkled with amusement. He appeared to watch a hidden part of me, hearing me think one thing while I was saying something else. He had a soft northern voice; I was entranced.

I said, "I really admire what you're doing."

He nodded shortly, as if that was boring. "What do you do?"

I hated that question, because I didn't do anything yet worth talking about. "I'm back in school." He didn't react negatively. "I'll finish in June and I'm going on to graduate school in the fall."

"Where?"

"I don't know exactly. The University of Arkansas maybe, or Purdue. I've been offered fellowships both places." I was lying, not about the fellowships, but about going. Fred would never let me go as far as Purdue. He hadn't even said yes to Arkansas.

Bruce looked at me hard without saying anything. "You've got either the world's most understanding husband or a marriage that's in trouble."

I felt myself redden and looked around. No one was listening. I wasn't used to men penetrating the veneer of southern courtesy, where things were allowed to be as they appeared.

"I have a very understanding husband."

He looked dubious. I changed the subject. "I just read a wonderful book. Solzhenitsyn's *One Day in the Life of Ivan Denisovich*." I pronounced it *Deneesovich*.

He smiled. "That's Denisovich."

I blushed again. "Have you read it?"

He nodded.

Was he right about the pronunciation? What did people in Mississippi know? "I think it's an incredible book. How could Stalin have done that to his own people?"

"He did what he had to. He was trying to bring a torn country together."

"Surely you're joking."

"No."

I couldn't tell. He could be joking. He was the first man I'd known who read Russian novels. "What are you working on now?"

"Voters' rights. We're establishing a statewide pattern of discrimination that occurs when people try to register to vote, depending on whether they're black or white."

"How do you do that?"

"We send people in to test-register in different counties. First we send in a white man and they give him an easy section of the state constitution to interpret. Then we send in a Negro and he'll be given something a Supreme Court justice would have trouble with."

"That's hard to believe."

"Believe it. You should know about these things. This is your state."

I ducked my head. He was right. I should know.

"Never mind. I'm just giving you a hard time." He touched my hand.

My face burned. I made parallel lines in the tablecloth with the tines of my fork, afraid if I looked at him he would see the jolt that touch gave me. "What will happen?"

"There will be a class action suit. Hopefully the federal government will send marshals down and we'll hold mass registrations all over the state. When we try that now, they claim the courthouse is only open an hour a day for registration and arrest everyone for loitering."

"Have you been arrested?"

He looked at me wryly. "Lawyers don't get arrested. We wait across the street."

I raised my eyebrows. "Oh, sure."

"Somebody has to be on the outside to get people out of jail." We laughed.

He leaned closer. "I have been arrested."

"What for?"

"Resisting death." He had a neighing laugh, which tickled me.

"What did you do?"

"I had a date with a young Negro lady and a car full of rednecks started following us. They pulled up alongside, yelling, 'Nigger lover,' and pelting the car with soft drink cans. There was one real fat boy. He threw diet sodas. I ran a red light to get away from them and got arrested."

"What happened?"

"I sent my date home in a cab. The police followed me to city hall and while they were booking me, I looked out the window. The same guys were turning my car upside down."

"And?"

"They arrested the guys and made me pay a fine for running a red light. I had to call a tow truck to get my car right side up."

He was talking to me like a person, not flirting, or not just flirting.

All the way home, I pictured Bruce's face and went over our conversation. "Wasn't that guy interesting, the civil rights lawyer?"

"He was all right." Fred drove silently.

Did Bruce like me? He seemed to like talking to me, but he didn't flirt. He challenged almost every statement I made.

Carmen called the next day. "What did you think?"

"He's nice."

"He's a dream. Didn't you love the lisp?"

"I didn't notice."

"You didn't? He has a little lisp when he says his s's."

I thought about him all that day and all day Sunday. I wanted to hear his voice again. On Monday morning I called the Lawyers' Constitutional Defense Committee where he worked. He sounded strange and curt on the telephone. My heart pounded and I wished I hadn't done it.

"It's Norma. Norma Craig. I met you Friday night."

"Yes."

I swallowed. "I wondered, I have two tickets for *The Fantasticks* at New Stage. I thought two of your staff might like to go."

There was a silence.

"That's not why you called."

I felt my throat close. "What do you mean?"

"I mean that's not why you called. You called because you want to see me again, right?"

"I guess so." My voice sounded tiny.

"I'd like to see you, too. Let's have lunch."

"Okay." My heart thudded. He seemed to think nothing of it.

"Meet me at the zoo, at the top of that path that goes around the park. Bring lunch. Friday noon."

I put down the phone gently. I was still in my own kitchen, standing on the brick floor, staring at the pumpkin Formica, but everything looked different. Friday I didn't have carpool or school. Marie would be at the house when the children got home. I was free.

I drove to the zoo feeling that every car on the road knew I was a wife going bad. I'd brought tuna fish sandwiches, put together when no one else was in the kitchen, and potato chips. We sat on a grassy bank. It was early spring, but warm, the trees out in pale green.

I felt expansive, as if I had made this day and presented it to him. Bruce took off his tie. His shirt was embroidered with a small "B.R." where a pocket would be. He ate his sandwich and watched me.

My mouth was dry. I had forgotten to bring anything to drink and had a hard time swallowing. "I like your shirt."

"Thanks. I have them made."

"You don't have a pocket."

"I despise pockets on dress shirts and the kinds of things men carry in them."

"Me, too." Actually, I had never given pockets a thought until this moment. *Have them made.* Outside of a British novel, I'd never known a man who had his shirts made. I filed this new information away. "Tell me more about what you do."

"Do you want law stories or story stories?"

"Either one."

"When I was on the Gulf Coast not long ago, I had a date with a nice young Negro lady."

"Is that all you date?" I thought about what my father said about the reason civil rights lawyers came here.

"No, but on that particular night I was with this attractive young woman and we went to a bar on the beach. They can't refuse to serve you anymore. It's against the law, but we got a lot of looks. We ordered a fancy drink, the kind that comes with a parasol and fruit."

I nodded.

"We drank it together out of two straws with our heads together, you know?"

I knew. I shivered at the nerve of it.

"All over the room, people were staring. Just staring, as if they couldn't believe their eyes, as if the ceiling were going to drop. The woman was beautiful. I knew half those men would trade places with me in a minute if they dared. We just sipped our drink and talked real low. I heard one woman say, 'That's disgusting,' but what could they do? A one-night lesson in race relations."

I grinned in admiration, shaking my head. "I would never have the nerve."

We finished and brushed the crumbs away. I stood up. There was nothing to do now but leave. "I hope you can come over to dinner one night. I'd like for you to get to know my family."

"I don't want to get to know your family. I don't care about that. I want to know you."

My heart gave a lurch. Nothing was working. All the men I'd liked came over, got to know Fred, ate my meals, played with my children, became seventh members of the family so that I could see them. Sometimes they stole a kiss or a hug. Occasionally I slept with one. No one had ever refused the invitation.

I found my voice. "What do you want to do?"

"I want to see you again. Can you get out?"

"It depends."

"Meet me here again next week."

"All right."

He bent and kissed me lightly. Just a brush of his lips on mine, but I got another one of those jolts. I got back into my car, a navy blue Pontiac convertible. It had been an early graduation gift from Fred. I thought I wanted a car; I thought a custom convertible with red leather upholstery might change things, until I got it. I realized it wasn't a car I wanted, it was a new life.

The next Friday, after Bruce and I ate our second picnic, chicken salad with walnuts, he stood up and brushed the crumbs off his pants. "Might as well go back to my place."

My heart raced like a rabbit's. "It's too soon."

"Why?"

"We've only been together twice, three times if you count that dinner."

"Counting is childish. I don't have time for that."

I felt both threatened and exhilarated. This man was not going to play by the rules.

"Do you want to come or not?"

I left my car and went in his, a faded blue Triumph convertible. He lived in the colored part of town. As we drove down shaded streets, faced with small, neatly painted wooden bungalows, I felt uneasy. Unless you were bringing your cook home, this was forbidden territory. "I didn't know you lived here."

"Where else? We have all kinds of visitors, Negro and white. What other part of town could we live in?"

The house was white like its fellows, but the paint was worn. There were no shade trees. It had a threadbare, rented look. Bruce pointed out a scorched place in the grass.

"People came by one night and burned a cross." He said it calmly.

"No." I was horrified.

"We've had them throw firecrackers, big ones. We thought they were dynamite. They drive by, carloads of them, and scream, 'Nigger lover, nigger lover.' One night they knocked on the door and left plastic lilies with a ribbon that said, 'Rest in Peace.'"

"Weren't you scared?"

"I have a dog. You'll meet him." Bruce opened the screened door and unlocked the door behind it. A large gray Weimaraner leapt to meet us, jumping on Bruce, wriggling in delight, yellow eyes gleaming.

"He's only a puppy. He won't hurt you, but when people bother us, like the ones that brought the lilies, I go to the door with Yossarian on a leash, and I say sternly, 'Don't kill, boy, don't kill.'"

I laughed. "Does that work?"

"It gives them something to think about. They never heard anyone tell a dog *not* to kill."

"Did you like *Catch-22*?"

"I thought it was fantastic."

"Me, too." A tickle of elation. We read the same books. Enough reason right there to sin.

But I felt strange walking into his house, tentative and alert, aware of the chance I was taking. Closing the door behind me, I realized that first day I might never be able to return to my old life. I was Alice entering the looking glass.

The living room was empty, with wooden floors, painted walls, and a fireplace with a gas heater. Three bedrooms, each small and plain, opened off the hall. The kitchen was white with an old-fashioned sink on legs. The floor had faded green and black squares of linoleum. A green Formica table stood against one wall, with three white painted chairs around it. When Bruce opened the refrigerator, an old one with the ice compartment inside, there was nothing in there but milk and an open can of tomato juice.

"It doesn't look like anyone lives here." This was only about the fourth time I'd ever been inside a Negro house, and I caught myself appraising it with white eyes, thinking how bare and poor things appeared.

Bruce drank from the milk carton. "We don't spend much time here. We work long days and eat out. We only sleep here. A lot of movement people come through town and stay with us. The living room is usually filled with sleeping bags."

I liked that word "movement." Maybe I could be part of the movement.

He led the way to his bedroom, which had a double bed with a white cotton spread pulled up over the pillows, a small chest and a closet with no door. I could see his clothes, two suits, one sport coat, and a dozen starched shirts.

"You have a lot of shirts."

"I have to wear a clean one every day, two if I'm going to court in the afternoon."

"Nice." I was practically twitching with nervousness. There was nowhere to sit except on the bed. I wondered how many other women he'd had in this room and what color they had been. I was ashamed to even be thinking about that.

Bruce hung his coat on the corner of the door and began unbuttoning his shirt. "Sit down. Make yourself comfortable."

I sat on the bed, leaving my sandals on the floor, and pulling my legs beside me to show how comfortable I was. I folded my blue cotton sundress carefully over my knees. I felt numb, part of me watching him, wanting to touch him, while a hard, judgmental place warned that I might be ruining a perfectly good life. He hung his shirt over the coat and I stared at his chest. It was broad and tan, covered with black curly hair. There were brown freckles on his shoulders. Fred had a narrow chest with small reddish freckles on his pale skin, and no chest hair. Was Bruce going to take off every

263

stitch while I watched? I could still change my mind and ask him to drive me back to the car.

He stopped with the top half. In his trousers, he sat on the bed and kissed me gently. Misgivings moved back to a part of my brain that quit listening to reason. I wasn't doing anything I hadn't done before. I could end it anytime. His tongue reached deep in my mouth, his brown eyes gleamed through hooded lids. This remarkable man wanted *me*. The world closed in. His arms were warm. I wanted my skin next to his. Desire spread heat all the way to my bones, warmth from our lips, from my back where his arms grasped me, from our chests pressed together and from my aching groin. He pulled back and began unbuttoning my dress. I waited, flushed, breathing hard, watching his fingers. I stopped thinking. He pulled the straps off my shoulders. I reached back and unfastened my brassiere. There was a rush of cooler air on my breasts and I felt the nipples harden.

He put one breast in his mouth, moaning. I lay back, abandoned to sin. Bruce stood up, watching me while he unzipped his pants, folding them neatly at the foot of the bed. He hesitated a moment. He wore jockey shorts, a foreign thing. In the South, small boys wore them, but men, nice men, wore boxers. I stared at the lump in them, and at the way his torso widened above the waist. He slipped his shorts off and let them drop on the floor. I watched them lying there empty instead of looking at him. I didn't want to stare. Bruce bent and slid my dress and underpants down over my hips. I lifted myself to help him. He lay beside me, put his arms around me, and buried his head in my hair.

"You smell nice."

"What do I smell like?"

"Just nice."

"You smell like a foreigner."

He lifted his head and laughed, delighted. He looked me up and down, resting on his elbows. "You have a beautiful body."

"So do you."

264

"You look like a girl. I didn't expect that."

"What did you expect?"

"A mother."

We laughed. I messed up his hair. He didn't seem to mind. He traced a line down my arm. "You don't have much hair on your body."

"It's my Indian blood."

His eyes lit up. "Are you part Indian? Which tribe?"

"Choctaw." This was a lie as far as I knew, but I often told it. Being part Indian sounded exotic; you could never be part colored.

He kissed me and I could feel his skin against mine, from my chest to my feet, warm and heavy, hairy and male. I wanted him inside me. I wanted not just to have him, but to become part of him, the way Mrs. Johnson described it back in Latin class. He kissed me again. I held him tighter, feeling the terrible pleasure of longing, a single-minded rush of desire. He held me, letting me feel the hot length of him, turning us until I was on top. His body felt big and solid. He felt strong enough to save me.

He whispered into my hair. "I don't think we can make love today."

"Why not?" Was there someone else? Was something wrong with me? Was I too old?

He raised his eyebrows apologetically. "I guess I'm nervous."

I pulled back and gave him a forgiving smile. "Don't worry. It doesn't matter. There's plenty of time." He must care about me. Fred could always do it. He could have sex the same way he fell asleep, anywhere, in thirty seconds.

"It's happened to me before, the first time." Bruce stroked my hair. "When I want someone too much. Are you sure I can't help you?"

I didn't know what he meant. "I'm fine. I like lying here against you. I'd like to lie here for the rest of my life."

He kissed my closed eyes and pulled my head against his chest. "Me, too, but I have to get back to the office." We sat up and dressed,

265

watching each other, pleased with what we saw. I felt wonderful, grateful to be wanted, relieved not to have been had. I wasn't lost yet.

He drove me back to my car. "I'd like to see you again."

"Me, too."

"I don't want to wait a week."

"Me either."

"And I don't want to come to dinner."

We laughed.

"Let me check my schedule." He kissed me.

"You can call me at home during the day." I closed my car door, then rolled down the window. "Maybe I'd better call you." Fred might be home for lunch.

I drove home singing as if I weren't almost an adulteress again. If Fred and the children noticed anything during dinner, it was my quiet and kindness. I was not so much Miss Hosford the corrector.

Inside, I was a jumble. I'd met a man who read and listened to me, who told stories as well as my father, a man who not only believed change was possible, but was willing to fight for it. Laws and lawyers could change the human heart. I didn't want to examine what this meant. I didn't know. I couldn't see past our next meeting, the next phone call.

Fred sat at the end of the table, being patient and funny with the children. Every night, he bathed the two youngest, read to them, listened to their prayers. He was a wonderful father. Except for the silences, the inflexibility, his bigotry, and the awful sex, he was an exemplary husband. For someone.

25

During April and May, I saw Bruce as often as I could get away. He never came to the house, never saw Fred again, and never met my children. I drove across town to his place when I was supposed to be doing research at the library.

The experience was enormously exciting. Making love, I'd think, maybe that was an orgasm. I couldn't be sure and, to be truthful, I didn't care. After years of my not being looked at, his attention was so penetrating, his touch so ecstatic, the question had fled my mind.

There was no particular moment when I admitted to myself that I had fallen in love, but what you give energy to thrives. Gradually, Fred became less substantial, a ghostly presence in my life. I was nice, perfectly pleasant, but nothing we did together seemed real. It was as if I had a role in a play called marriage. I knew the lines perfectly, but I was walking through my part. If I had been the slightest bit introspective, I might have stopped to think I was doing to my husband precisely what my father had done to my mother. It shames me still to admit my selfishness. At the time, I had no room in my head to examine where my actions might lead. I was filled with Bruce. He was the person I thought of when something happened during the day. It was Bruce I phoned when I finished my college orals.

"I cried."

"You shouldn't let those people upset you."

"That professor I told you about, Aunt Marguerite, the grammar freak? She asked me to name the ways a pronoun must agree with its object and I said, 'Number, person, and gender,' but I was nervous so my voice came out in this little squeak and she said, 'Speak up, Norma' real loud, and I started crying. Silently, no sobs, but tears ran down my face and my nose dripped. It was horrible. I didn't have a Kleenex and I kept wiping my face on my sleeve."

"Poor baby."

"I couldn't stop. The other professors pretended it wasn't happening. They went on asking my partner and me questions, and we answered and I cried. Finally, my aunt handed me her handkerchief. I would rather have put my hand in a dragon's mouth than take it, but my cuffs were soaked."

I could laugh at myself now and Bruce laughed, too.

"I won't get summa. That did it."

"Forget summa. We know how smart you are. Meet me outside the Italian place tonight and we'll talk."

When I drove into the darkest corner of the parking lot at a restaurant on the far side of town, Bruce was waiting with fried catfish and hush puppies to comfort me. We sat in his car with the top down and ate.

"I want you to come away with me."

I stopped breathing. "What do you mean?"

"I've taken a job in Florida. I have to leave in June, early July at the latest. I want you to come."

"I can't leave here." This wasn't part of the plan. Not that I had a plan. I thought we'd go on the way we were until—I had never considered a next step.

"Why not? You don't love him."

I was silent.

"Do you?"

"Not the way—" I trailed off.

"Not the way you love me, right? Not the way I love you. We're lucky, don't you see, extremely lucky to have found each other. We can't afford to throw that away."

Bruce had never come right out and said he loved me. I went soft inside with happiness. "Maybe I could come in the fall."

"If it's going to work, we have to do it together. I want you to come with me now."

"I can't leave my children."

"We'll send for the children. They can go to school next fall in Miami."

"And I would go to graduate school?" I couldn't believe I was contemplating this.

"Of course. There's nothing we can't do together."

This would be the man I crawled into bed with every night. These arms would hold me. My heart was beating so hard my eyes didn't work right. The restaurant's red neon sign shivered and I blinked to make it stop. Obviously I couldn't do it. I could never leave my family or the people I grew up with. I couldn't walk away from my entire life. Why was I even considering it?

I don't remember much of the trip home. I drove automatically past Bailey Junior High and the park. On the hill, I saw the boarded-up swimming pool where I used to race, a visible signature of my father's victory over integration. My mind whispered: you could. You could leave.

On May 14, I graduated from Millsaps with honors in English. I got an award as the most creative senior. My family gave me a party. All my friends and relatives came. They took pictures of me in my robes with the four children clustered around. I smiled, every tooth a lie. I had never felt like such a fraud.

The University of Mississippi gave me a fellowship for graduate school. Sensing my withdrawal, Fred's feelings about advanced education switched from reluctance to enthusiasm. As far as I was concerned, Ole Miss was a bad last choice. I had no desire to return to gray winters in Oxford. When Fred talked about how I could drive home every Friday, or maybe some weekends he would bring the children up, I nodded and withdrew further.

I spent the next weeks abandoning the terrifying idea of leaving and being propped up again by Bruce's assurances. I tried to think it through. I hated it here. I loved my children and hated my marriage.

I pretended to be a good person, working for the church bazaar and the Junior League, but I wasn't a good person. Sooner or later I would either get caught or go crazy trying to keep the layers of my life separate. This was a way out. I would never have the courage do it on my own. Bruce was my spine, my crutch.

In June, I tried to go to the Meredith march. James Meredith had graduated from Ole Miss and was marching, almost alone, from Memphis to Jackson to support Negro voters' rights. He only made it as far as Hernando, Mississippi, before someone blasted him with a shotgun. Injured, he was taken to a hospital. Civil rights leaders from all over the country rose up in protest and came together to complete the march: Martin Luther King, Ralph Abernathy, Stokely Carmichael, with thousands of others. Meredith recovered from his wounds and rejoined them. On the last day, fifteen thousand marchers would arrive at the state capitol in Jackson for a rally.

I didn't have the nerve to actually march, but I wanted to see them arrive at the capitol. I wanted to honor their courage. I drove downtown, parked the car, and walked toward the capitol. The whole area was ringed with wooden barricades. Behind them stood white people carrying signs that read, "Go Home Niggers" and "White Power Forever." Far down the street, I saw the marchers coming, singing and carrying banners. I stood uncertainly in the middle of the square.

A policeman approached, eyes hidden by mirrored sunglasses. "Are you with them?" He pointed to the marchers.

"No."

"Are you with them?" He indicated the spitters and yellers behind the barricades.

"No. I just want to watch."

He shook his head. "Lady, either you're with them." He pointed. "Or them. You can't stand here in the middle."

I went home. I was trapped in a state with no middle.

26

Bruce planned to leave town on Friday. This was Monday, and if I were truly going, I had to tell Fred. And not just Fred. I wouldn't sneak away. I wanted to do my dishonorable deed in an honorable way. I had this crazy idea that, if I did it right and explained my reasons for going, the family wouldn't mind as much. Another example of my misplaced belief in the power of reason.

Fred was first, and fear over what was to come made my stomach hurt. I fed the children breakfast, rehearsing silently. I would say nothing about Bruce. I wasn't crazy; I didn't want to be murdered. I would use the female excuse: I was exhausted. I went through my reasons: the strain of school and graduation, volunteering, the children.

One by one, all but Thomas left for school. I put their dishes in the sink. In half an hour Fred would walk in the door, back from checking his jobs. The thought made my heart jump so bad I had to sit down. I kept going over my hollow-sounding excuses. It was true I was tired, but it was Fred and the marriage I was tired of, that and the bigotry and my hateful state. I was sick of being afraid to do the right thing, of being too scared to even say what was right.

Fred came in the way he did every morning, sensing nothing amiss, which was another reason these last weeks felt surreal. My entire life was a lie, from the moment I woke up to my last conscious breath, and no one noticed. Not one person looked at me and said, what's wrong? If you could live undetected inside such an enormous falsehood, maybe you could walk away from it and hardly be missed.

I fed him breakfast. He talked. I made noises back, my chest so tight I couldn't manage words. Thomas was in Clay's room watching *Captain Kangaroo*. I went back to make up the bed. Fred followed me, saying he was off. He'd be home for lunch at the usual time.

Pulling the avocado velvet spread over the pillows, I took a breath, which didn't keep my voice from shaking. "I've got to go away and think. I need to get away from everything." I couldn't look at him. "I don't know when I'll be back." Another ragged breath. "Or if I'll be back." It was as if I stood at the far end of a long tunnel. The words echoed.

Fred acted as if he hadn't heard right. He made me say it again. "I have to get away."

"Where are you going?"

"I don't know." Lying, heart bumping against my ribs.

His thin face went white with anger. I took a quick look and kept thumping the pillows.

"If you're thinking about a divorce, I'll make sure you never see these children again." A hard, new voice.

I was too afraid to answer. Could he do that?

"Because if you divorce me, you're divorcing all of us. You're no longer a member of this family." He turned without another word and left.

I started crying before the door shut behind him. This did not feel like an idle threat. The Craigs were great haters, elephant-memoried grudge holders. Fred's father boasted of never speaking to his best friend after he refused to enlist and fight alongside him in World War I. In 1966, in the South, men held the power. Women didn't have jobs or money. As far as I knew, Fred could make good on his threat.

I called and told Bruce.

"Don't let him scare you. No judge would keep a woman from seeing her own children."

Beginning that night, Fred and I didn't sleep in the same bed. I moved to the spare bed in Thomas's room. Lying there, I heard Fred sobbing through the wall, desolate wracking sobs. I had never heard a man, or anyone, cry like that. I steeled my heart against it. All the things I yearned to do—go to him, give him hugs, tell him everything would be okay—the things I'd done during every calamity in our ten years together, I couldn't do. I was the cause of the pain. My determination was like the thinnest of eggshells. If the slightest crack opened, everything would collapse.

On Tuesday, I went to Fred's parents, Fredibel and Raymond. I said my little piece, the words coming out of that tunnel where I now lived.

After raising two sons, Fredibel loved having a daughter. Over the years, she called on me to help her pick out everything from new furniture to presents for other relatives. In spite of my early resentment at being forced to eat there every week (down from twice after the children were born), they were ideal grandparents. Fredibel played the piano and sang to my children. Their backyard had been remade for a child's pleasure with swings and a sandbox. The two of them were happy to keep all four any weekend we asked.

I saw her face change as I spoke. I watched as whatever she felt for me drained away. I realized her fondness had depended entirely on my being married to her son and the mother of her grandchildren. Not me the person, but my roles. Her face and body grew stiff. By the time I got to "Or if I'll be back," I was a stranger.

Raymond kept saying, "What? What's she saying?" I wasn't speaking loud enough for him to hear.

"Be quiet, Raymond," Fredibel said. When he kept asking, she shouted. "She's leaving." Two words from pressed lips, as if she'd been secretly expecting this day. Ten years of model daughter-in-law behavior hadn't fooled her.

We didn't hug. I didn't dare. She told Fred later that I had faucet love—turn it on, turn it off. She said going back to school had done it. I got overeducated and it made me crazy.

If she meant that education encouraged independent thinking, she was right, but I didn't have the sense or nerve to think that back then. Every terrible thing people said about me felt richly deserved.

The next day I went to see Mother. She screamed and stomped her tiny feet, which was somehow easier to take than Fredibel's silence.

"You cannot do this. You are throwing away everything I've worked for. You will ruin me in this town." She started crying, the birthmark burning red on her forehead. Only my age and my greater height kept her from hitting me. I could see she wanted to.

Annie hugged me and cried. Marie shook her head in disappointment as if I were still four.

I made two stops to tell my friends Kay and Patricia Derian. I said I was tired, fed up with everything in the South including my marriage. I said I was going away to graduate school. Kay's eyes went wide with disbelief. We'd spent years bitching about our lives, but was I really walking out of mine? She'd never heard of anyone wanting an education that bad. Patricia said when she told me to find the courage of my convictions, she hadn't meant I should leave. With each person I told, departure became more inevitable.

I told nobody about Bruce except the Episcopal priest. I wanted one person to know the truth, in case. A priest was sworn to secrecy. He drove me forty miles to Vicksburg trying to talk me out of leaving. When he finally parked the car, we were in the Vicksburg National Cemetery, home to seventeen thousand fallen Union soldiers. How appropriate, since that war had ended slavery and begun the Jim Crow hell I was fleeing.

"You don't realize what you're doing."

I stared at my hands. "I know it sounds horrible, but I have to."

"A lot of people have unhappy marriages. They don't leave. You say you hate the state. What are you helping by running? You're tired; you've admitted that. Take some time; think it through. You're being rash, and you can't possibly understand the consequences."

Pecking, pecking at the shell of my determination. I closed my ears.

I wondered if he were one of those people not leaving an unhappy marriage. At the last Junior League fund-raiser, he'd danced with me, and close.

He started the car. "You will suffer from guilt for the rest of your life."

It was like a curse.

For five days, I lived in a kind of fugue state. Words came into my tunnel from the outside. I answered in the echoing voice that nobody noticed. I tried to prepare for not being there. I cooked meals, labeled and froze them. I wrote up a month's worth of dinner menus and left them next to *The Joy of Cooking*.

I spent the long days padding my arguments. If I were determined to leave, it was better for the children to stay here where they had familiar surroundings, grandparents, friends, school, and Marie. Fred was a good father and he had the money to provide. I would be going to graduate school, and I could never manage that with four children to raise.

I reminded myself that I was leaving a bigoted state. Working with someone like Bruce, away from this place where I was so afraid, so hamstrung by family and expectations, courage might rub off on me. Once I was free, I would be able to do more. I wasn't sure what the "more" would be, but opportunities for change had to be better than here.

I had almost no money: a hundred and fifty dollars for being Most Creative Senior, and sixty dollars in old traveler's checks. On Thursday night after dinner, which we still ate together, except Fred never spoke directly to me, I got up my nerve and asked for money to leave him.

He wrote me a check for five hundred dollars and handed it over with a look of such disgust I haven't forgotten it to this day.

Seven hundred and ten dollars didn't feel like enough to start a new life, but Bruce wasn't concerned. He was used to living on nothing. In Mississippi, civil rights lawyers were paid ninety dollars a week.

I spent a lot of time during those last four nights worrying that Fred might kill me. Lying in Thomas's room, listening through the wall, I remembered the knife. Fred carried a small pocketknife, innocent looking, but long and sharp enough to reach my heart. After the sobbing stopped, I waited for him to come up the hall and stab me. He never came. He was a decent man married to a bad woman.

I didn't let myself look at how bad I was. I didn't allow myself to think about how much I would miss my children's arms around me, their trust, or the way we made each other laugh. I chose to believe Bruce. The children would come and live with us in Miami. Fred might be brokenhearted now, but he wouldn't want to be married to someone like me if he knew the truth. First I would get away. The rest would straighten itself out later. That's how dumb, numb, and scared I was. I got those green velvet drapes from Tara for my wedding, and I had turned into Scarlett. I would worry about everything tomorrow. Leaving was too enormous to contemplate. The consequences were unknowable. Doing it required a sabotage of reason.

On Friday morning before school, I told the children that I would not be there when they came home.

Only Clay fully understood. His brown eyes brimmed with tears. "When will you be back?"

I had to tell the truth. "I don't know."

He wept in earnest. "How will I talk to you?"

"I'll call you, sweetie, I promise. I'll call all the time." I bent and tried to hug them all at once. Allison took a step back, watching me with darkened eyes.

Clay gulped. "But that means you won't be here for my birthday."

I caught my breath at the pain of not remembering. "If I'm not,

I'll send you nine presents, one for each year. And I'll write. I'll write each of you a letter every week, with pictures."

"Of dogs," Linden said.

"Filled with dogs," I promised.

Fred left without breakfast and without a word.

I went and sobbed into the velvet bedspread so that Thomas wouldn't hear. Then I got up, wiped my swollen face, and packed.

27

On Friday afternoon, July 1, 1966, I left. I put my suitcase in the trunk of the car that morning before Marie arrived. Thomas was down for his nap. I looked in on him, blonde curls damp against the pillow. I tried to swallow, but regret was a knot that wouldn't go down. I walked out of the house and my marriage with only a purse, as if I were going for a loaf of bread. I saw Marie watching from the kitchen window.

The plan was to meet Bruce on South State Street in front of the Pontiac dealership. I refused to take my new car. Bruce thought that was stupid. The Pontiac convertible was new and in much better shape than his Triumph. It had been a gift, he pointed out. It *was* mine, the first car I'd ever owned. But I couldn't take it any more than I could have taken the dishes or silver. I didn't want to carry off anything that belonged to Fred Craig except me. And books. I did take those. I packed the college novels, Shakespeare, my copy of *Gone With the Wind*, and shipped them by bus to Miami.

All the way up North State, I watched the rearview mirror. Someone might be coming after me. I didn't know who to look for—Mother maybe. My teeth were so clenched with fear my jaw ached, and my hands were slippery on the steering wheel. I kept thinking, what are you doing? Are you out of your mind? I watched the road, keeping to the speed limit. Fred might have sent the police. I reminded myself that he didn't know which way I was headed or where we were meeting. He didn't know I was meeting anyone, but the thought of him finding out about Bruce made my heart and the car lurch. I straightened the wheel and told myself to calm down. I took deep breaths, but it didn't help. I couldn't believe a woman, a wife in 1966 Jackson, Mississippi, could ride away from her life without being stopped. I kept listening for a siren, expecting to be pulled over and jerked out of the car like a bad child.

At the Pontiac dealership, I sat in the car for a few minutes trying to slow my breathing. I got out and walked into the office. "I've brought the car in for a tune-up." The car was only two months old. It didn't need a tune-up. My voice sounded as fake as my excuse. "Would you call my husband when it's ready?"

"Will do. Shouldn't take more than an hour," the man said.

I was seized by a new fear. "On second thought." I could hardly get the words out. "He'll call you." Fred might come get the car and I'd still be standing on the sidewalk waiting for Bruce.

The man watched suspiciously as I got my suitcase out of the trunk and walked to the corner. The sun beat down on my head. I had worn a plain gray cotton dress, the kind of dress nobody would give a second glance. I used my purse as a shade and tried to look businesslike, gazing out into Friday afternoon traffic as if I knew exactly what I was doing. I was shaking so bad, I thought my knees would give way.

In my journal the night before, I'd written: "I'm leaving Mississippi, Fred, my children, and everyone I know. I'm making a statement against bigotry." I crossed that last part out. It sounded like a lie, even to me. "I'm going to get an education." That sounded better. The next line was hard to admit. "I'm in love with Bruce, a handsome civil rights lawyer, defender of the downtrodden and the Constitution of the United States." The "defender of the downtrodden" part sounded pretentious, but it was true.

I was scared to death. I didn't write that.

In this town where my family had lived for a hundred years, I felt like a criminal. Someone would scoop me off the corner and return me to Fred like the chattel I was. Minutes passed. Nothing happened. No one even honked. Bruce pulled up. The top of the Triumph was down.

"Could we put the top up?" Anyone could see us.

He gave me a quizzical look, but hauled it up and loaded my suitcase in the back with the dog. I got in.

He smiled, genuine joy on his face. "Here we go."

I tried to smile back. He was the most beautiful man I'd ever seen. He was taking me away to a new life, something I would never have the courage to do for myself.

I thought I might be sick.

We pulled away. It felt unreal. Surely I wasn't going to go through with this. I would say, "Stop." I would get out of the car, take my bags, catch a cab home, apologize to Fred, and start supper. I remembered the meals I'd frozen, the menus with the pages marked in *The Joy of Cooking*. I was a crazy woman, believing if meals appeared they wouldn't notice I was gone.

I thought of Clay's eyes when he said, "How will I talk to you?"

In the car, riding through West Jackson, I cried, wiping my eyes on the back of my hand and trying to keep Bruce from seeing. There is a good person inside me, I told myself, but I felt frozen. There must be a good person who will speak up now and refuse to let me do this. I waited. The good person kept quiet. If I didn't say, *Stop*, out loud, right now, the deed was done. Everything would change. Life as a good southern wife was over.

I looked at Bruce. His dark hair blew in the wind.

"The Episcopal priest said that I will suffer from guilt for the rest of my life."

He reached over and patted me on the knee. "If you're unhappy, you can always go back."

That was true. I took a breath and felt the pain in my chest ease. This wasn't irrevocable. I was just taking a trip, going away for a rest like I'd told my parents and in-laws. It was no different from having a lover. I'd done that before. Except now I was driving south with a man who liked me enough to carry me away, a knight in a blue Triumph. In spite of the fear that sat in my chest like a wet toad, I felt too flattered to turn back yet.

He saw me watching him and tapped a book on the seat between us. "I bought this for us to read on the road. Do you feel like reading?" The book was *The Past That Would Not Die* by Walter Lord.

I opened the book and began. I had to shout over the wind. It was about civil rights and the Meredith case. On page one, I read, "John F. Kennedy was appealing to them to accept on their campus at Oxford a young Negro Air Force veteran. . . ." I pronounced the word "Nigra," which was what everyone in Mississippi said if they didn't say colored or, for the openly bigoted, nigger.

Bruce corrected me. "That's Neegro."

I tried again. "Neeeeegro." I said it several times to get it right. It was my first Yankee word. I would not talk like a bigot. The miles sped by. With every page, I was reminded of why I left. My throat got sore. On page 142, the book described my father: ". . . a dynamic attorney whose offices in Jackson could well have been found in any urban center."

I felt proud. My father might be on the wrong side, but he was no hick.

"I wonder what your father would say if he knew I was leaving town with his little girl?"

My heart began banging around my chest. I didn't want to think about that. Underneath, a dark thought swam: was this the real reason Bruce wanted to take me away?

"I couldn't save the whole state, so I settled for you." He laughed and pulled me over for a kiss.

I turned around to look. Nobody was following us yet. I took another breath, but the pain was stuck under my heart.

I had waited until last to tell Daddy. He was the only person outside of Annie and Marie who seemed to understand. We were in the living room. He was fifty-six now, still trim, but softer around the middle. The blond pompadour had almost imperceptibly turned silver.

He listened to my stumbling explanation about needing to get away and looked at me hard. "Baby, do whatever you feel you have to."

I thought of the time he left Mother and was forced to return. I thought of the silences in that house. I remembered my son's tears earlier today, and our desolate feelings in the hall so many years ago when Daddy told us he was leaving. Mildred, the one-time girlfriend, was still Daddy's secretary. He spent every night in the twin bed under the single headboard, next to a wife he never touched. I had no idea what bargain the three of them had made, or how they endured.

Daddy had pulled me into a hug. "Whatever happens, you know I love you."

I hadn't told him about Bruce. He wouldn't love me if he knew that part.

We'd put the top down south of Jackson. Dusk fell around the open car. My arms were burned and dry from so much sun. It grew too dark to read. The book had taken my mind off the dreadful thing I was doing, but in the silence dread came rushing back. We'd gone too far for me to go back tonight.

I kept taking deep breaths, trying to ease the weight in my chest. I used to think growing up meant finding some kind of peace, but this didn't feel like peace. I might call myself enlightened, compared with bigots in Mississippi, or claim I was fleeing a horror I had no power to change. I could tell myself I was leaving for an education, for a world where I could be a person instead of a female. I could claim any number of things, but the truth was, I was running away—and leaving my children behind.

I loved them, but not enough to put them ahead of my own desires. In my fear of turning out like my mother, drinking myself into oblivion out of loneliness and disappointment, I neglected to notice I had become my father.

I saw myself at nine, holding his hand at the station, jumping up and down, begging to go to New Orleans. I was finally on that train, pulling out of the only life I knew. The timing was rotten; I should have gotten aboard at nineteen instead of thirty.

I thought of Miss Hosford standing in the ashes of Allison's Wells. She believed when one thing didn't work out, you picked yourself up and tried the next. She would not consider this the next best thing.

Bruce reached over and squeezed my hand. Our headlights moved up the road, cutting the dark around us. There was seeing and there was nothing. I was either being saved or condemned.

Epilogue 1970

My father called. Mother was in the hospital. She'd been in twice before for an intestinal blockage. Each time, they'd cut out the blocked portion, got things working, and sent her home. Each time, it collapsed again and now, after a third surgery, she was very weak. I flew to Jackson.

I went back with fewer qualms than in the past. Bruce and I had been married for three years. I did not get my children; Fred was right about that, but Clay came to live with us when he was thirteen. The other three visited Florida twice a year and I flew to Jackson twice to see them. We were as close as phone calls, letters, and four visits a year could keep us. I had my master's degree. I was an assistant professor of English at Miami-Dade Community College, where I taught women's literature and black literature. I went home these days feeling, if not vindicated, pretty pleased with myself.

At Baptist Hospital, my sister Mary Elizabeth and I stood in the hall with the doctor. Adhesions, he said. Bands of fibrous scar tissue from her hysterectomy were causing the blockages. He shook his head. There was nothing more they could do. I thought about that long-ago operation, the one Daddy said made him stop loving Mother. She had that done so she wouldn't die in childbirth. Now she was dying from the operation instead, hastened, I was sure, by an absence of love, evenings of alcohol, and mornings of black coffee and Bufferin.

Mother lay in the bed like a tiny white-wrapped package. She had shrunk to a size she'd always longed to be. I went to Jackson's best women's store, Francis Pepper, and bought her a dress in her new size, black silk with a white ruff. She loved it. We hung it in the hospital room closet. She said she couldn't wait to wear it.

She was heavily drugged and kept coming in and out of sleep. I stood on one side of the bed patting her hand. Mary Elizabeth, whom we now called M.E., stood on the other, frowning.

"Stop patting her like that. She's not a pet."

Startled by the anger in her voice, I took my hand away. My sister's blue eyes were filled with rage. "Sorry." Apologizing as if it were her hand I'd been caressing. Her look said she and Mother were together in this business of dying; I was an intruder.

Mother's eyes opened. I leaned down to kiss her.

"Don't come too close," she said. "I smell bad."

My feelings about my mother were a stew of love and exasperation, but this broke my heart. I wrapped the hand without tubes in mine and kissed her forehead. "No you don't."

She had an "Archie Manning" button pinned to her hospital gown. Manning was the starting quarterback for Ole Miss. Mother was a rabid Rebels fan. She attended every Jackson game, and once they were televised, watched from our living room couch, cigarette in one hand, drink in the other, criticizing the choice of plays and cussing the coaches.

"Wearing your hero over your heart, I see."

She grinned with a hint of her old spirit and gave my hand a squeeze.

After work, Daddy came and sat beside the bed. He took her hand. "I love you, Norma." She turned her head and gave him the sweetest smile, as if these were words she'd waited a lifetime for.

Did he love her? He sounded sincere. Maybe he'd loved her all along in some hands-off way, or maybe he loved her now, for dying and setting him free.

None of us mentioned the word death. That wasn't done in the South. Mother was going to get up and dance in that new dress. Until her last breath, there was always a chance for improvement.

She died early one morning when none of us were there. The

Methodist minister told us that the two of them had often spoken of death. When I burst into tears, he tried to comfort me. "She wasn't afraid." But I was crying over the lie, the way we'd kept fooling each other with our bright talk, sparing her feelings while she spared ours, which seemed like a metaphor for our lives in this town. In death, she looked as fragile as porcelain.

I was relieved that she didn't have to hurt anymore and sad that we'd never been better friends. She might have forgiven me for leaving, but she didn't actually like me. I never praised her enough for her very real attributes: the wonderful food, the beautiful clothes she created, her charm and talent for friendship. I blamed her instead, for the drinking and the double chin, for being bigoted and not able to hold onto my father's love.

In the local paper, her obituary appeared on the page opposite the funny papers. She was "Wife of Prominent Attorney." Even in death a woman got no recognition.

After the ceremony at the church and the burial in the Watkins plot at Greenwood Cemetery, we gathered at the house, where relatives and friends ate the ham, fried chicken, cakes, and pies they'd brought by earlier, and the women began eying my father speculatively, as if measuring him for a new wife. Everyone said how smart and darling Mother was, and what a shame she'd gone so soon. She was fifty-nine.

You *leave* in the South. You *depart*. Nobody dies.

All signs of this gathering had vanished when Daddy called us together in the living room. He sat on the couch with Mother's will in front of him on the glass-topped table. He slid on his black-rimmed reading glasses. My two sisters and I sat in a circle around him, our faces serious, showing no signs of expectation or greed. The will was not long; Mother had little of her own to leave.

My father put on his courtroom voice. "I leave my emerald dinner ring and the diamond bracelet to my daughter Mary Elizabeth." My middle sister wore her little closed-mouth smile. She was the proper daughter: debutante, Junior League member, and possessor of a single husband. In my opinion, she was also enormously troubled, maybe mentally ill. Being southern, we didn't talk about that either.

"I leave the dining table, chairs, and buffet, a gift to me from my family, to my daughter Sydney." Sydney was the youngest, our baby, Daddy's last chance for a son. Everyone loved her best. That part about "my family," might have been in there to remind Daddy that things he had taken for granted, the very table he ate from, had never been his.

Did my sister plan to take away an entire roomful of furniture, leaving Daddy to have supper in the kitchen with Annie on the red Formica table? He didn't appear to mind. Mother was dead and he was free to live as he chose. We could have all the furniture.

A share of an oil well went to Mary Elizabeth and another to Sydney. There was a diamond stickpin for Sydney and a silver tea service for Mary Elizabeth. I was starting to get the picture. The silver flatware went to one of my children, the mahogany secretary in the corner to another.

"That's it." Daddy shuffled the pages.

I had been disinherited.

My sisters looked at the floor, embarrassed for me. I identified the pressure in my chest as hurt.

Daddy cleared his throat. "She loved you, baby. This will was drawn up years ago. She just forgot to change it."

I didn't believe that for a minute and neither did he. I could tell from the way he kept straightening the pages and wouldn't look at me.

Four years ago I had given up the life Mother groomed me for—the house, the husband, the children, the days filled with tennis, bridge, and church bazaars, the tasteful, noncontroversial volunteer work for the Junior League. To her, I must have seemed like Esau, selling my birthright for a mess of pottage.

But that was in the early days. After things settled, I thought the past was forgotten. I married a lawyer. A lawyer was nothing to be ashamed of. I became a college professor. I might look different with my straight hair, long skirts, and no makeup, but I lived a life of probity.

Mother seemed charmed by Bruce. She acted as if she'd forgiven me for leaving. When I flew home for each of the other operations, she was genuinely glad to see me and grateful I'd come.

But I realized—sitting there trying not to weep, telling myself it didn't matter—there were deeds that could never be forgiven. People pretended to your face, the uncles and cousins smiled. They gave me hugs and teased me as they always had. But under the façade of southern courtesy, they remembered and they minded. I had torn the fabric of the family. Whatever satisfactions I managed to find out there in the world with strangers, I was welcome to them. I could not have the thing I longed for: to be accepted here at home, and loved as I once had been.

Annie cried in the kitchen, wiping her eyes on her apron. Mother overworked and underpaid her. In that house during the long hours Daddy spent at the office, Annie was often her only company. Mother scolded, flattered, condescended, and confided in her. Annie had not been left anything either, but she loved my mother. Her grief came from a place of pure loss.

My sisters and I were in Mother's room, our hands in her jewelry box.

"You pick first." What Mary Elizabeth meant was, since I didn't get left anything.

I fingered a strand of pearls.

She said, "You already have pearls."

My hand retreated. "I don't want anything." I wanted to be a thousand miles from here, in our cabin in the woods, back in my other life. I'd chosen it and if at times like this it hurt, so be it. I lived around people I didn't have to lie to. I was no longer afraid. I could talk about civil rights, or rail against the war in Viet Nam without being called a Communist.

Sydney said, "She did love you." Her blue eyes filled with tears.

She wanted everyone to get along. She wanted this to get over with so she could pour herself a big glass of wine.

I felt my eyes sting. Pity was worse than being disinherited.

Sydney said, "Take the gold beads."

I picked up the necklace, the beads cool in my hand. I couldn't let myself cry. Crying would make them think I cared, that I was sorry I left, and that I missed being part of what once felt like an unbreakable circle.

NOTE TO READERS: If a class or book club reads *The Last Resort* and would like the opportunity to speak with the author by phone, check her Web site, normawatkins.com, for contact information. Appointments can be made between 8 a.m. and 6 p.m. (Pacific time).